Remembered

The Men on the War Memorials of Witney, Crawley and Hailey

Volume 1: 1914-1919

By

Jeff Clements

Cover photograph: *The Witney War Memorial between the wars.* From a contemporary postcard.

In memory of my best friend
Phil Gittins

1971-2011

R.I.P.

Contents

Introduction

In the summer of 2009 my father and I, along with a group of our friends, visited some of the First World War battlefields of France and Belgium. We had been before and have subsequently been again, but I remember that it was upon returning from that one particular trip that for the first time I began to think about the men whose names appear on my local war memorial in Witney. I wondered who they were and where they had lived and worked. I wanted to know the stories behind the names.

Initially I imagined that a quick search of the internet would reveal all I wanted to know – perhaps a history of the memorial itself, a detailed list of names, dates and battles fought, maybe even some pictures of the men who had been lost almost a century ago. In the event, apart from a few pictures of the memorial, I found none of these things. I extended my search to include the memorials of Crawley and Hailey, Witney's neighbouring townships[1], and still nothing. Surely this couldn't be right. I had just come back from visiting numerous military cemeteries, museums and battlefields, all places where you could not help but be immersed in an atmosphere of respect and remembrance for those who had participated and yet back home there was nothing but three memorials coldly commemorating those who appeared to have been largely forgotten.

I felt that something needed to be done. Other communities had researched their local memorials why not the people of Witney? I believed that this was something I could do. It could be my act of remembrance; a way to give something to the people of Witney, Crawley and Hailey – to put them in touch with the men who had once walked our streets and who had left here all those years ago. I never imagined it would take so long – that was four years ago.

---

[1] Curbridge, Witney's third township, surprisingly has no war memorial despite several local men being lost during the Great War.

My intention at first was to research each name on the memorials of Witney, Crawley and Hailey, from both World Wars and to then put all the information together in one publication. However, as the project grew and the centenary of the beginning of the First World War was fast approaching I decided to deal with each conflict separately and hopefully produce two publications. This then is the first of those publications and charts the movement to remember the local men who fell in the Great War 1914 – 1919.

Context

When Britain went to war with Germany in August 1914, the whole country was swept up in a wave of patriotism as thousands of young men clamoured to enlist, all desperate to get into the fight as quickly as possible, fearing it might be over all too soon. In an outward display of civic pride Rolls of Honour - lists of the men who had volunteered for military service or who were already serving - began to be compiled locally in the press, individual communities, schools, factories, businesses and clubs. This was to be a brief campaign, sure to be over by Christmas, or so it was said.

As the early days of the war turned into weeks and the weeks into months the casualty lists began to grow ever longer. Faced with a logistical nightmare and mindful of the adverse effect that large numbers of coffins arriving at ports would have upon morale at home, in early 1915 the military authorities banned the repatriation of all dead servicemen. Henceforth all fallen servicemen would remain in the immediate vicinity of their death, their graves becoming, in the words of the war poet Rupert Brooke, '...that corner of a foreign field that is for ever England'. For the families left at home, bereft of their loved ones, there arose an intense desire to establish local shrines and memorials to give a focus for shared grief and mourning. In 1917 the Imperial War Graves Commission was established to oversee the construction of official military cemeteries and later to commission the building of monuments, especially for those casualties who had been classed as 'missing' and had no known grave.

At the same time the government began to encourage local communities to form committees and raise funds for their own local memorials. They imposed very few restrictions and gave little guidance, so that following the cessation of hostilities in 1918, thousands of memorials, of varying size and type began to be erected.[2] Some communities chose to remember their dead through the provision of services for the living; dedicating hospitals and other public amenities in their memory whilst others chose more traditional monuments to effect their remembrance.

In Witney this whole period was covered in the pages of the local paper; the *Witney Gazette*. Appearing then, as it does now, on a weekly basis and carrying a mixture of local, national and international news. From the 12th September 1914 until the 12th February 1916, when paper shortages forced the paper to be reduced in size, it produced a weekly roll of honour, listing all the local men who were either serving, had become casualties, or had been taken prisoner of war.[3] The following stories of the War Memorials in Witney, Crawley and Hailey are drawn primarily from contemporary reports as they appeared in the *Witney Gazette*.

---

[2] It is estimated that in this country there are around 36,000 memorials to the dead of the Great War.

[3] The task of compiling a full and up-to-date roll of honour for Witney specifically was resurrected in September 1916 by Edward Early, Chairman of the Witney Urban District Council. By November 1917 the roll listed 533 names and continued to grow.

The Witney War Memorial

Calls for a permanent memorial to the town's fallen servicemen first began to appear in the local press in late 1916. However, despite the establishment of some temporary 'war shrines' in places such as schools and churches, it was not until the conflict entered its final stage that a formal War Memorial Committee was convened to investigate a suitable scheme of remembrance. At the end of October 1918, at a meeting of the Witney Urban District Council (W.U.D.C.), the Committee presented their preliminary report. They recommended that a public meeting be held to debate the various schemes already suggested and that in the meantime '... *a list of those who had fallen or had been discharged, and those still fighting should be drawn up and placed upon a public building in the town.*' It was further suggested that this list of names should be inscribed on a permanent board which '... *could afterwards be removed to the permanent memorial.*' The Council members agreed unanimously.[4]

The well attended public meeting duly took place in the Corn Exchange, on the evening of the 19th November 1918. Mr E.C. Early, Chair of the W.U.D.C, said in his opening address that '... *they* [the townspeople] *were met that night to take in hand something that they were all agreed upon – to consider a memorial for those who had fallen in the war, but when it came to the question of what form the memorial should take he thought there would be a good many opinions.*' Nevertheless, he believed that they would all agree upon two things; the first being the inscribed board – as previously discussed and agreed at the earlier Council meeting, and the second was for the permanent acquisition of some German artillery pieces as '... *he felt that their Witney men had earned them*' - to which statement he received a round of applause. He then went on to present to the meeting the various suggestions for a memorial that had already been submitted, these were for '...*a drinking fountain in the market place,*

---

[4] *Witney Gazette*, 2nd November 1918.

purchase of the recreation ground for the town, a war museum, endowment of the YMCA for the men when they return, a cottage hospital ..., a fund for enabling sick people to go to a convalescent home,' and for an endowment to be made to the town's Nursing Association. Whilst the suggestion from the Council was for the purchase of *'... a motor ambulance* [to provide transport to the Radcliffe Infirmary in Oxford] *and the erection of a monument on Church Green.'* Despite the range of the suggestions proposed it was the cottage hospital scheme which aroused the most debate with strong arguments for and against. As the meeting ended it was left to the War Memorial Committee to canvas wider public opinion before a definite proposal could be made.[5]

As Christmas 1918 approached the views of the townspeople were sought and, despite a public debate in the press and on the streets about whether or not the nature of a suitable memorial should be to honour the dead rather than to be an institution for the living,[6] it soon became apparent that the cottage hospital scheme was by far the most popular choice. At a second public meeting, held on the 13th February 1919, the hospital scheme - to include the erection of a separate monument, was formally proposed by the War Memorial Committee and after some debate, adopted by the town. The Committee estimated that the total cost of the scheme would be approximately *'... £1000 for a monument, £4,500 for building a hospital, and £6,500 for an endowment fund* [for its future upkeep]*'* and with pledges having already been made by twenty five local individuals this left a balance of £5000 for the townspeople to raise. Mr C. Viner noted that whilst this was still a large sum of money they (the Committee) *'...wanted every man women and child in the town to have a share in this War Memorial* [and that] *if they were going to make the scheme a success they must give to the point of sacrifice. After all what sacrifice could they make compared with those who had sacrificed their lives.'*[7]

By early September 1919 not only had more than £9,000 been pledged – this being the sum originally identified as the minimum needed to get the scheme underway, but a suitable site for the hospital had also been secured when Mr C.W. Early agreed to donate, free of charge, part of the Cricket Field in Newland. It was at this point though that the spectre of post-war inflation first

---

[5] *ibid.*, 23rd November 1918.
[6] *ibid.*, 14th December 1918.
[7] *ibid.*, 15th February 1919.

began to be noted in the local press. The *Witney Gazette* carried a piece discussing the general increase in prices since the war's end and urging donations of a further £1,000 to enable the hospital project to begin.[8]

During the first week of October 1919 the first of the town's allocated war trophies arrived in the form of a German field gun which the Council decided would be best placed, albeit temporarily, under the Town Hall.[9] Unfortunately the gun was soon found to be an irresistible draw to the local boys and, within a couple of weeks, it was taken off display and withdrawn to the security of the Council yard, behind the Corn Exchange, where it was planned that it would remain until the War Memorial was completed.[10] Further trophies were offered to the town in the spring of 1920 but the Town Clerk, having travelled to inspect them, was of the opinion that '...*they were not worth the carriage from Oxford*'.[11]

On the 2nd January 1920 the W.U.D.C., having been assured of the required funds and building plots, '*unanimously decided to proceed with the erection of :- (a) A Cottage Hospital on a portion of the Cricket Field in Newland, and, (b) A Monument on Church Green, in accordance with the plans and design submitted to and approved by the meeting*'.[12] Although it had been decided to site the memorial on Church Green, the exact location was not agreed until several months later when the War Memorial Committee, '*having considered various sites* [recommended] *a position at the northern end of the row of lime trees on the west side of Church Green*', with the exact position to be decided by a small committee in consultation with the architect, Mr Thomas Rayson of Oxford.[13]

It is important to note at this stage that whilst the planning was well underway for the Witney War Memorial, a separate memorial was also being planned by another committee in Cogges. Long considered to be distinctly separate from Witney, the parishioners of Cogges and Newland chose to organise their own tribute to the local men who had served during the war. The

---

[8] *ibid.*, 6th September 1919.
[9] *ibid.*, 11th October 1919.
[10] *ibid.*, 1st November 1919.
[11] *ibid.*, 17th April 1920.
[12] *ibid.*, 10th January 1920.
[13] *ibid.*, 5th June 1920.

resultant stone memorial today stands in a tiny square garden on Oxford Road. It bears no specific names, being simply dedicated 'To all who served'. Later, following the end of the Second World War, the names of the men from Cogges and Newland who had been killed during the Great War were inscribed upon a stone tablet which was then affixed to the east side of the Witney War Memorial.[14] Today a wooden memorial within St. Mary's Church, Cogges, records the dead of the parish from both World Wars.

By the end of May 1920, as the list of names for inclusion on the memorial was closed, it became clear that rising prices had outstripped the original estimates for the construction of the planned hospital and that the £12,000 which had initially been called for was not going to be enough. It was estimated that a further £5,000 would be required to undertake and maintain the original scheme and, with only £9,800 of the original target having been promised at this point, it was felt that the hospital scheme would have to be abandoned. The memorial would be erected as planned but the War Memorial Committee was left in the unenviable position of having to devise an alternative scheme, one which they hoped would continue to have the support of the original subscribers and townspeople alike.

On Saturday June 19th 1920 the *Witney Gazette* reported the abandonment of the hospital scheme and informed its readers that '*the Committee now invite the subscribers to support a scheme for the purchase of the Recreation Ground* [known as 'the Church Leys'], *and the granting of substantial aid to the Witney Nursing Association and the Radcliffe Infirmary...* [it is hoped] *that the new scheme will meet with general approval, and that a good deal of money promised for the Hospital scheme will be available for this one. Whatever may be thought of the purchase of the Recreation Ground, the Nursing Association and the Infirmary are closely connected with the old scheme and although the more ambitious scheme has fallen through the present one holds out great possibilities of helping the suffering, which we maintain is an ideal form of War Memorial.*'[15] Although seemingly meant with the best of intentions the decision

---

[14] Thereby duplicating the names of three men: Albert Haggitt, Thomas Keen and George Stanley who, due to them having family connections in both Witney and Cogges, are remembered on both the original Witney memorial and the subsequent Cogges plaque.

[15] *Witney Gazette*, 19th June 1920.

to scrap the hospital scheme, a scheme that so many who could ill afford it had contributed to, was one which was to cause resentment within the town for many years to come.

As the summer of 1920 began to wane the construction work on the town's war memorial neared completion and the date set for its formal unveiling. The dedication service was to take place on the afternoon of Sunday 12th September - Feast Sunday, although the town's people were advised that '... *if wet, the service will be postponed to the first fine Sunday*'. They need not have been concerned. In the event the weather was fine and the service took place as planned. One week later, on Saturday 18th September 1920, the *Witney Gazette* carried the following report on the occasion:

'The beautiful memorial cross which has lately been erected on the West side of Church Green, was dedicated on Sunday afternoon in the presence of some two thousand people. The time chosen was particularly appropriate for it was feast Sunday – a red letter day in the lives of all Witney people, and many of these lads which the cross commemorates had happy memories clustering around their annual festival. It was a lovely September afternoon reminding one of the beautiful weather of September 1914, when so many of Witney's heroes marched away to fight for the honour of their Country. The school children and other youthful organisations of the town – the Boy's Brigade, Boy Scouts, Boy Reserves, Girl Guides, Brownies &c, marched to the Green and formed an inner cordon round the Cross, while in the centre were the Ministers of the town and the Witney Band who led the singing. The large space was crowded with townspeople, and many from the surrounding villages. At the close of the service a large number of beautiful wreaths were placed at the foot of the Cross. It was an impressive sight and the historic occasion will live in the minds of all who were present.

The service commenced with the singing of "Praise to the Holiest in the height", followed by the opening sentences and Psalm xivi, read by the Rev. O.F. East, concluding with the Lord's prayer. The Rev. L. Martin followed with the reading of prayers after which there was an interval of silence, "O God of Love, O King of Peace" having been sung.

The Rev. R. Unsworth delivered an address as follows:- "Six years ago today, on just such a beautiful September day, the armies of England and France, after weeks of a terrible retirement, with almost incredible losses on the part of France, stood at last at bay on the banks of the Marne, and there they turned on the relentless foe and threw him back and won what will be for all time one of the greatest and most decisive battles of the world, and saved Europe. We can remember those days of terrible anxiety and we can also recollect that the young men of England were pouring out to go to the rescue of the stricken armies of France and rally to the standard of England in her hour of need. You remember the days when these young soldiers drilled without uniform and without rifles; they learnt their soldiers' life in an incredible space of time and went out to meet the trained and disciplined armies of Central Europe. They crossed the narrow sea and poured over France and Belgium and eventually over the seven seas to Italy, Africa, Mesopotamia and Egypt to uphold the honour and glory of England and to save their Motherland. Numbers have come back, thank God they have done their duty and added to the undying fame of England's Glory. Many, alas, are sleeping their last sleep in strange lands and many are sleeping nobody knows where; out of sight but not out of the memory, and love, and regard of their Country. At the base of this memorial you will see the names inscribed of those who went from Witney in the promise of their splendid youth and gave their lives that we might live. Their names will remain enshrined forever. Long after we have passed away people will move round this stately column and read the names of those who were born in this place and went out to die for England. To this generation they are far more than names, they are tender loving persons still fresh in the memory of those who knew and loved them. They have many times passed this place where this cross stands as they have gone to school with all the promise of their life in front of them. You all remember their last journey to the station, you saw the smile in all their faces and you heard the encouraging words that they would soon be back again. At home many of you number amongst your richest treasures the last letter they wrote to you, or a little memento reaching back into childhood. So just because we owe them so much we have tried in our small feeble way to erect for all time in the heart of the town a memorial to their memory as a pledge of our gratitude to them. For they gave up, as every man who went out was prepared to give up, their life that we might walk through these streets as free men and women. They went through terrible trial and suffering for four weary years and some have gone never to return. There is coming out, I can hear it, a message from the dead, ringing out to us so that everyone can hear it, "We have given" the message says, "our lives for you that you might have a better, happier and nobler England. What is the meaning of this murmuring, this unrest and dissatisfaction which is going on all round. Have you forgotten those splendid days at the beginning of the war when we realised we were all one family, and threw down the barriers between class and class, when we were ready to go and endure all things for the sake of England. Through our suffering you have won a magnificent victory and here you are today unhappy and restless through the length and breadth of the land.[16] Have we died for you in vain?" Now men and women listen to the message they give to you. The only way of getting back to the best which life holds out for you is through the sacrifice which this cross commemorates. It is eternally enshrined because of those who have sought not their own but laid down their lives that you and I might have the chance of living a life today, such as our forefathers never dreamed of. But it must be based on self sacrifice, not on greed and class prejudice, but surrendering yourselves for the benefit of the whole. Take that message and carry it home. The highest thing we can do to the sacred holy memory of the illustrious dead is to do what they would want us to do, to follow in their steps, and live a life of sacrifice and make the lives of others happier and more blessed."

The remainder of the service was conducted by the Rev. Ernest D. Green and consisted of extempore prayer, a special benediction and the singing of "O God our help in ages past." The "Last Post" was sounded by four buglers from the 1/4 O. & B.L.I. [1/4th Battalion, Oxfordshire and Buckinghamshire Light Infantry] A muffled peal was ringing on the bells of St. Mary's., and the flag at the Church and at the Town Hall were at half-mast.

Most beautiful wreaths were placed on the Cross including many from the Friendly Societies and other organisations.

The Cross which is 25ft in height with a width at the base of 13ft is of Portland stone and is a limestone of fine grain and great durability. The whole work stands on a cement concrete bed, and the wrought stone is backed by local

---

[16] A reference to the social and political unrest affecting much of the country at this time. See Marwick, A., The Deluge, British Society and the First World War, MacMillan, London, 1991.

rubble. The stone cross in the niche is of Mansfield stone, a close grained sandstone of Nottinghamshire. The work has been carried out by Messrs. W.H. Axtall & son, of Oxford, from a design by Mr T Rayson, ARIBA of the same city.[17]

Originally inscribed with 119 names commemorating the dead of the First World War the four base panels of the Witney War Memorial now display 125 names (although one of those is actually of a Second World War bomber pilot, inscribed here due to the lack of space on the two stone plaques which were added in 1950 to commemorate the town's dead from 1939-45), whilst the later addition of the Cogges plaque has brought the total number remembered from the Great War to 143. Though, in the absence of any real criteria for a person's original inclusion upon the war memorial, it is not surprising to learn that the total number of names inscribed upon the town's cenotaph is not complete nor is it an accurate reflection of all those connected with the town who gave their lives during the Great War. There may have been numerous reasons for these omissions but most commonly it was due to families moving away from the area either before or during the war. An incomplete list of some of these names appears at appendix (i).

For each of the men who are remembered on the memorial I have written a brief biography, with each one following a similar format – beginning with the man's name, as inscribed on the memorial, followed by his full name, rank, service number and the unit he was serving with at the time of his death or discharge. A paragraph or two concerning his domestic background is then followed by details of his military service and eventual demise, including place of burial and/or commemoration. For just a few I was able to draw upon rich and detailed records whereas for the majority I had to piece together their individual lives from sources such as decennial census data, approximate records of births, deaths and marriages and snippets of information gleaned from the contemporary local press.

These then, in alphabetical order, are the men commemorated on the Witney War Memorial:

---

[17] *Witney Gazette*, 18th September 1920.

F.J. Amery
Sergeant, Francis John Amery, 700383,
'C' Company,
1/23rd (County of London) Battalion,
London Regiment

Francis Amery was born in the Somerset village of Bishop's Hull during the spring of 1897, the eldest son of John, a cowman, and his wife Laura (née Willis). Following the birth of the couple's second son, Gilbert, in 1900, the family moved to a farm at Waterperry near Oxford. Here the family remained for a number of years before moving again, probably at some time during the First World War, to Downs Farm, west of Witney.

When war was declared in August 1914 Francis was amongst the first to volunteer for military service. He was posted to the 1/23rd (County of London) Battalion of the London Regiment, part of the 2nd London Division, which at the time was encamped near St. Albans, Hertfordshire. On the 14th March 1915 the 1/23rd Battalion left St. Albans en route to Southampton and from there onto Le Havre, France. The battalion got its initial taste of trench warfare, and suffered its first casualties on the 12th April 1915 and from this point onwards, for the remainder of the war, it was to remain on the Western Front.

On the 21st March 1918 the Germans unleashed a series of massive offensive operations on the Western Front. In a move code-named 'Operation Michael' seventy two German Divisions from three armies, supported by an intense artillery bombardment and aided by poor weather conditions, punched a hole sixty miles wide through the Allied front-line on the Somme. In a little over a week they had succeeded in capturing several key Allied-held towns in the battlefield area including Peronne, Albert and Bapaume. The initial German success came at a price. Casualties had been high and the speed and depth of their advance was frustrated by an inability to remain adequately supplied. On the 5th April the German military commander, General Ludendorf, terminated the offensive and his dispirited and disorganized forces were left to consolidate their gains.

The Allied counter offensive on the Somme began on the 21st August 1918 with the battle to re-take the town of Albert. It was here, at 3:20 a.m.[18] on the morning of the 22nd August, that Francis Amery prepared to lead the men of his unit in an attack against the German positions. At 5:00 a.m., 'Zero Hour', the order was given and 'A', 'B' and 'D' companies went 'over the top' with 'C' company following up in support. By 8:05 a.m. the assaulting companies had succeeded in advancing and making contact with the 1/24th Battalion on their left and the 1/22nd on their right. Casualties had been, in the words of the battalion diarist, '...moderately heavy'[19]. At 4:35 p.m. the Germans counter attacked and the 1/23rd was forced to pull back. They were eventually relieved at 10:35 p.m. that night when they moved into reserve positions near Marett Wood to the south west of Albert.

The estimated battalion casualties resulting from this one action were 12 Officers and 261 Other Ranks, one of whom was 21 year old Francis Amery. Today his grave can be found in the Bray Vale British Cemetery, Bray-Sur-Somme. France.

S.G. Beale
Corporal, Sydney George Beale, 11274,
6th Battalion,
Oxfordshire & Buckinghamshire Light Infantry

Sydney Beale was born on the 4th July 1892 in a little house on Broad Hill, Witney, and baptised on the 18th September at Holy Trinity Church on Woodgreen. The youngest son of Robert, a blanket finisher, and his wife Jane (née Haley), he was educated at St. Mary's Church School. At the time of the 1911 census he was working as a mill hand and by 1914, when he volunteered for the Army, he was employed as a fettler[20] at Early's factory.

Sydney volunteered for military service within the first few weeks of the war and was posted to the newly formed 6th Battalion of the Oxfordshire and

---

[18] Note the 24hr clock was not officially adopted by the British Army until 1918 therefore the times quoted throughout all use the contemporaneous 12hr clock.
[19] WO 95/2744
[20] A machine cleaner.

Buckinghamshire Light Infantry (OBLI), part of the 20th (Light) Division. By June of the following year the battalion had been fully trained and equipped and, following an inspection of the entire Division by King George V at Knighton Down in Wiltshire, it was deemed ready to go to war. The battalion landed in France on the 22nd July 1915. Throughout the remainder of the year and into the winter of 1915/16 the men of the 6th OBLI took their turn in the front line. Sydney, later described by one of his officers as '... *a quiet retiring lad who said little but who had a large personal influence amongst the men...*'[21], elected not to take any leave until the end of the war, preferring instead to remain with his unit. His dedication to duty was rewarded in short time with promotion to the rank of Lance Corporal.

In July 1916 the huge Allied offensive began on the Somme. The 6th OBLI did not take part in the early engagements but, due to the length of the operation and the cost in human life, it was only a matter of time before it was to be called upon to take its turn. At 8:30 p.m., on 16th September 1916 Sydney, recently promoted to the full rank of Corporal, and the rest of his battalion which had been billeted between the villages of Corbie and Meaulte, to the south west and south respectively of Albert, started a gruelling six hour journey to the front. At 2:20 a.m. on 17th September the men took up their positions opposite the enemy in the front line trench near High Wood, Longueval, and were immediately ordered to 'dig in' and consolidate the trench line. However, although they did attempt to comply, the men were exhausted from their march and their officers allowed them '... to sit about or lean on their spades, or even to stand up and fall asleep against the side of the trench'[22].

During the morning of the 17th the Germans began shelling the battalion's position. It was during this barrage that a shell exploded in the trench wall near to where Sydney was sheltering, burying alive himself and six others. Without delay their comrades in the trench began to dig them out. One of the first two men pulled alive from the debris was Sydney's friend and fellow Witney man, William Miles. Who, upon being rescued began immediately to search for Sydney. He soon found him and managed to get his face clear of the mud but

---

[21] Lieutenant D.S. Bensen, 6th OBLI, from a letter published in the *Witney Gazette*, 7th October 1916.

[22] The words of Captain Graeme West, 6th OBLI. in; Gilbert, M., Somme, John Murray, London. 2007. (p.194).

by this stage he had been rendered unconscious. The frantic activity was halted just moments later when a second shell hit the trench, re burying the soldiers and killing Sydney and five others.

Miles was himself rendered a casualty as a result of the second bomb blast and was evacuated from the battlefield to a military hospital. He went on to make a full recovery and was later returned to his unit. In a letter written a short time after to Sydney's mother, he explained the circumstances of her son's death and consoled her that her son had been dug out and re buried '... *as respectable as the circumstances would allow'*[23]. William Miles was later killed in action on the Western Front in 1917, his name also remembered on the Witney War Memorial.

It is not known where Sydney Beale was originally buried as for many years the site of his grave was lost. But in June 1938 the following article appeared in the Witney Gazette:

> **'A Witney man, who was killed in 1916, during the Great War, has only recently been buried. He was Corporal S.G.Beale, of Corn Street, Witney, whose name appears second on the list in Witney's Roll of Honour.** *A few months ago his family received notification that his body had been found by workmen while excavating, and was to be buried, the number of the grave and the name of the cemetery at Lonegueval, in France was also given. They were asked if they would like to put an inscription on his grave.*
>
> *His sister, Mrs Smith, of Corn Street, Witney, has her brother's watch, which was found on his body and was sent at the same time as the notification from the War Office. It is a silver watch and shows marks of having been subjected to great heat, one hinge is broken but the glass and the works of the watch are intact...It is believed that Corporal Beale was buried in a dug-out after an explosion with a number of his companions, as other bodies were also found.'*[24]

His body now lies in the London Cemetery, Longeuval, France.

---

[23] From an unpublished letter sent from W. Miles to Sydney's parents following the death of their son.

[24] *Witney Gazette*, 3rd June 1938.

16

F. Bennett
Private, Frank Bennett, 193452,
42nd Battalion,
Canadian Infantry (Quebec Regiment)

Frank Bennett was born in Corn Street on the 7th February 1886, the youngest son of Charles, a carriage painter, and his wife Zilpah (née Williams). His parents had married in Brighton and it was there that their first child, Alice, had been born. In the mid 1870's the family moved to Leafield, Oxfordshire, the village of Zilpah's birth and in the late 1870's, into Witney. By the time of the 1901 census Charles and Zilpah had moved back to Leafield and Frank was living and working as a 'general barman' at the New Inn, Minster Lovell.

In October 1905 Frank's father died and by 1911 Frank and his mother were living in a flat in Fulham, London, where Frank had a job as a grocer's shop assistant. However a fresh start beckoned for both and within twelve months Zilpah Bennett had moved to Reading and Frank, in March 1912, left England to start a new life in Canada. Despite his stated aim, at the time of emigration, of hoping to secure agricultural work near Hamilton, Frank was to end up working in a bar in Toronto.

On the 13th September 1915 Frank, still employed as a bartender, volunteered for military service overseas with the Canadian Expeditionary Force (CEF). Following basic training he was assigned to the 92nd Battalion, CEF and on the 20th May 1916, aboard the troop transport *S.S. Empress of Britain,* Frank left Canada bound for Liverpool. Once in England Frank and the men of his draft continued their training in preparation for service on the Western Front. On the 17th August 1916 Frank was transferred to the 42nd Infantry Battalion and the following day he landed in France, destined to play his part in the Allied offensive on the Somme.

At 6 p.m. on the 15th September 1916, as part of a major Allied offensive action on the Somme, later to be known as the Battle of Flers-Courcelette, the Canadian Corps launched an attack on the German held village of Courcelette. The men of the 42nd Infantry Battalion, attacking the German front line trench to the west of the village, secured their initial objective without heavy casualties and immediately began work to consolidate the captured trench and reverse the parapet to face the enemy's second trench line. That night, and through the following morning, the Canadians came under heavy enemy shelling which accounted for a large number of casualties. Depleted in numbers they were ordered to advance again at 4:55 p.m. on the 16th. This time they were not successful. The artillery barrage which had been planned to subdue the German defenders was inadequate and, as the Canadians advanced, they could plainly see the unmolested Germans standing shoulder to shoulder, in their trenches, firing into the advancing ranks. The attack faltered and ultimately failed as the number of casualties increased. The survivors of the 42nd fell back to their initial positions before being relieved several hours later.[25]

Frank Bennett fell during the attack on the 16th September 1916. His body was never identified and today his name is recorded on the Vimy Memorial, Vimy Ridge, France, alongside the names of over 11,000 Canadian troops who were posted 'missing presumed dead' on the Western Front.

J. Berry
Corporal, James Berry, 26484,
6th Battalion,
Oxfordshire & Buckinghamshire Light Infantry

James Berry was born in High Street, Witney, in the fourth quarter of 1883, the youngest son of James, a former fellmonger turned baker,[26] and his wife Amelia (née Long). In 1893 Amelia died and the couple's eldest daughter Alice, aged 20 at the time, appears to have taken responsibility for the running of the house and the care of her younger brothers and sisters. By the time of the 1901 census James had left school and had entered into a carpentry apprenticeship which he obviously completed successfully as ten years later, in 1911, he was employed by a local builder as a joiner. On the 10th May 1911 he

---

[25] Battalion diary accessed at www.collectionscanada.gc.ca

[26] Recorded in the census of 1881 as a fellmonger (a dealer in skins or hides) employing two people and by 1891 as a baker. The bakery itself was situated on the High Street, opposite the entrance to Gloucester Place, in a building which was later demolished during the construction of Witan Way.

married Maud Hadland, of Leafield, and the couple lived in Witney. In the spring of 1914 their only child was born; a daughter they called Kathleen.

It is unclear when James enlisted for military service. However, at the time of his deployment to France in 1916/17 he was already a Corporal in rank so it is likely that he had served for some time on home service prior to his transfer to front-line service. Once in France he was attached to the 6th Battalion of the Oxfordshire and Buckinghamshire Light Infantry, part of the 20th (Light) Division.

It was on the 20th November 1917, during the opening day of the Battle of Cambrais, that James was killed. Reportedly a victim of stray artillery fire.[27] His body was never identified and he has no known grave. Today his name is remembered on the Cambrais Memorial, at Louveral in France.

In 1921 James's widow, Maud, was married to Robert Boggis a local man who had himself suffered the loss of a brother, Herbert, killed in action on the Somme in 1916.

A.I. Bishop
Private, Alfred Isaac Bishop, S/43403,
1/4th Battalion,
Seaforth Highlanders

Alfred Bishop was born near the village of Asthall in 1883, the eldest son of Edward, a mill hand, and his wife Emily (née Mills). By the time of the 1901 census the family had moved into Witney and Alfred was working as a carter for a local coal merchant. In 1903 he married Eliza Rowles, a local blanket weaver, also originally from Asthall. The couple's first child died in infancy and in 1910, following the birth of their second child, named Alfred after his father, the family moved to Cannock in Staffordshire where Alfred had found work labouring at a colliery. It is unclear exactly how long the family remained away from Witney but it could not have been for too long as their daughter, Ivy, was born in the town in late 1913. On Tuesday the 16th February 1915,

---

[27] *Witney Gazette*, 15th December 1917.

Eliza Bishop died and Alfred was left to care for their two young children on his own.

In the absence of any surviving records it remains unclear when Alfred originally volunteered for military service. However, a newspaper report indicates that he had enlisted, at the latest, by the autumn of 1916 because on the 24th December 1916 he was deployed to France and the Western Front. Initially he served with the Army Vetinary Corps but was later transferred, first to the West Riding Regiment and subsequently to the 1/4th Battalion of the Seaforth Highlanders.

In October 1918, during the period known as 'The Last Hundred Days', the Allied armies on the Western front were engaged in a series of skirmishes with units of the German Army as they pushed them further and further back. The Germans for their part, although a demoralised and broken force, were retreating in a controlled fashion and still able to mount limited counter attacks. It was during one of these engagements, near the village of Aulnoy in northern France, that Alfred was killed.

The details of his fate were at first unclear, and his family were initially informed that he had been posted as 'missing in action' but on the 12th February 1919 they finally received confirmation from the War Office that Alfred had indeed been killed on, or around, the 24th October 1918. Today his body, along with a number of his comrades, lies in the Aulnoy Communal Cemetery, Aulnoy, France.

Upon Alfred's death his orphaned children were left in the care of his family; eight year old Alfred with his uncle Mark, his late father's younger brother, and five year old Ivy with her paternal grandmother.

H.F. Boggis
Lance Corporal, Herbert Frank Boggis, 3149,
9th Battalion (Queen Victoria's Rifles),
London Regiment

Herbert Boggis, known by his middle name of Frank, was born in Sudbury, Suffolk in the spring of 1892, the eldest son of Herbert, a draper by trade, and Annie (née Drake). In 1897 the family moved to Witney when Frank's father went into partnership with William Cook, a local draper and clothier. The business they established went simply by the name of *Cook and Boggis* and for many years it traded from premises at the Market Square entrance to the High Street.[28] Frank, having received his education at the Wesleyan Day School and thereafter at the Witney Grammar School, was by 1911 working in his father's business. Shortly afterwards he moved to London where he became engaged in business for himself.

In October 1914 and still living in London, Frank volunteered for military service joining the 1/9th (County of London) London Regiment (Queen Victoria's Rifles).[29] He was still in basic training when his battalion deployed to France in early November 1914 but on the 20th January 1915 he rejoined his unit on the Western Front. The 1/9th was part of 13th Brigade, 5th Division until February 1916 and as such was involved in the following notable engagements: The capture of Hill 60 (17th-22nd April 1915); the battle of Gravenstaffel (22nd-23rd April 1915); and the battle of St. Julien (24th April-5th May 1915).

In February 1916 the old pre-war 'London Division' of the Territorial Force, having been broken up a year earlier to reinforce other units, was reformed at Hallencourt on the Somme and designated the 56th (1st London) Division of which the 1/9th was to form one element. Once established, the 56th Division remained on the Somme in readiness for the planned Allied summer offensive which, it was anticipated, would break the stalemate of trench warfare on the Western Front and punch a hole right through the German front line. The prelude to what became known as 'the Battle of the Somme' began in the last week of June 1916 with a week long, massive artillery bombardment of the German front line trench system. The object of this was to smash the German barbed wire and annihilate any resistance before Allied troops were committed to cross 'no-man's-land'. As part of the plan the 56th and 46th (North Midland) Division were assigned to attack the heavily fortified German held village of Gommecourt, on the northern most extremity of the Allied assault.

The village in actual fact held very little strategic value to the Allies but its position, which formed a bulge or salient into the Allied front line, had been

---

[28] The shop and business remained on the same site until destroyed by fire in 1964.

[29] In the *Witney Gazette* of 22nd July 1916 he was wrongly reported as having served with the 'London Scottish', more officially known as the 1/14th London Regiment, although both battalions were engaged at Gommecourt on 1st July 1916.

considered to be a nuisance and as it represented the furthest westward advance of the German Army it was believed that its capture would strike a blow to the enemies' morale. The intention of Allied commanders was simple enough. The 46th Division would attack the northern shoulder of the salient whilst the 56th Division would attack the southern shoulder. The attacking forces would then meet behind the German lines to the east of Gommecourt and effectively cut off the fortified village and its defenders from the rest of the German Army to the east, forcing them to surrender and effectively shortening the British front line. The battle plan was purely diversionary with no intention of exploiting a success at Gommecourt. The British commander, General Sir Douglas Haig, felt that the German's could be confused into believing the Allied attack would be further north and on a much narrower front than it actually was. Thus their heavy guns would be directed towards Gommecourt and away from the real thrust of the offensive further south. To further aid this plan the two Divisional commanders were ordered to make their preparation for an assault on Gommecourt as obvious to the Germans as possible.

At 'zero hour', 7:30 a.m. on 1st July 1916, the lead units of the 56th Division, including Frank, now promoted to Lance Corporal, and his unit went 'over the top' from a freshly dug trench half-way across no-man's-land, 400 yds from the German front line. Attacking through a smoke screen, over uncut German wire and under heavy fire, they quickly swept over the first two enemy trench lines before being held in check by the defending forces. Engaged in fierce hand to hand fighting the Londoners began taking heavy casualties and with no sign of the troops from the 46th Division, whose attack from the north had completely failed, they were forced to pull back. By the early evening the situation for the attacking force had become intolerable and at 8:20 p.m., having been beaten back towards no-man's-land by German trench mortars and bombing parties, the order was given to retreat.

The attack at Gommecourt had ultimately failed in its aim to seize the fortified village and remove the salient. However it did succeed in drawing heavy German artillery fire, which would otherwise have fallen on the main attack further south.[30] At the end of the day the British casualties were

---

[30] A contemporary account of the battle can be found in Liveling, E.G.D., Attack, Macmillan, London, 1918.

calculated to have been 182 officers and 4,567 men killed, wounded and missing. One of those killed was Frank Boggis. His body was never identified and he has no known grave. Today his name is remembered on the Thiepval Memorial to the missing of the Somme, near the village of Thiepval, France.

F. Boswell
Private, Frederick Boswell, 238210,
13th Battalion,
Duke of Wellington's (West Riding Regiment)

Frederick was born in Paddington, London around 1890 and as a child he was brought to the village of Sutton, near Eynsham to live with 'adoptive' parents; James Boswell, a shoemaker, and his wife Emily (née Smith). In 1901 the family were living at *The Sparrow* public house in the village. Ten years later, at the time of the 1911 census Frederick, was recorded as living alone in Sutton and working as a jobbing gardener. At some point within the next few years he married Elizabeth (surname unknown) and the couple moved to Church Green, Witney.

It is not known when Frederick enlisted in the Army nor is it possible to say when he first arrived on the Western Front but his record of medal entitlement indicates that it would have been after 1st January 1916. What is clear is that upon his arrival in France he was initially assigned to a battalion of the Dorsetshire Regiment and that he was later transferred to the 13th Battalion, Duke of Wellington's (West Riding Regiment). He continued to serve with this unit until the cessation of hostilities on 11th November 1918.

Having served and fought, avoiding injury and death on the battlefield, Frederick fell ill with bronchial pneumonia and died on the 9th February 1919. His body was laid to rest in Les Baraques Military Cemetery, Sangatte, France.

After his death his widow, Elizabeth, moved to a house in Lowell's Place, Witney and later, in 1921, she married James Temple.

J. Brice
Aircraftman 2nd Class, James Brice, 89509,
Royal Air Force

James Brice was born in Witney during the third quarter of 1883, the eldest son of Joseph, a plumber and glazier (later to be a house painter), and his wife Ellen (née Ilott). At the time of the 1901 census the family were living in Corn Street and James was employed as a house painter, working for his father. He married Ellen Brook in the fourth quarter of 1906 and the couple's first child, a son they named Alfred, was born a year later. A second child, Kathleen, was born in 1909. By 1911 James and his family were living in West End where he had established a business as both a house painter and picture framer. The couple's third child, Elsie, was born in 1912.

In the early stages of the war James joined the local Volunteer Battalion of the Oxfordshire and Buckinghamshire Light Infantry (OBLI) and in 1917 he was called up for regular military service in which his four younger brothers were serving in either the Navy or the Army. Within a short time he found himself attached to the fledgling Royal Air Force as an Air Mechanic.

By all accounts this genial man was as popular and well liked by all ranks within his Section in the RAF as he had been by the townspeople of Witney.[31] But unfortunately in late 1918 he, like so many others at that time, was struck down by influenza and despite the best medical attention he died on New Year's Day 1919 at the Milton Hill Military Hospital, Abingdon. His body was brought back to Witney where, on Saturday 4th January 1919, he was buried at Holy Trinity Church, Woodgreen. Full military honours, including a firing party, being provided by the Witney Platoon, 'A' Company, 2nd Volunteer Battalion of the OBLI under the command of Lieut. H.A. Steptoe. The *Witney Gazette* reported that the service was well attended by both family and friends.[32]

James Brice's grave, which can be found to the rear of the churchyard, is today marked by a Commonwealth War Grave headstone.

---

[31] *Witney Gazette,* 4th January 1919.
[32] *ibid*, 11th January 1919.

W.R. Bridgman
Private, Walter Richard Bridgman, 17299,
2nd Battalion,
Hampshire Regiment

Walter Bridgman, or 'Blackie' as he was known to his family and friends, was born in High Street, Witney, in the spring of 1892. He was the third son of Frederick, a blanket finisher, and his wife Prudence (née Pratley). At the time of the 1911 census the family were living in Ducklington and Walter was recorded as working as a woollen spinner in a blanket mill but by 1914 the family had returned to Witney and were living in a house on Bridge Street.

Although Walter's Army record has not survived, it is clear that he was amongst the first to volunteer for military service as he was deployed to France on the 29th November 1914. Initially he was assigned to a battalion of the Oxfordshire and Buckinghamshire Light Infantry but once his training had been completed, at a base depot in France, he was redeployed to the 2nd Battalion of the Hampshire Regiment and returned to England, in early February 1915, to join his new unit. Transfers of this kind were commonplace especially if, at the time of completing basic training, a soldier's designated battalion was already at full strength and another unit in was in need of replacements. The 2nd Hampshires, as part of 88th Brigade, 29th Division, had originally been intended for service in France but had subsequently been selected to take part in the ill fated attempt in the Dardanelles. On 12th March 1915 the entire Division was paraded for inspection by King George V, at Stretton-on-Dunsmore, Warwickshire. It then moved to Avonmouth, Bristol, where, on 16th March, it embarked aboard troop ships bound for Gallipoli.

On the 25th April 1915 Walter's unit, along with the rest of the 29th Division, landed under heavy fire from the Turkish defenders at Cape Helles. The resistance they encountered was so fierce that an Allied naval bombardment of the enemy positions was called for in order to extricate the attacking force, which for nearly twenty-four hours had not been able to advance further than the water's edge. Following the bombardment, the infantry began their advance and infiltrated the Turkish defences. By the evening of the 27th April the Allies had managed to occupy the toe of the Gallipoli Peninsula to a depth of about two miles, with a further beachhead being established to the north by the

Australian and New Zealand Army Corps (ANZAC's). From this point on repeated attempts to break out of the Helles beachhead and join up with the ANZACs was continually thwarted by the Turks, who stubbornly refused to give up any ground.

During their time at Gallipoli the men of the 2nd Hampshires were engaged in the battles for the fortified village of Krithia and the Achi Baba Heights, a prominent hill feature close by the village - the possession of which was felt at the time to be the key to any further Allied advance. The campaign in the Dardanelles lasted until December 1915 when the military authorities, pressured by public opinion, realised the futility of a continuation of the operation and ordered a full evacuation. The last British soldiers left the peninsula on the 9th January 1916.

There was never any official confirmation as to how Walter Bridgman was killed. His medal roll index card merely records his demise as *Presumed dead 6/8/15*", the day on which the Allies launched a fresh offensive. His body was never identified and he has no known grave. Today his name is recorded on the Helles Memorial, at Gallipoli, alongside the names of over 21,000 other British and Commonwealth soldiers, who died during operations on the peninsula.

A.E. Brooks
Private, Albert Edward Brooks, 23803,
7th Battalion,
Oxfordshire & Buckinghamshire Light Infantry

Albert Brookes was born in Cogges during the third quarter of 1887, the youngest son of Thomas, a former woodsman and his wife Ann (née Gardner). At the time of the census of 1891 the family were living at *The Royal Oak* public house in High Street where Thomas was the landlord. In the late spring of 1900 Albert's father died and responsibility for the pub passed to his widowed mother. As a young man Albert was also engaged in the brewery trade, being recorded in the census of 1901 as a maltster[33]. On the 19th December 1905, in the village of Fawkham, Kent, he married Laura Hollands, a

---

[33] One who prepared the malt for the later stages of brewing beer.

domestic servant and native of Fawkham. Following their marriage the couple came to Witney and, by 1911, were living in the town's Market Square. At this time Albert was employed as a domestic gardener. They had five children: Mary born in 1906, Laura 1908, Albert 1911, Hubert 1913 and Iris in 1916.

It is unclear when Albert first enlisted in the Army but it is clear from his record of medal entitlement that he was not deployed overseas until some point after January 1916 when he was sent to Salonika in northern Greece as part of a draft to reinforce the 7th Battalion of the Oxfordshire and Buckinghamshire Light Infantry, who had been in that theatre of operations since November 1915.

On the 22nd April 1917 the British launched a large scale offensive operation against the Bulgarian forces towards Varder and Dorian. The aim was to smash through the Bulgarian defences and affect a major breakthrough in the Balkans. The attack, which had been preceded by a four day artillery barrage, was initially successful but an enemy counter attack soon forced the British to retreat with heavy casualties. The fighting continued intermittently and on the 8th May the British, under pressure from their High Command, launched a second large scale attack. At 9 p.m., following an intense artillery barrage, the British troops went 'over the top'. Four attacks were made against the Bulgarian positions during the night of the 8th/9th May 1917 and each one was repulsed with huge loss of life.

One of those killed that night was Albert Brooks. His body was never identified and he has no known grave. Today his name is remembered on the Dorian Memorial, Northern Greece, alongside the names of more than 2,000 Commonwealth soldiers who died on the Macedonian Front and who have no known graves.

Albert's widow, Laura, married again in 1919 to Percy Andrews in Watford, Hertfordshire.

F.R. Brooks
Driver, Frederick Reginald Brooks, 616392,
158th Brigade,
Royal Horse Artillery
(Nephew of Albert Brooks, killed in action, Salonika, 9th May 1917)

Frederick Brooks was born in Witney during the first quarter of 1897, the eldest son of Jesse, a brewery worker, and his wife Elizabeth (née Prior). At the time of the 1911 census Frederick was living with his family in Market Square and working as a gardener's labourer.

Frederick's date of enlistment is unknown, however, it is clear that having joined the army and completed his basic training he was posted to the 2/1st Berkshire Battery of the Royal Horse Artillery – a territorial unit first established in 1914 and based in the UK. The 2/1st, along with several other Territorial batteries, was incorporated in April 1917 into the newly formed 158th Brigade which was despatched to France on the 24th May 1917.

On the 9th July the 158th Brigade took up positions, two and a half miles south-east of Ypres, near Zillebeke Lake - an area prone to persistent enemy shelling. The official account of Frederick's fate states that it was here, on the 12th July 1917, that he was killed in action. But if this was the case it is surprising that he was not buried in one of the cemeteries more local to his battery's position. Instead he is buried in the Lijssenthoek Military Cemetery in Poperinge, six miles west of Ypres, where all but 41 of the 9,901 burials are of men who died whilst being treated at the nearby medical facilities. Therefore it is more likely that he died as a result of wounds received in action.

T. Broom
Private, Thomas John Broom, 9037,
2nd Battalion,
Oxfordshire & Buckinghamshire Light Infantry

Thomas Broom was born in Witney during the summer of 1881, the second son of Thomas, a blanket weaver, and his wife Sophia (née Beechey). By 1901 Thomas was working in the town as a grocer's assistant. In the summer of 1910 he married Gertrude Cottrill of Cheltenham and on 27th December that year their first child was born, a son they named Leonard. In the 1911 census Thomas, who was by then employed as a groom, was recorded as living with his young family in Corn Street. In early 1913 the couple's second child was born, a daughter they named Ivy.

Thomas volunteered for military service upon the outbreak of war in August 1914 and on the 4th January 1915 he landed in France to be attached to the 2nd Battalion of the Oxfordshire and Buckinghamshire Light Infantry, part of the 2nd Division, alongside many of his fellow townsmen. The battalion took its turn rotating through the front line and support trenches with regular periods spent 'out of the line' and away from the front, in reserve. But in May 1915 the 2nd Division was chosen to participate in a large support operation, assisting the French in their offensive near Arras. The British were to launch their first night attack of the war along a three mile front from Neuve Chapelle in the north to the village of Festubert in the south. The aim of which was to draw the German forces away from the area currently being attacked by the French. The assault, planned to commence on the night of the 15th May, was to be preceded by a 60 hour long artillery bombardment of the German lines.

It was during this preliminary bombardment, that Thomas Broom, in all probability a victim of retaliatory German shell fire, was mortally wounded. He died on the 13th May 1915. The site of his final resting place is unknown but it is probable that it was on, or very near to, the battlefield upon which he was due to fight. Today his name is recorded, alongside over 13,000 other British soldiers who fought in the area, on Le Touret Memorial, near the village of Festubert, France.

Towards the end of 1916 Thomas's widow, Gertrude, was married to Gordon England in the district of Banbury, Oxfordshire.

E.G. Brotherton
Corporal, Ernest George Visto Brotherton, 11603,
2/4ᵗʰ Battalion,
Oxfordshire & Buckinghamshire Light Infantry

Ernest Brotherton was born in Stepney, London, during the autumn of 1895, the only son of George, a native of Leafield and former Royal Navy sailor, and his wife Esther (née Bull). At the time of the 1901 census Ernest's father, who had originally found work as a labourer upon his discharge from the Navy, was working as a fireman at the Fire Station in Tabernacle Square, Shoreditch. But within ten years he had left the Fire Brigade and had brought his family to Witney where, by 1911, they were living on the Burford Road. At the time of that year's census both Ernest and his father were recorded as working in the blanket factories, his father as a weaver and Ernest as a spinner.

Ernest volunteered for military service on the 1ˢᵗ September 1914 and was posted to 'A' Company of the newly formed 6ᵗʰ Battalion of the Oxfordshire and Buckinghamshire Light Infantry (OBLI), part of the 20ᵗʰ (Light) Division. After an extensive period of training and equipping the Division was inspected by King George V on 24ᵗʰ June 1915, at which time it was deemed ready to go to war.

On 23ʳᵈ July 1915 the 6ᵗʰ OBLI landed at Boulogne and, within several days, the entire Division was concentrated in the Saint-Omer area. Following a brief period of trench familiarisation and further training in the Fleurbaix area the Division went into the line. It was to remain on the Western Front for the rest of the war being involved in many notable engagements including the Somme Offensive of 1916; the German retreat to the Hindenburg Line; the Third Battle of Ypres and the Cambrai Operations in 1917. In February 1918 the 6ᵗʰ OBLI was disbanded and its soldiers redeployed to the Regiment's 2/4ᵗʰ and 5ᵗʰ Battalions with Ernest, by now a Corporal, one of two hundred men joining the 2/4ᵗʰ OBLI, part of the 61ˢᵗ (South Midland) Division.

By the end of March 1918 the 61ˢᵗ Division was engaged in covering a huge British withdrawal on the Somme as the Germans launched what was to become their final offensive of the war. During the Battles of the Lys (9ᵗʰ – 29ᵗʰ April) the Division took many casualties but as the tide of war turned, the British began once again to advance against the Germans. By the middle of

October the 61st Division was in action during the Final Advance in Picardy. As the Germans retreated on a line from Verdun to the sea they needed to protect their centre from being pierced and their flanks attacked, consequently the German rear-guards put up stiff resistance, and every village and hamlet had to be fought for. On the 24th October 1918 the men of the 2/4th OBLI, advancing rapidly in artillery formation[34] from Haussy, attacked and took the high ground east of Bermerain[35]. It was during this encounter that Ernest Brotherton was killed in action.

Ernest was originally buried on the battlefield but after the Armistice his grave was moved to the Romeries Communal Cemetery Extension, in the village of Romeries, France.

F.E. Buckingham
Driver, Frank Ernest Buckingham, 177422,
'B' Battery,
190th Brigade,
Royal Field Artillery

Frank Buckingham was born in the summer of 1890 at the family home in Buckle's Yard – opposite the bottom of Narrow Hill, Witney – the youngest son of John and his wife Sarah (née Buckle). Frank's father, a native of Eynsham, worked for many years as a porter at the Witney railway station but, during the first decade of the twentieth century, he took up farming. Frank's older brother, Frederick, had, like his father, begun working for the railway, initially as a clerk and by 1911 as Station Master at the small railway station in Shipston on Stour, Warwickshire. Frank however, was to follow a different path. Having completed his education at the Witney Grammar School he started working for his father on their farm, *High Croft*, in Hailey. After 1911 the family moved to *Holly Court* farm, which lies just to the north of North Leigh,

---

[34] A method of deploying a formation of men in a dispersed but organised fashion to decrease the unit's vulnerability to enemy artillery and machine gun fire.
[35] Rose, G.K., The Story of the 2/4th Oxfordshire & Buckinghamshire Light Infantry, B.H. Blackwell, Oxford, 1920. (p.218)

and it was whilst he was living there that, in 1915, Frank volunteered for service with the Army.

Following his basic training Frank was posted to 'B' Battery, 190th Brigade, Royal Field Artillery, part of the 41st Division, which landed in France during the first week of May 1916. By the 8th May the entire Division was concentrated in an area between the towns of Hazebrouk and Bailleul, approximately twelve miles south-west of Ypres. From this point onwards it remained in action on the Western Front until October 1917, taking part in the latter phases of the Somme offensive during the late summer of 1916, the Battle of Messines in the following June and then phases of the Third Battle of Ypres, or "Passchendaele" as it is more commonly known, which began in July 1917.

On the 9th August 1917, within the first few weeks of the Passchendaele Offensive, Frank Buckingham was killed in action. His body now lies in La Clytte Military Cemetery, in the village of De Klijte (formerly La Clytte), five miles west of Ipres, Belgium.

After the war Frank's parents moved back into Witney and in the early 1920's they were living at *Woodside*, on Woodgreen.

G.W. Burford
Lance Corporal, George William Burford, S/1547,
13th Battalion,
Rifle Brigade (The Prince Consort's Own)

George Burford was born in Witney around May 1892, the youngest son of William, an engineer's store keeper, and his wife Harriett (née Usher). In 1901 the family were living in Cape Terrace, in Gloucester Place and by the time of the 1911 census they had moved to a house in the Crofts. In that same census George, still living with his parents, was recorded as working for the Witney Gas Company as a gas fitter.

When the war started in 1914 George was quick to enlist. He was attested at Warwick on the 3rd September 1914, posted to the Rifle Brigade and, following his basic training, assigned to 'C' Company of the 10th Battalion. His unit was deployed to France on the 22nd July 1915 as part of the 20th (Light) Division but in February 1916 he was sent back to England for medical treatment, after suffering from the effects of the cold and damp in the trenches. When he returned to France in July 1916, he was re deployed to the 13th Battalion, Rifle Brigade, part of the 37th Division and was to remain on the Western Front for the next two years, fighting with his unit.

As the war entered its final phase in the autumn of 1918 the Allied forces on the Western Front were pushing the German Army back ever further. Following on from their success at the earlier Battle of the Selle, the Allied commanders planned a final advance to end the war and on the 4th November 1918 the 37th Division assaulted the German positions in the Forest of Mormal, near the Franco-Belgian border. It was during the ensuing battle that Lance Corporal George Burford was killed. He was buried alongside thirty of his Battalion comrades in the Ghissignies British Cemetery, near the village of Ghissignies, France, which had been taken by the 37th Division just a week earlier.

George's older brother, John, had also volunteered and served with the Oxfordshire and Buckinghamshire Light Infantry. He survived the war and returned home to Witney with the rank of Regimental Quartermaster Sergeant, having been earlier mentioned in despatches for gallant conduct and awarded the Meritorious Service Medal whilst on active duty. He died in Witney in 1979.

A.C. Busby
Gunner, Alfred Charles Busby, 154293,
87th Battery,
2nd Brigade,
Royal Field Artillery

Alfred was born the illegitimate son of blanket weaver Mary Ellen Busby, at his grandparents' home on Woodgreen, Witney, during the summer of 1897. In the spring of 1910 his mother married William Broom and the couple set up home in a small three roomed house on the Crawley Road. Alfred however remained with his elderly grandparents, Thomas and Jane, in the larger house where he had grown up. After leaving school he found work as an errand boy at a local grocer's shop.

He joined the Army in 1916 and was posted to the Royal Field Artillery. In December of that year, following his basic training, he was deployed to France where he was attached to the 87th Battery, 2nd Brigade, part of the 6th Division. He remained with his battery on the Western Front through numerous actions, until the ceasefire on 11th November 1918, at which point his unit became part of the occupying force within a defeated Germany.

In February 1919 Alfred was allowed home on leave but upon returning to his unit at Euskirchen in Germany he fell ill with influenza. This developed into pneumonia and on Thursday the 23rd February 1919, several days after his admission to the 42nd Stationary Hospital in the town, he died. His mother was later informed that he had been given a full military funeral and buried in the small cemetery just outside the town.

In 1922 it was decided to consolidate the burial sites of all the Commonwealth soldiers who had died in Germany into four large permanent cemeteries. As a result, in 1923, Alfred's remains, along with all those from the Euskirchen Cemetery and those from 182 other sites, were moved to the Cologne Southern Cemetery, Koln, Germany.

J. Chapman[36]
Private, George Chapman, L-481,
17th (Duke of Cambridge's Own) Lancers

George Chapman was born at Newland in the first quarter of 1886, the eldest child of James, a general labourer, and his wife Alice (née Radburn). By the time of the 1901 census both George and his father were employed within the town's woollen industry; George as a wool spinner and James as a blanket finisher. A former member of the 1st Witney Company of the Boys Brigade, George joined the Army around 1905 and was posted to the 17th (Duke of Cambridge's Own) Lancers, which throughout George's pre-war service was based in India.[37]

---

[36] Wrongly inscribed on the Memorial.

[37] At the time of the 1911 census the 17th Lancers were stationed at the Edward Barracks, Sialkot, in the Punjab, India.

Within the first weeks of the war the 17th Lancers were deployed from India, as part of the 1st Indian Cavalry Division, arriving in France on the 8th November 1914. However George Chapman had arrived in France a month earlier on the 6th October, along with a number of his comrades. It is likely that these men having served their time with the colours, had passed to the Army Reserves and, upon the declaration of war, had been mobilised to join their parent unit when it arrived in France.

On the 21st October 1914, two weeks before his old unit arrived on the Western Front, George Chapman was killed in action. He has no known grave and today his name is remembered on the Ypres (Menin Gate) Memorial, Ieper, Belgium.

H. Churchill
Private, Harry Churchill, SS/23077,
206th Labour Company,
Labour Corps

Harry Churchill was born in Reigate, Surrey, on the 18th November 1864, the only child of Samuel, a shoemaker, and his wife Mary (née Ellis). Records show that Mary died towards the end of 1864, possibly as a result of childbirth or complications arising directly afterwards and Samuel, left to raise his baby son alone, gave the child up to be cared for by another couple. Adoption, during this period was largely a localised, unregulated practice conducted between family members or people of the same town or district. With no records to confirm the ensuing events we must look forward several years to the census of 1871 where we find Harry Churchill, described as an orphan, still living in Reigate but with his 'adoptive' family; Thomas Amor, a whitesmith[38] originally from Bromham in Wiltshire, his wife Jane and their two sons; George aged 3 and Thomas aged 10 months.

By 1881 the family had moved to Witney and were living in the Crofts where Harry, aged 16, was in employment as a whitesmith's assistant to Thomas. In the spring of 1898 Harry married a Witney girl, Alice Bennett and

---

[38] One who works with 'white' or light coloured metals such as tin or pewter.

the couple moved to the industrial area of Llandudno in South Wales where Harry found work, probably in the Iron foundries there. The couple's two children, both daughters, were born during the brief time that they lived in Wales; Emily in late 1898 and Ellen in the summer of 1900. By the spring of 1901 the family were back in Oxfordshire, living in Cowley and Harry was working as a fettler[39] in an ironworks. A decade later, at the time of the 1911 census, Harry, now living near the Iffley Road in Oxford, was recorded as being employed as a domestic gardener. By August 1914 the family had moved once again, this time to Brighton on the south coast where Harry, now aged 50, was employed as a painter. In the autumn of 1914 Alice died and following her death Harry volunteered for military service.

After his basic training he was posted to the Army Service Corps and on the 13th December 1915 he left Southampton aboard the *SS Lydia* bound for France. Upon his arrival there Harry was attached to 206th Labour Company of the Labour Corps which at that time was based in and around the port of Le Havre. It was whilst he was working in the port on the 4th June 1917, moving a consignment of heavy ammunition that some of it fell on top of him. Seriously injured, Harry was immediately taken to the No2 General Hospital in the town where it was discovered he had sustained a fractured pelvis and severe rupturing of a number of internal organs. The surgeons operated and were able to stabilise his condition. Following surgery he remained at the hospital in Le Havre for almost three months before being transferred on the 30th August 1917 to the King George Hospital in London.

On 10th January 1918 a panel of the Army Medical Board met at the hospital and deliberated Harry's future in the Army. It was clear, given the terrible internal injuries he had sustained and the fact that he required constant care, that he would never be fit for either home or active service again. It was recommended by the panel that he be medically discharged from the Army and that he be provided with a water bed to ease his discomfort. The panel's recommendation, concerning his future in the Army, was accepted and Harry was officially discharged on the 31st January 1918. He remained a patient of the King George Hospital for a further eight months before finally being discharged on 16th October 1918 into the care of his adoptive parents, Thomas

---

[39] A machine cleaner.

and Jane Amor at their home on Church Green, Witney. It was here, on the 21st October 1918, sixteen months after that fateful accident, that Harry finally succumbed to his injuries.

He was buried in the town's cemetery where today his grave can be found marked by a Commonwealth War Graves Commission headstone.

T. Clack
Private, Thomas Clack, 18461,
5th Battalion,
Oxfordshire & Buckinghamshire Light Infantry

Thomas Clack was born in Witney during the third quarter of 1879, the youngest son of Thomas, a general labourer, and his wife Ellen (née Lewis). In the spring of 1898 Thomas married Harriett Wright and their only son, Albert, was born later that year. At the time of the 1901 census the couple were living in Lowell's Place and were both employed in the blanket industry; Thomas as a mill hand and Harriett as a blanket weaver. By 1911, still living in Lowell's Place, Thomas was recorded as a general labourer.

Thomas volunteered for military service in May 1915 and, following his basic training, he was deployed to France on the 18th September to join the 5th Battalion, Oxfordshire and Buckinghamshire Light Infantry (OBLI), part of the 14th (Light) Division. His unit fought through the winter of 1915/16 and then on the Somme during the great Allied offensive of the following summer. In the spring of 1917 the 5th OBLI were deployed in the Arras offensive and it is likely that during the opening phase of the offensive, now known as the First Battle of the Scarpe (9th – 14th April 1917), Thomas was wounded.

He was taken to the 32nd Casualty Clearing Station, sited between the villages of Warlincourt and Saulty, west of Arras, where he died from his wounds on the 13th April 1917. His body was buried in the Warlincourt Halte British Cemetery, Saulty, France.

G.W.C. Clanfield[40]
Driver, George William Clanfield, 94298,
'D' Battery,
65th (Howitzer) Brigade,
Royal Field Artillery

George Clanfield was born in Cumnor during the third quarter of 1891, the eldest son of Jesse, an agricultural stockman, and his wife Maria (née Costar). In the mid 1890's the family moved to Water Eaton and from there, around 1898, to High Cogges where, by the time of the 1911 census, George was working on a local farm as a 'horseman'.

Soon after the war began George volunteered for military service and following his basic training he was posted to 'D' Battery, 65th (Howitzer) Brigade, Royal Field Artillery, part of the newly formed 12th (Eastern) Division. The entire Division went into training near Aldershot from where, on the night of the 29th May 1915, it began its deployment to France. Travelling from Southampton the whole 65th Brigade, embarked aboard three troop ships to be ferried across the Channel to Le Havre.

Once in France the Brigade was ordered to en train for Wizernes and from there it was to move by road to Dohem for Divisional concentration. The first of the Brigade's trains left Le Havre at 10.25 p.m. on the 31st May and carried the brigade Head Quarters and 'A' Battery. Travelling via Abbeville, Boulogne, Calais, and St. Omer it arrived at Wizernes in the early hours of the 1st June. 'B' Battery followed, arriving shortly after at 5 a.m. and 'C' Battery around 11 a.m. However when 'D' Battery arrived at 7.30 a.m. it was reported to the Brigade Commander that George Clanfield had fallen from the moving train somewhere between Calais and St. Omer.[41]

Seriously injured from his fall he was taken to the No. 13 Stationary Hospital in Boulogne where on the following day (2nd June 1915), in the hospital's No. 6 Ward, he died. He was buried in the Boulogne Eastern Cemetery, Boulogne, France.

---

[40] Wrongly inscribed on the War Memorial.
[41] WO 95/1838

George's mother died in 1938 and his father in 1941. Both are buried in the Churchyard at Cogges. Upon their shared headstone George is remembered, albeit rather misleadingly, as having been *'killed in action in France 2nd June 1915, aged 23 years.'*

On the 27th May 1918, George's younger brother, Francis, who had enlisted a month before his brother's death, was captured by the Germans whilst serving with the 6th Battalion of the Royal Berkshire Regiment in France. Interned in a prisoner of war camp for the remaining months of the war he returned home to Witney in December 1918 and remained living in the local area until his death in 1988.

H.W. Clements
Private, Herbert William Clements, M2/097969,
No.1 General Headquarters,
Reserve Mechanical Transport Company,
Army Service Corps

Herbert Clements was born in Hailey during the third quarter of 1882 the eldest child of William, a labourer, and his wife Kate (née Dore). By the time of the 1891 census the family had moved into Witney where they were living in the High Street. They had moved again by 1911 when, in the census of that year, they were recorded as living in Bridge Street. At this point, Herbert, still living with his family, was working as a porter in a grocer's shop.

Herbert volunteered for military service within the first few months of the war and was duly posted to the Army Service Corps (ASC) – a huge and vital organisation responsible for keeping the army moving and adequately supplied. He deployed to France and the Western Front on the 22nd July 1915. Unfortunately no full record has survived detailing where he served and with which units, but it is known that at the time of his death he was attached to the No.1 General Headquarters (GHQ), Reserve Mechanical Transport Company, ASC. This unit, along with many others, came under the direct command of GHQ and not of any other subordinate unit such as a Division or Brigade.

Despite the lack of information it is likely, from the place of Herbert's burial, that he was wounded somewhere to the east of Peronne during the Allied pursuit of the German Army as it retreated in the closing weeks of the war. His wounds were serious enough for him to have been evacuated to, in all probability, the nearest Casualty Clearing Station, in this case one of a number operating on the site of the destroyed village of Tincourt, and it was here that he died of his wounds on the 9th October 1915. Today his grave can be found in the Tincourt New British Cemetery, in the village of Tincourt, several miles east of Peronne, France.

S. Cooper
Private, Sidney Cooper, 29403,
1st Battalion,
(Prince Albert's) Somerset Light Infantry

Sidney Cooper was born in Corn Street, Witney, during the summer of 1898, the ninth son of James, a stonemason, and his wife Susan (née Simpson).

In April 1917 Sidney joined the army and was posted to the Somerset Light Infantry (SLI). Following his basic training he was deployed to France in January 1918 to join the Regiment's 1st Battalion, part of the 4th Division, on the Western Front.

When the Germans unleashed their major spring offensive on the 21st March 1918 the 4th Division were holding the line on the northern bank of the River Scarpe, three and a half miles east of Arras. Although not attacked directly, the Divisional front was subjected to a concentrated artillery bombardment for several days, until the Germans attacked in force on the morning of the 28th March. The fighting lasted all day but eventually the Germans were beaten off. They attacked again the following morning and this time managed to breach the British front line. The men of the 1st SLI, who hadn't taken part in the fighting on the 28th, were pushed in to 'plug the gaps' and a number of men from the battalion managed to eject the attackers before following up with a counter attack of their own. This brave act came at a price and the casualties were high.[42]

---

[42] Majendie, V.H.B. Major D.S.O., <u>A History of the 1st Battalion The Somerset Light Infantry</u>, Goodman & Son, Taunton, 1921. (pp. 70-71)

Whether or not Sidney Cooper was one of those brave men who went 'over the top' in that small counter attack is not known, but his family were notified that on the 29th March he had been posted as 'missing in action'. Their hope was that in the absence of any further information he may have been taken prisoner by the Germans, but these hopes were dashed six months later when, at the beginning of October, they received official confirmation from the War Office that Sidney had in fact been killed in action on the 29th March 1918. His body was never identified and he has no known grave. Today his name is remembered on the Arras Memorial, Arras, France.

J. Cox
Private, James Cox, 54658,
13th Battalion,
Welsh Regiment

James Cox was born in Newland during the summer of 1883, the youngest son of Henry, a general labourer, and his wife Fanny (née Smith). At the time of the census of 1891 the family had moved and were living in one of several cottages in Gas Yard, off the High Street. Around 1899 James found employment working as a gardener at the Witney Grammar School, a job he was to retain until he later volunteered for military service. In the spring of 1907 he married Matilda Sollis and the couple's first child, a daughter, Ethel, was born on the 5th November that same year. In 1910 the couple's first son, Cecil was born, and he was followed by Florence in 1912, and George in 1915.

In June 1916 James joined the Army, initially being posted to the Worcestershire Regiment and then subsequently to the Herefordshire Regiment. In June 1917 he was deployed to France and transferred to the 13th Battalion, the Welsh Regiment, part of the 38th (Welsh) Division. In February 1918 he was allowed to return home to Witney on a brief period of leave before returning to France and re-joining his unit.

During the fighting of the 20th October 1918, in what was later to become known as the Battle of the Selle, James was both seriously wounded and gassed. He spent six weeks in hospital in France before being transferred to the Metropolitan Hospital in London. Where, shortly after his arrival, surgeons had to operate and amputate one of his legs. Unfortunately his wounds became infected and he died from septic poisoning on the 19th January 1919.

His body was brought home to Witney and on Thursday 23rd January 1919 he was buried with military honours in the town's Cemetery.

W. Cox
Private, William Alfred Cox, 200312,
'B' Company,
1/4th Battalion,
Oxfordshire & Buckinghamshire Light Infantry

William Cox was born at Southleigh during the summer of 1892, the son of Francis, a farm worker, and his wife Sarah (née Paine). At the time of the 1911 census William, living with his parents at Hill House in the village, was recorded as being employed as a farm labourer.

When war broke out in August 1914 William was quick to volunteer for military service and was posted to the newly formed 1/4th Battalion of the Oxfordshire and Buckinghamshire Light Infantry (OBLI), part of the 48th (South Midland) Division. On the 29th March 1915, following training and equipping, the Division was deployed to France and the Western Front where it was to remain until the spring of 1918. The 1/4th OBLI fought through the great Somme offensive of 1916 and the Third Battle of Ypres, or "Passchendaele" as it is more commonly known, in 1917.

In March 1918 the 48th Division was redeployed to northern Italy where it, along with another two British Divisions, had been sent to relieve Italian troops who had been holding the relatively quiet front line against the Austrians between Asiago and Canove. However, the comparative peace was short lived. On the 15th June 1918 the Austrians launched a large scale assault against the Allied forces in the area and, in what later became known as the Battle of Asiago, they penetrated the Allied line to a depth of 1,000 yards. It was during this attack on the 15th that William Cox was killed in action. The following day the Allies counter attacked, forcing the Austrians back and retaking the lost ground.

William was buried on the battlefield and today his grave can be found in the Boscon British Cemetery on the Asiago Plateau in Northern Italy.

C.H. Davis
Private, Claude Harry Davis, 6/1826,
1st Battalion,
Canterbury Infantry Regiment,
New Zealand Expeditionary Force

Claude Davis was born in the High Street, Witney, during the spring of 1889, the sixth son of Charles, a watchmaker, and his wife Rebecca (née Holliday). He received his education at the town's Wesleyan School and in the 1911 census he was recorded as working for the Great Western Railway as a booking clerk. In 1912 Claude emigrated to Christchurch, New Zealand where, by 1914, he had entered into business for himself.

On the outbreak of war Claude volunteered for military service and was duly posted to the 1st Battalion, Canterbury Regiment of the New Zealand Light Infantry. On the 17th April 1915, having completed his basic training, Claude, as part of the 4th Reinforcements,[43] left Wellington bound for Egypt. His unit was deployed at 'ANZAC Cove'[44] in the ill fated Dardanelles campaign where casualties amongst the Allied troops were high; indeed when the 1st Battalion were evacuated in December 1915, less than thirty of Claude's original Company left the peninsula with him.[45]

After Gallipoli the 1st Battalion returned to Egypt where they were used briefly in the defence of the Suez Canal Zone before being transferred to France in April 1916. Within a month Claude and his unit went into the line on the Western Front. In June 1916 Claude was granted his first period of leave since

---

[43] It was usual for detachments of colonial reinforcements to be deployed under a collective, non-operational, title, in this instance the '4th Reinforcements'. It was only after their arrival in theatre that the soldiers would have been attached to their operational units.

[44] Named after the colonial troops occupying the area - Australian and New Zealand Army Corps (ANZAC).

[45] *Witney Gazette*, 12th August 1916.

43

joining the army and he used it to visit Witney and his family. Upon returning to France he rejoined his unit at the front but within a very short time was fatally wounded in action. He died on the 30th July 1916.

Today his grave can be found in the Cite Bonjean Military Cemetery, Armentieres, France.

G.C. Dix
Leading Seaman, George Charles Dix, J/14543,
H.M.S. Hydra

George Dix was born in Witney on the 29th March 1896, the only son of John, a sailor, and his wife Annie (maiden name unknown). At the time of the census in 1901 George was recorded as living in Gosport with his mother, his father being away at sea. By 1911 the family had moved to Witney where they had all secured jobs within the town's blanket industry: George, his mother and elder sister all working for W. Early & Co. whilst his father, in addition to drawing a small naval pension, had a job with W. Smith & Co. But life as a mill hand in the spinning shop of Early's mill was not enough for George. On the 5th October 1911 he joined the Royal Navy at Portsmouth, as a Boy 2nd Class. In March 1914, upon reaching the age of 18, he transferred to the adult service and signed on for a period of twelve years.

On the 17th August 1914 George joined *HMS Dryad*, a minesweeper, which operated as part of the Royal Navy's 'Northern Patrol' off the coast of Scotland during the period October 1914 to February 1915. Whilst serving aboard the *Dryad* he gained promotion from Ordinary Seaman to Able Seaman and eventually, in February 1917, to Leading Seaman. It was around this time also that he was married to Emma Louisa Beckett of Lowestoft, Norfolk. On the 6th June 1917 George joined his new ship at Devonport Naval Base - *HMS Hydra*, a 990 ton Acheron Class Destroyer, part of the Navy's 3rd Battle Squadron.[46]

The *Hydra* put to sea on the 1st September 1917, bound for the Mediterranean, where she was to remain until the end of the war. However George did not make it that far. He fell dangerously ill with influenza and died

---

[46] ADM 188/676

on the 13th October 1918. His body was buried in the Staglieno Cemetery in Genoa[47], Italy.

In 1922 George's widow, Emma, married Henry Linder at Norwich.

G. Eaton
Private, George Richard Eaton, T/202272,
3/4th Battalion,
The Queen's (Royal West Surrey Regiment)

George Eaton was born at the family home in Church End, Standlake, during the autumn of 1882, the youngest son of Alfred, a farm labourer, and his wife Sarah (née Hanslow). In the census of 1901 he was recorded as working as a groom and gardener but during the following decade his occupation changed and by the time of the next census in 1911 he was described as a bread baker although on census night itself it was noted that he was actually out of work. At some point during the next few years George moved out of his parents' home in Standlake and came to live in Witney.

It is unclear exactly when George joined the army but it is known that when he was deployed to France and the Western Front he went as a member of the 3/4th Battalion, The Queen's (Royal West Surrey Regiment). The Battalion landed at Le Havre on the 1st June 1917 and following attachments to several Divisions was, on the 9th August 1917, eventually incorporated into the 21st Division in preparation for the Third Battle of Ypres, or "Passchendaele" as it is more commonly known.

On the 1st October 1917 the battalion was at Zillebeke, approximately 1½ miles south east of Ypres. From here they moved into the front line near Polygon Wood and in the early hours of the 4th October, advancing behind a creeping barrage, they attacked the German lines and despite fierce resistance were successful in gaining ground. An enemy counter attack was repelled and over the following three days the men of the 3/4th, under almost continuous and heavy artillery fire, held on. Relief came on the night of the 7th October when

---

[47] Genoa was a base for Commonwealth forces and three military hospitals were posted in the city. It is unknown if George Dix was brought ashore for burial or whether he died after having been transferred to one of the military hospitals in the city.

their section of the line was taken over by a company of the 1ˢᵗ Royal Welch Fusiliers.

The 3/4ᵗʰ were withdrawn to the southern bank of Zillibeke Lake where they spent the night of the 8ᵗʰ in, as the battalion diarist recorded, '...*appalling weather conditions*' where the '...*men suffered from lack of shelter*'[48]. On the 9ᵗʰ the battalion moved further out of the line to the village of Sercus where they were given more comfortable billets in the farms on the edge of the village. The battalion diary entry for the 10ᵗʰ October 1917 records that the '*day devoted to rest & cleaning up. Casualties O.R.* [other ranks] *4 killed 3 wounded*'[49]. One of those killed that day at Sercus was George Eaton, although the exact nature of his death is unknown.

Today his grave can be found in the Tyne Cot Cemetery near the Belgian village of Passchendaele. In addition to his name being recorded on the Witney War Memorial he is also remembered on the war memorial in his native village of Standlake.

E. Elliott
Private, Edwin Elliott, 2631,
2/4ᵗʰ Battalion,
Oxfordshire & Buckinghamshire Light Infantry

Very little is known about the E. Elliott recorded on the Witney War Memorial, and the information that is available appears contradictory and confusing. From the list published in the *Witney Gazette* at the time, he was one of the original 'Witney Company', that gallant group of young men who marched through the town to the railway station on 1ˢᵗ September 1914 in order to travel to Oxford and enlist.[50] That same list indicated those volunteers who were refused for medical reasons but it did not include E. Elliott, therefore one has to assume that he was accepted into the Army at that time.

The Commonwealth War Graves Commission (CWGC) holds the records of two men named 'E. Elliott' who were killed whilst serving with the

---

[48] WO 95/2156/1

[49] *ibid.*

[50] *Witney Gazette*, 5ᵗʰ September, 1914.

Oxfordshire and Buckinghamshire Light Infantry during the First World War. The first was Edgar Elliott, whose parents lived in Brixton, London and the second was Edwin Elliott whose father is recorded as living in Chickerell, Dorest. Research completed earlier by Jacqui Broome of the CWGC[51] seems to favour Edwin Elliott as being the man recorded on the Witney memorial. His service details are as listed above and he was killed in action on the 25th June 1916. However the surviving records suggest that Edwin enlisted at Chickerell in Dorset and not at Oxford.

Despite the lack of evidence it is clear is that E. Elliott did qualify for inclusion upon the Witney War Memorial and therefore further research is needed.

A.W. Englefield
Private, Alresford William Englefield, 9205,
2nd Battalion,
Oxfordshire & Buckinghamshire Light Infantry

Alresford Englefield, known as 'Will', was born in Brimpton, Berkshire, in the spring of 1879 the son of William, a labourer and former soldier, and his wife Flora (née Butler). When Will was just two years old his elder sister, Harriett, died. A tragedy which was compounded by the death of his mother around the same time. William was left to bring up his young son alone and did not remarry until 1886 when Mary Chaplin became his second wife. Will left school and initially worked as a gardener but on the 14th December 1897, aged 18½ years, he enlisted in the Army to serve with the Oxfordshire Light Infantry.

Far from being a model soldier, it appears that Will did not take to Army life as well as he may have hoped. Within six months he had deserted, been recaptured and imprisoned. He was *'released to his duty'*, whilst awaiting his trial, but insubordination towards a senior officer put him back in prison. He was duly punished and allowed to remain with his battalion, although his total

---

[51] Broome, J.A., <u>Roll of Honour of Servicemen and Women from Witney and Cogges who lost their lives during the 1914-1918 and 1939-1945 World Wars</u>, unpublished, copy held at the Witney and District Museum.

period of service was recalculated to start from the date of his recapture. It was not an auspicious start to a military career but, to use a well worn cliché, his experiences seem to have made a man of him and, following his poor start, Will settled down and applied himself to being a good soldier.

In October 1899 he was posted with his battalion to India where he studied for his third and then second class certificates of education. When his battalion returned to the UK in early 1906 Will was promoted to the rank of Lance Corporal, a rank he had held temporarily and unpaid for the previous eighteen months. In the summer of 1906 he transferred to the reserves having completed his initial engagement and in August 1910 he was officially released from his military obligation having served both his time with the colours and with the reserves. However, he chose to extend his term of reserve service for another four years - a term due to expire on the 4th August 1914.

Following his military service Will moved to Witney and by the time of the 1911 census he was living in West End, Witney, working as a postman. When the declaration of war came in 1914 his time as a reservist had just expired but, eager to do his duty, Will re-enlisted as a private in the Territorials and, on the 9th November 1914, he landed in France to join his old unit; the 2nd Battalion of the Oxfordshire and Buckinghamshire Light Infantry (OBLI), 2nd Division.

During the next eight months Will fought with his battalion on the Western Front through the First Battle of Ypres and through the winter of 1914/15. Despite the privations that he must have suffered alongside his comrades in the trenches he appears to have retained his sense of humour as this letter, sent to the Witney Gazette in February 1915, testifies:

> *"**Football at the Front**. The following account of a football match at the front will be of interest to our readers:-*
>
> *British v Germans.*
>
> *Played on neutral ground, Feb 6th 1915. Our opponents were the first to take the field. At once welcoming us with a few of their "Jack Johnsons", our left wing was knocked out. At 2pm we kicked off, making a fine rush down the field to the Barricade. Having a tussel in the mid-field for a short time. It was a bit of "ding-dong" sort of passing, but with the help of our (Field Guns) halves, and our (Long Toms) backs, we began to press home the forwards, making a*

48

demonstration which held them in check for a time. Then with a rush,
our "right wing" got well away, capturing the "triangle". This was
the one and only goal of the day, Result:

> *British   1 goal*
> *Germans   nil*

Proving a clear win for the "contemptible little army". The losing
side, to show no ill feeling, gave us a splendid display of "fire works"
at night, and when it is too light for any more of their "fireworks" we
are giving them a hearty send off.
Now! Are we disheartened? No.
From A.W. Englefield, a Witney postman, with the Oxford & Bucks
Light Infantry- "doing his 'wee bit' at the front"[52]

Life in the trenches continued much as before for the men of the 2nd OBLI
with spells in the front and support lines and in reserve. However in May 1915
the 2nd Division was chosen to participate in a large support operation to assist
the French in their offensive near Arras. A night attack, the first one of the war
undertaken by British troops, was to be made along a three mile front from
Neuve Chapelle in the north to the village of Festubert in the south. The aim of
which was to draw German forces from the area currently being attacked by the
French. The assault, which had been preceded by a 60 hour long artillery
bombardment, began on the night of the 15th May and, although much of the
German defences remained intact, some progress was made. But casualties
were high.

Private T. Gregory of the 2nd OBLI, writing home to his mother after the
battle, described the event:

> *"...We lost nearly all our officers and about half of the men in our*
> *regiment, but we took the trenches away from the Germans. The*
> *slaughter was terrible. We knew what we had to face before we*
> *started, and our chaplain read a prayer. The attack started at 11 p.m.,*
> *and it was hot work for 48 hours. The Germans were driven out and*
> *mown down by rifle fire. The 2nd Oxford and Bucks were*

---

[52] *Witney Gazette*, 20th February 1915.

complimented afterwards for their good work ... We shall never forget it as long as we live. We lost about 22 officers and 500 men killed and wounded. Since that attack we have kept the enemy on the move and we don't think the war will last much longer; at least we hope not. At present we are out of the trenches for a rest, and we have been relieved by troops fresh from home; let them have a go at it, I wish them luck. There was not a man amongst us, I should think, who did not think of those he had left behind that night. There were dozens of regiments in that attack; we all had different parts to take, and we did more than the Generals expected us to do. We thank God we got through all right...[53]

Unfortunately Will Englefield did not get through. At the time it was thought that he had been wounded in the early stages of the battle but his body was never recovered and therefore it is only presumed that he was killed on the 16th May 1915. His name, alongside the names of over 13,000 other British soldiers who fought and died in the area and whose bodies were never identified, is recorded on Le Touret Memorial near the village of Festubert, France.

H.F. Evans
Private, Herbert Frederick Evans,
6th Battalion,
Oxfordshire & Buckinghamshire Light Infantry

Herbert Evans, or 'Bert' as he was known, was born in Corn Street in the third quarter of 1894 the only son of Frederick, a 'cattle doctor and castrator', and his wife Emma (née Harris). In the census of 1911 Bert was recorded as being employed as a grocer's assistant.

Exactly when Bert enlisted is unknown but it is evident that he had joined and served with the Queen's Own Oxfordshire Hussars (QOOH) for some time before he was sent abroad in 1916. He was deployed to France around September 1916 to join the QOOH but was transferred to the 6th Battalion,

---

[53] *ibid*, 29th May 1915.

Oxfordshire and Buckinghamshire Light Infantry (OBLI), part of the 20th (Light) Division, at the beginning of October.

On the 7th October 1916, during the Allied offensive on the Somme, the 6th OBLI engaged with the enemy in what was later to become known as the Battle of the Transloy Ridges. During the attack Bert Evans, at the front for just a week, was fatally wounded. He died later that day.

He has no known grave and his name is recorded on the Thiepval Memorial to the missing of the Somme, France.

A year later, on the 6th October 1917, a brief and touching message appeared in the *Witney Gazette*:

> *"In loving memory of my dear pal, Pte. Bert Evans, who died in France October 7th, 1916 – Jack Groves, Tank Corps, France."*

H.J.H. Foreshew
2nd Lieutenant, Henry John Hulbert Foreshew,
6th Battalion (attached to 3rd Bn.),
Rifle Brigade

Henry Foreshew was born on Church Green, Witney, during the third quarter of 1884, the seventh child and second son of Thomas, a brewer, and his wife, Rachel (née Clinch). Educated at the prestigious Berkhamsted School, by the time of the 1911 census he was living in Wanstead, north-east London and working for a firm of drug (pharmaceutical) merchants.

When war was declared in August 1914 Henry, still living in Wanstead, volunteered for military service, and was posted to the newly formed 10th Battalion of the Royal Fusiliers, part of the 18th (Eastern) Division. At the same time, back in Witney, his two brothers, Thomas and Charles, also volunteered and were both selected to undergo officer training[54]. When the 10th Battalion was deployed to France on the 30th July 1915 Henry had been promoted to the rank of Lance Corporal and, whilst in France, his ability to command was noted

---

[54] In March 1915 they were both gazetted as Second Lieutenants in the 3rd Battalion of the Oxfordshire & Buckinghamshire Light Infantry.

by his Commanding Officer. He was recommended for a commission and returned to England to undertake officer training at Cambridge. Upon successful completion of his training he was gazetted as a 2nd Lieutenant in the 6th Battalion of the Rifle Brigade, a depot unit based throughout the war in the UK.

At some point before April 1917 Henry was posted back to France and the Western Front, where he was attached to his regiment's 3rd Battalion, part of the 24th Division. In the spring of 1917, during the Arras Offensive, the 24th Division fought in the Battle of Vimy Ridge (9th – 12th April). Two days after the battle, on the 15th April 1917, Henry Foreshew was killed in action. His body was never identified and he has no known grave. Today his name is remembered on the Arras Memorial, Arras, France.

His two brothers survived the war. Charles, who was awarded the Military Cross for gallantry on the Western Front, returned home to Witney with the rank of Captain whilst Thomas ended his military career a Lieutenant. He too returned home to Witney, married and had children of his own. His only son, Thomas, served with the Rifle Brigade during the Second World War and was killed in action in June 1944. He is also commemorated on the Witney War Memorial.

E.J. Fowler
Private, Ernest Joseph Fowler, 200439,
'C' Company,
1/4th Battalion,
Oxfordshire & Buckinghamshire Light Infantry

Ernest Fowler was born in Witney during the early summer of 1897 and baptised at the Holy Trinity church, Woodgreen, on 1st August that same year. He was the sixth child and second son of Job, a brewer's labourer and former inn keeper, and his wife Emma (née Painter). At the time of the census of 1901 the family were recorded as living in the Crofts. Ernest was educated at St. Mary's School before being admitted to the town's Grammar School in January

1908. However, and despite having a four year exemption from fees, he left after 18 months and returned to elementary school.[55]

Ernest volunteered for military service on the outbreak of war and was assigned to the newly formed 1/4th Battalion of the Oxfordshire and Buckinghamshire Light Infantry (OBLI), part of the 48th (South Midland) Division. In April 1915 the Division was deployed to France and the Western Front. However Ernest, still only eighteen years old and therefore not old enough to be sent on active duty overseas, was left behind. It was not until he had turned nineteen, two months later that he was allowed to join his unit. Once on the Western Front he fought with his battalion throughout the great Allied offensive on the Somme in 1916 and during the German retreat to the Hindenburg Line[56] in the spring of 1917.

On the night of the 5th/6th August 1917 the 1/4th OBLI moved into the trenches along the line of a ditch known as the 'Steenbeeck', near Pilckem, in the Ypres Salient[57]. For the following three days the men holding the line were almost continually shelled by German artillery. Relief came during the early evening of the 8th August when the 1/6th Battalion of the Gloucestershire Regiment came into the line and the 1/4th OBLI moved back to Dambre Camp behind the line. The casualty list for the Battalion following their three days in the front line included 18 soldiers killed. One of those men was Ernest Fowler.

Several days later the Officer Commanding 'C' Company wrote to Ernest's father, describing his son as *"...one of the best fellows in the Company, knowing no fear, and willing to undertake any task no matter how dangerous"*. He had, the officer continued, been *"...instantaneously killed by a German high explosive shell..."*[58] during the battalion relief on the evening of the 8th August 1917. He was buried in a hastily arranged British cemetery and the hope was that in the future a proper cross would be put up to mark his grave. But this was not to happen. His grave was lost and today his name is remembered on the Ypres (Menin Gate) Memorial, Ieper, Belgium.

---

[55] Cavell, J., The Henry Box School – Its Place in History, The Henry Box School, Witney, 2009. (p.93)

[56] A vast system of pre-prepared German defensive positions in north-eastern France stretching from Lens to beyond Verdun.

[57] The bulge formed in the Allied front line as it skirted around the town.

[58] Letter published in the *Witney Gazette*, 25th August 1917.

J.H. Fowler
Private, John Henry Fowler, 54910,
3rd Infantry Labour Company,
Devonshire Regiment

John Fowler was born at Ironbridge, Shropshire, during the second quarter of 1882. By 1904 he was in Witney where, in the spring of that year, he married Ada Haley. The couple had two children; John, born in 1907 and Cyril in 1909. At the time of the 1911 census the family were living in Church Lane, Cogges, and John (senior) was employed in the town's woollen industry as a blanket fuller.

John enlisted before 1916 and was posted to the Oxfordshire and Buckinghamshire Light Infantry. In early 1917 he was transferred to Exeter where he joined the newly formed 3rd Infantry Labour Company of the Devonshire Regiment. In March 1917 this unit, along with the Regiment's eleven other Labour Companies, went to France whereupon they were all incorporated into the Labour Corps and re-designated, with John's unit becoming the 168th Labour Company.

The exact movements of the 168th Labour Company whilst on the Western Front in 1917 are unknown as are the details surrounding when and where John received the wounds which were to prove fatal. Nevertheless, given the fact that he is buried in the Lijssenthoek Military Cemetery, situated approximately seven miles west of Ipres, in Belgium it is likely that having been wounded he was evacuated there to a Casualty Clearing Station where he died on 30th October 1917.

H.T. Gardner
Private, Harry Thomas Gardner, 25347,
105th Company,
Machine Gun Corps

Harry Gardner was born in Witney during the fourth quarter of 1897, the fourth son of John, an ostler,[59] and his wife Elizabeth (née Poole). At the time of the 1901 census the family were living in Gas Yard, off the High Street. By 1911, when the next census was taken, they had moved to Corn Street and thirteen year-old Harry was recorded as being in employment as an errand boy working for a local family.

Exactly when Harry first enlisted in the Army is unknown because his military record has not survived and his record of medal entitlement was only completed once he was deployed overseas. However, given his age, it is likely that he joined up around the end of 1915 and was posted to the Gloucestershire Regiment. By the end of 1916, having received his basic training and having reached the age of nineteen, he was deployed to France to join a battalion of his regiment. It was whilst he was in France that he transferred to the Machine Gun Corps, joining the 105th Company MGC, part of the 35th Division.

By 12th October 1917, during the Third Battle of Ypres, or "Passchendaele" as it came to be known, the British had successfully linked up with the French on the southern outskirts of Houthulst Forest, to the north west of the ruined village of Poelcappelle. For the next ten days the British consolidated their newly won positions and repulsed repeated German counter attacks before going on the offensive again on the 22nd October. However, two days prior to this, on the 20th October 1917, Harry Gardner, had been killed in action whilst fighting with the 35th Division on this fiercely disputed front line.

Although today his grave is in the large, concentration cemetery of Artillery Wood, near Boezinge, Belgium, it is probable that initially he had been buried in a smaller battlefield cemetery and transferred to his final resting place after the Armistice.

---

[59] Employed to look after horses at an inn, hostelry or stable.

E. Godfrey
Gunner, Ernest Godfrey, 69624,
6th Battalion,
Tank Corps

Ernest Godfrey was born in Corn Street, Witney, during the third quarter of 1893, the third son of Jesse, a mop maker, and his wife Susannah (née Hickman). At the time of the 1911 census Ernest was working in the town as a milk carrier.

Ernest's military service record has not survived, and the evidence that does remain is scant, but it is clear that after initially enlisting and serving with the East Kent Regiment he transferred to the Tank Corps. It was as a member of the Tank Corps that Ernest went to France, sometime around 1917, where he was attached to the Corps' 6th Battalion.

On 21st March 1918 the Germans launched their massive spring offensive on the Western Front. An all-out effort to smash through the Allied lines and win the war before the newly arrived American troops could be deployed. On the day the offensive began Ernest was with his battalion in an area approximately 5½ miles south of Arras. The events of that day are best described in the words of his Captain, John Dashwood, taken from a letter sent to Ernest's mother:

> *"Dear Mrs Godfrey, It is my sad duty to have to inform you of your son's death as a result of a shell burst on the 21st of March. The shell landed just outside my office where he was employed as a runner, and I am thankful to say that he can have suffered no pain as his death must have been instantaneous, for I entered the office about 10 seconds after the explosion and he had passed away. He was buried in a cemetery close to Ficheux. I may say that he worked most willingly and cheerfully all the time he was with me, and I feel his death to be a personal loss..."* [60]

The cemetery in which Ernest was buried is now known as the Bucquoy Road Cemetery, just outside Ficheux in the Pas de Calais, France.

---

[60] *Witney Gazette*, 20th April 1918.

J. Godfrey
Lance Corporal, James Godfrey, 10418,
5th Battalion,
Oxfordshire & Buckinghamshire Light Infantry

James Godfrey was born in the village of Asthall around 1888, the eldest son of Thomas, a general labourer, and his wife Elizabeth (née Martin). By 1901 the family had moved to Minster Lovell and were living at 'Upper Crescent', which formed part of the Charterville Estate. Within the following decade James left home and moved to Deddington, (possibly around the same time that his parents moved from Minster Lovell to Tower Hill in Witney). In the spring of 1910 he married Rose Bennett from the nearby hamlet of Bishops Itchington, where the couple's only child, Ellen, was born later that year. On census night 1911 James, working as a fishmonger, was in Witney staying at his parent's home whilst Rose and the baby were staying with relations in Clifton, another hamlet near Deddington. It was in Clifton that the couple were to take up permanent residence in the last couple of years of peace prior to 1914.

James volunteered for military service on the outbreak of war in August 1914 and was posted to the newly formed 5th Battalion of the Oxfordshire and Buckinghamshire Light Infantry, part of the 14th (Light) Division. Following training and equipping the 5th Battalion were deployed to France on the 20th May 1915, at which time James held the rank of Lance Corporal. The 14th Division was in action at Hooge in late July 1915 where it had the misfortune to be the first to face German flame throwers and later, on the 25th and 26th September, it was in action again during the Second Attack on Bellewaarde.

It was during this action at Bellewaarde that James Godfrey was mortally wounded. It is likely that he was evacuated from the battlefield to Etaples, which at the time was home to a huge concentration of Commonwealth troops, stores and depots as well as a number of military hospitals. He died from his wounds on the 29th September 1915 and was buried in the nearby military cemetery. Today his grave can be found in the Etaples Military Cemetery, just to the north of the town of Etaples, France.

As well as being remembered on the Witney War Memorial, James is also commemorated on the War Memorial in Deddington and upon an engraved brass plaque inside Deddington Church.

A. Grant
Captain, Arch Grant,
'Z' Company,
1st Battalion,
Essex Regiment
(Elder brother of Ernest Grant, killed in action at 'High Wood', France, 30th July 1916)

Arch Grant was born in Witney around 1887, the fourth son of James, a tailor, and his wife Ellen (née Gardener). Educated at the town's Wesleyan and Bluecoat schools, he went on win one of the Holloway apprenticeships, administered by the Governors of the Witney Grammar and Technical School. Having served his apprenticeship with a saddler in the town he left Witney in 1911 and moved abroad to find work on the tea plantations of Ceylon (modern day Sri Lanka).

When Britain went to war in August 1914 so did the various forces of the Empire. In Ceylon a locally raised militia, recruited from amongst the white settlers of the tea plantations of which Arch was a member, was mobilised. On November 11th 1914, 8 officers and 229 other ranks of the Ceylon Planters Rifle Corps (CPRC) arrived in Egypt where they were initially used in the defence of the Suez Canal. On the 8th December 1914 this small colonial unit was attached to the New Zealand Expeditionary Force and incorporated into the Australia and New Zealand Army Corps (ANZAC). On the 5th April 1915, whilst at Salonika, Arch received a commission and was later with the CPRC when they landed on 'Z' beach at Anzac Cove during the Allied offensive in the Dardanelles. Following the evacuation of the Gallipoli peninsular in 1916, Arch was promoted to the rank of Captain and, leaving the CPRC, returned briefly to England. It was whilst he was in England that news reached him of his younger brother, Ernest's death. He had been killed in action at 'High Wood' near Longeuval, on the 30th July 1916, during the great Allied offensive on the Somme.

Arch was sent to France on the 23rd July 1917 where he joined the 1st Battalion of the Essex Regiment on the 19th September. It was whilst commanding 'Z' Company, 1st Essex, at the battle of Cambrai on 30th November 1917 that Arch was killed. Private Charles Holman MM, interviewed many years after, recalled that on the 30th he, as the company runner had been given a message by Captain Grant to take to Battalion Headquarters. As Holman began to leave his officer's side he turned to see Arch Grant falling to the ground having been shot in the head. He later found out that it had been Arch who had recommended him for the Military Medal that he was subsequently awarded.[61]

Arch Grant's body was never identified and he has no known grave. Today his name is remembered on the Cambrai Memorial, Louverval, France.

E.J. Grant
Private, Ernest Jesse Grant, 25621,
8th Battalion,
Gloucestershire Regiment
(Younger brother of Arch Grant, Killed in action at Cambrai, 30th November 1917)

Ernest Grant was born at the family home in Gloucester Place, Witney, during the first quarter of 1890, the youngest son of James, a tailor, and his wife Ellen (née Gardener). A former pupil of the town's Wesleyan Day School, by the time of the 1911 census he was living and working at the Cross Keys Hotel, Market Square, as an ostler.[62] When war broke out he joined the Witney Volunteer Training Corps, a First World War equivalent of the later Home Guard. In December 1915 he enlisted in the Army joining the 15th (Reserve) Battalion of the Gloucestershire Regiment.

In the early part of 1916 Ernest was posted to France, to reinforce the Gloucestershire's 8th Battalion, part of 19th Division, as they prepared for the Allied summer offensive on the Somme. The 19th Division went into action on the second day of the offensive, 2nd July 1916, attacking and taking the German held village of La Boiselle. The Division were to go into action on numerous occasions over the following weeks in support of the offensive and on the 30th July they were used again in the assault on the German held 'High Wood'. In

---

[61] See www.hellfire-corner.demon.co.uk/holman.htm
[62] Employed to look after horses at an inn, hostelry or stable.

the early evening the infantry, advancing behind a creeping barrage, moved towards the enemy positions. Fierce fighting ensued and, despite some limited success, the attack was deemed to have been an overall failure. It was during this attack that Ernest Grant was killed.

Today his body lies in the Caterpillar Valley Cemetery, Longeuval, France, just south of 'High Wood' and the battlefield upon which he died.

On the 30th November 1917 Ernest's older brother, Arch, was killed in action at Cambrai, France.

H. Green
Private, Herbert Green, 267331,
2/1st (Bucks) Battalion,
Oxfordshire & Buckinghamshire Light Infantry

Herbert Green was born in Southleigh at the beginning of 1892, the youngest son of farm labourer, Charles and his wife Mary (née Green). In the census of 1911 Herbert, still living with his family in the village, was recorded as being employed as a horseman on a local farm. In the third quarter of 1915 he married Emily J. Gomm, a domestic servant from Wheatley.

In 1915 Herbert volunteered for military service and was posted to the 2/1st (Bucks) Battalion of the Oxfordshire and Buckinghamshire Light Infantry (OBLI), part of the 61st (2nd South Midland) Division. The Division was deployed to the Western Front in May 1916, with the 2/1st OBLI landing in France on the 24th of that month, and concentrated in the Merville area. The arrival of the Division allowed other units to move further south in preparation for the Allied summer offensive on the Somme, where the 61st was destined to take its turn during the winter of 1916/17.

At the beginning of July 1917, on the eve of the Third Battle of Ypres, the British forces in and around Ypres were again preparing for a great offensive operation to break out of the Salient and, advancing north-eastwards, take the village of Passchendaele and continue on to secure the Belgian coast. The Battle began on 31st July, after a two week long artillery bombardment, but failed to make any headway. The 2/1st OBLI went into the front line on the night of the 21st/ 22nd August in preparation for an attack, scheduled for the following morning, on the German positions near St. Julien.

The 2/1st Bucks went over the top shortly after 5 am, attacking on the right of the 2/4th OBLI, and advancing behind a creeping artillery barrage. Casualties were light in the initial advance but upon reaching their objectives the numbers being killed and wounded by enemy machine gun and sniper fire steadily increased. With their ability to advance further and their movement generally being severely hampered by enemy fire, the attackers, seeking refuge in shell holes, were grimly forced to defend their strategically insignificant gains until they were relieved on the night of the 23rd/24th.

One of those casualties on the field of battle on the 22nd August 1917 was Herbert Green. His body was never identified and he has no known grave. Today his name is remembered on the Tyne Cot Memorial, Zonnebeke, Belgium.

At the time of Herbert's death his widow, Emily, was living at 59 The Crofts. It is believed that in early 1919 she married again to John Pugh.

A. Groves
Corporal, Albert Groves, MM (Military Medal)**, 13096,**
2nd Battalion,
Kings Own Yorkshire Light Infantry

Albert Groves was born in Corn Street in September 1891, the only child of John, a house painter, and his wife Mary (née Bridgwater). Following his education at the town's Wesleyan School, where *'he won the affection of teachers and scholars by his wonderfully cheerful and happy disposition and kindness of heart',*[63] he entered into an apprenticeship with local grocer, R.L. Walker. He joined the 1st Witney Company of the Boys Brigade and regularly attended evening classes at the Witney School of Science and Arts. It is a testament to his commitment that upon completion of his apprenticeship he was chosen to receive the highest award of £5 from the Governors of the Witney

---

[63] *Witney Gazette*, 21st September 1918.

Educational Foundation. At the time of the 1911 census Albert had left Witney and moved to Yorkshire.

Within the first few weeks of the war Albert presented himself at a recruiting station in Huddersfield and enlisted. He was accepted into the King's Own Yorkshire Light Infantry (KOYLI) and, following his basic training, posted to the Western Front on the 31st August 1915 where he joined the Regiment's 2nd Battalion, initially part of the 5th but from December 1915, part of the 32nd Division. Demonstrating the same sense of duty and commitment to his military career that he had in his civilian life he was soon marked out for promotion and on April 29th 1917 Albert, now a Lance Corporal, was awarded the Military Medal for *gallantry and devotion to duty in action.*[64]

The Battle of Amiens, which opened on the 8th of August 1918, heralded the beginning of the final phase of the Great War. The Allied forces, operating under strict secrecy, launched a highly organised and well planned attack against the Germans near Amiens, on the Somme. The attack took the Germans completely by surprise and the Allies advanced seven miles on the first day. The men of the 2nd KOYLI joined the fight on the following day and by the 13th August the British were 12 miles into the German positions.

On the 19th August 1918, during the continued Allied advance, Albert Groves was killed in action. In letter sent to his mother (his father had died in 1912) Sergeant J. Mair, one of Albert's former comrades, recounted that...

> *'...he was killed by a sniper whilst gallantly carrying out his duties in action. I ... can readily understand how heavily the blow will fall upon you, his mother, of whom he often spoke to me. I knew him from the time he joined us in France in 1915. Our work brought us together a great deal, and we were inseparable chums. He was a first class soldier and a splendid chum. As a son he must have been perfect. All who knew the boy loved him well, and his loss will be felt by officers and men alike...'*[65]

---

[64] The citation giving details of the specific event is unavailable.

[65] *Witney Gazette*, 21st September 1918.

Albert's body was never identified and he has no known grave. Today his name is remembered on the Vis-en-Artois Memorial, France, alongside the names of over 9,000 British, Irish and South African soldiers who were killed between the 8th August 1918 and the date of the Armistice and who also have no known grave.

P.E. Gunter
Lance Corporal, Percy Edward Gunter, 8972,
2nd Battalion,
Oxfordshire & Buckinghamshire Light Infantry

Percy Gunter was the son of William, a bricklayer, and his wife Caroline (née Howe). He was born in the village of East Woodhay, Hampshire, during the late summer of 1891 and appears to have been known variously by his second name, 'Edward' and, more strangely as 'Charles'.[66] By 1901 his family had moved to Ash, near Aldershot in Surrey. In early 1909 Percy volunteered for military service and at the time of the 1911 census he was at Elham in Kent, serving with the 2nd Battalion of the Oxfordshire and Buckinghamshire Light Infantry. It was not long after the census that he married Laura Griffiths, a young waitress who had worked in a cafe in the vicinity of the Army camp. In 1912, following Percy's discharge from the Army, the couple came to live in the Witney area and Percy began work as a porter and shunter at the town's railway station. By 1914 they were living in the nearby village of Ducklington.

When the order for general mobilisation was issued in August 1914 Percy, as a reservist, was immediately recalled to his regiment and posted to his old unit

---

[66] Although named upon the War Memorial as 'P.E. Gunter', the Commonwealth War Graves Commission records him as 'C.E. Gunter' and his record of medal entitlement as 'Charles E. Gunter.' He is described as C.E. Gunter in the official records of the Great Western Railway. On the 6th November 1915 a letter appeared in the Witney Gazette from a 'Private E. Gunter' of the 2nd Bn. Oxfordshire and Buckinghamshire Light Infantry. His obituary in the *Witney Gazette* (26th May 1917) described him as 'P.E. Gunter', a man who had formerly worked at the town's railway station. Throughout the records the date of death and the service number are the same, indicating that all the records relate to the same man.

which, by then, was part of the 2nd Division. Within days of war being declared the 2nd Division received orders to deploy to France, becoming one of the first formations to do so and Percy, alongside his comrades, landed at the port of Boulogne on the 14th August 1914.

During their time on the Western Front the units of the 2nd Division saw action in many of the major engagements of the war. In 1914 they were at Mons, and the subsequent retreat; in the battles of both the Marne and the Aisne in September and later, in October, at Ypres. By the end of the following year, having seen action at the battles of Festubert and Loos, Percy had been transferred to his battalion's Machine Gun Section. In 1916 the Division took part in the Allied summer offensive on the Somme and by the spring of 1917 it formed part of a pursuing force as the Germans retreated to their pre-prepared positions on the Hindenburg Line.

On the 9th April 1917 British and Commonwealth troops attacked the German lines near the French city of Arras. The aim of the attack was to draw German forces away from an area fifty miles to the south where the French launched the Nivelle Offensive. During what became known as the Battle of Arras, which lasted until the 16th May, the British were able to make a number of small scale gains, but at considerable cost in casualties, whilst the Canadians managed to take the strategically important Vimy Ridge.

It was during this operation that Percy Gunter, who had earlier in the war been wounded, became a casualty for a second time. This time his wounds were to prove fatal. He died at a casualty clearing station near the village of Aubigny on the 3rd May 1917 and was buried in the nearby Aubigny Communal Cemetery Extension, Aubigny-en-Artois, France.

A.E. Haggitt
Private, Albert Ernest Haggitt, 8621,
2nd Battalion,
Oxfordshire & Buckinghamshire Light Infantry

Albert Haggitt was born near Witney during the fourth quarter of 1887, eldest son of William, a general labourer and his wife, Elizabeth (née Gould). At the time of the 1891 census the family were living on Razor Hill[67]. Ten years later, in the census of 1901, they had moved to Newland and Albert was recorded as working as an errand boy to a local carrier. In the spring of 1907 he married Fanny Robinson and the couple's first child, a daughter, Mabel, was born the following year. In 1910 a second daughter, Florence, was born and by 1911 the family were living in Newland where Albert was employed as a fish hawker.

It is unclear when Albert first joined the Army, although there is evidence to suggest that he enlisted following his marriage. Indeed his regimental number, issued sequentially and therefore reasonably easy to date, points to the fact that he originally enlisted around the beginning of 1908. His appearance as a 'civilian' on the 1911 census for Witney suggests that by the spring of that year he had served a minimum of three year's regular service, been transferred to the Reserves and had returned home. When the order for general mobilisation was issued at the beginning of August 1914 Albert, as a reservist, was recalled to the colours and on 13th September 1914, he moved to France to join the 2nd Battalion of the Oxfordshire and Buckinghamshire Light Infantry (OBLI), part of the 2nd Division.

On the night of the 15th/16th May 1915 the 2nd OBLI participated in the first British night attack of the war. In a move designed to drain German forces away from a planned French offensive near Arras, the British attacked along a three mile front from Neuve Chapelle in the north to Festubert in the south. Despite some limited success, and the fact that the attack had been preceded by a 60 hour long artillery bombardment, the German defences remained largely intact which resulted in the British taking heavy casualties[68].

---

[67] The area around modern day Beech Road, off of Tower Hill.

[68] See also T. Broom, T. Purbrick and A.W. Englefield, who were all killed in the same action.

65

It was during the attack on the 16th May 1915 that Albert Haggitt was killed. His body was never identified and he has no known grave. Today his name is commemorated on Le Touret Memorial, near the village of Festubert, France.

W. Hall
Private, George William Hall, 34690,
1st Battalion,
Duke of Cornwall's Light Infantry

George Hall, known by his second name of 'William', was born in Lowell's Place, Witney on Christmas Day 1897, the eldest son of George, a general labourer, and his wife Ellen (née Pearce). At the time of the 1911 census the family were still in Lowell's Place and William was working as an errand boy.

William enlisted for military service around 1916/17 and was initially posted to the Oxfordshire and Buckinghamshire Light Infantry. However upon his deployment to France he was transferred to the 1st Battalion of the Duke of Cornwall's Light Infantry (DCLI), a unit which had been on the Western Front since August 1914 and which, in November 1917, was transferred to Italy before returning to France in April 1918.

It was whilst in action on the Western Front on 31st May 1918 that William Hall was killed. Today his body lies in the Thiennes British Cemetery, France.

On 22nd June 1918 in the *'In Memoriam'* column of the *Witney Gazette*, George Hall, William's father, was remembered – he had died from a diabetes related condition in June 1915. However it was cited that he had been serving with the DCLI when he died, as was William three years later when he was killed. However, the lack of evidence found to date suggests that George Hall did not serve during the war and his name is absent from the Witney War Memorial.

J.T. Hanks
Private, James Thomas Hanks, 10999,
5th Battalion,
Oxfordshire & Buckinghamshire Light Infantry

James Hanks was born in Witney during the first quarter of 1897, the eldest son of Thomas, a traction engine driver, and his wife Mary (née Gould). At the time of the 1901 census the family were recorded as living in Lowell's Place and by 1911 James was working in the town's woollen industry as a blanket spinner.

When war came in August 1914 James was one of the first to enlist and was posted to the newly formed 5th Battalion, Oxfordshire and Buckinghamshire Light Infantry, soon to be part of the 14th (Light) Division. In May 1915, following training and equipping, the Division was deployed to France although its move to the front line was delayed due to a lack of rifle and artillery ammunition. During the summer of 1915 the 14th Division was engaged at Hooge, in the Ypres Salient[69], where it became the first formation in the war to be attacked by Germans using flame throwers.

On the 25th September, James, whilst fighting with his unit at Bellewaerde near Hooge, was killed in action. His body was never identified and he has no known grave. Today his name is remembered on the Ypres (Menin Gate) Memorial, Ieper, Belgium.

C.S. Harris
Private, Charles Stanley N. Harris, 200424,
5th Battalion,
Oxfordshire & Buckinghamshire Light Infantry

Charles Harris was born in South Leigh on the 12th October 1895, the eldest son of Jonathan, a cattleman, and his wife Ellen (née Pickett). At the time of the census in 1911 Charles and his younger sister, Elsie, although still living in the village, were both working in one of Witney's woollen mills, Charles as a spinner and Elsie as a 'tier on'.

---

[69] The 'bulge' in the Allied front line to the east of Ypres.

When war was declared in August 1914 Charles was quick to volunteer for military service and was posted to the 1/4th Battalion of the Oxfordshire and Buckinghamshire Light Infantry, part of the South Midland Division. Following training and equipping the Division was deployed to France on the 30th March 1915. At some point during the following three years Charles transferred from the 1/4th to the Regiment's 5th Battalion (part of the 14th (Light) Division). When this transfer occurred is unknown as his service record has not survived. But it is known that he was serving with the 5th Battalion in March 1918.

The German High Command had decided by the end of 1917 that the primary target for their spring offensive would be the British Forces on the Western Front. They had gauged that the British, exhausted and under strength following four major offensive operations earlier in the year, could be beaten before the newly arrived American troops could be effectively deployed in an offensive role. On the 21st March 1918 seventy two German Divisions from three armies were unleashed against the British forces on the Somme and succeeded in punching a sixty mile wide hole through their thinly defended front line. Within a week the Germans had steam-rollered across the old battlefields of 1916 and taken several key Allied-held towns.

Charles Harris's father was initially informed that his son had been posted as missing in action on the 21st March 1918, the first day of the German offensive. But within days it was confirmed that he had in fact been killed in action on that day. His body was never identified and he has no known grave. Today his name is remembered on the Pozieres Memorial, Ovillers-La Boisselle, France.

G.H. Harris
Private, George Henry Harris, 1348,
'D' Company,
37th Battalion,
Australian Infantry,
Australian Imperial Force

George Harris was born in Witney around March 1893, the eldest son of George, a hairdresser, and his wife Amy (née Townsend). His mother died in the spring of 1897 and in 1899 George's father married for a second time to Louisa Brooker. At the time of the census in 1911 George, was living with his family on the Woodstock Road, and working as a hairdresser in his father's shop on Bridge Street. In 1912 he emigrated to Australia and by early 1916 he was farming in King Valley, near Wangaratta, north-east Victoria.

On the 1st March 1916 George presented himself at the Army recruiting station in Wangaratta and volunteered for military service. One month later he was despatched to the military training camp at Seymour and attached to the recently formed 37th Battalion, Australian Infantry, part of the 3rd Australian Division. After two months of basic training the Battalion moved to Melbourne and on the 3rd of June 1916 the men of the 37th boarded the troop transport, *HMAT Persic,* and left Australia bound for Europe. The *Persic* docked in the UK on the 25th July 1916, whereupon the Australians were moved to Larkhill Camp on Salisbury Plain for further training. It was during his time at Larkhill, just before he was sent overseas, that George was granted leave during which time he was able to return to Witney to visit his family.

On the 22nd November 1916 the 37th Battalion (soon to be nicknamed the "Larkhill Lancers" by the men of the other three infantry divisions of the Australian Imperial Force, due to their late arrival at the front) and its sister battalions of the 3rd Division were deployed to France. Within a week of their arrival they were occupying trenches in the Armentieres sector on the Western Front. The severe winter weather of 1916/17 did not make things any easier for the new arrivals and between the 6th and 9th of January 1917 George was a patient in the 10th Australian Field Ambulance, where he was treated for tracheitis.

On the night of the 26th/27th January 1917 the 37th Battalion were ordered to Chapelle-d'Armentieres to take over a section of trench line from a battalion of the Northumberland Fusiliers. By 3.50 a.m. on the 27th the relief had been completed, and the men of the 37th settled down to another spell in the trenches. The battalion diary records that the 27th January was without event but that on the 28th the Germans began shelling gun positions near the battalion headquarters and two guns were hit and put out of action. The diarist also recorded that on that day the battalion suffered just one casualty.[70] This entry must relate to George who on the 28th, according to his military record, was wounded by gunshot wounds to his right buttock and leg. He was evacuated from the battlefield, first to the 10th Australian Field Ambulance and from there to the 1st Canadian Casualty Clearing Station at Bailleul. It was here that George died of his wounds at 2.30 a.m. on the morning of the 30th January 1917. He was buried in a nearby cemetery later that same day. Today his grave can be found in the Ballieul Communal Cemetery Extension (Nord), Ballieul, France.

In addition to being remembered on the Witney War Memorial George Harris is also recorded on the Honour Roll of Trinity Cathedral, Wangaratta, Victoria, Australia.

H.T. Harris
Corporal, Harold Thomas Harris, 200659,
1/4th Battalion,
Oxfordshire & Buckinghamshire Light Infantry

Harold Harris was born in Witney during the third quarter of 1891, the illegitimate son of Ann Harris. In 1901 he and his mother, who was by then working as a blanket weaver in the town, were living in the High Street with his widowed grandmother, Harriet. Educated at the town's Wesleyan Day School Harold was one of the original members of the 1st Witney Company of the Boys Brigade, eventually holding the rank of Staff Sergeant. At the time of the 1911 census he was living in Oxford, at the home of his Uncle Albert, and

---

[70] AWM4, 23/54/7 (January 1917)

working as a printer's apprentice at the print works where his uncle was an overseer.

In 1912 he moved to London to study journalism under the direction of Walter Cranfield, a prominent social commentator of the time who wrote under the pseudonym "Denis Crane". Whilst in London Harold regularly wrote pieces for the *'Methodist Recorder'* and continued his work with the Boys Brigade, becoming an officer of the 102nd London Company. It was in this capacity that in May 1914 he acted as a standard-bearer in the guard of honour, at the funeral of Sir William Alexander Smith, the founder of the Boy's Brigade.

Upon the outbreak of war in August 1914, Harold returned home to Witney to enlist alongside his friends and fellow townsmen and on the 1st September he joined forty other local men - the 'Witney Company' as they were proudly referred to, as they marched through the town midst cheering crowds to the train station and onwards to Oxford to volunteer for military service. Harold was accepted and posted to the newly formed 1/4th Battalion of the Oxfordshire and Buckinghamshire Light Infantry (OBLI), then part of the South Midland Division – later re-designated the 48th (South Midland).

By the spring of 1915 the 1/4th OBLI, along with the rest of South Midland Division, had been fully trained and equipped and deemed ready for war. On the 29th March 1915 the battalion was landed at the French port of Boulogne and by the 3rd April it had been joined by the rest of its division near the town of Cassel. It was to remain on the Western Front until late 1917 when it was transferred to the Italian Front.

For many months after his arrival in France Harold was employed on special work at Brigade Headquarters, work which kept him away from the front line. However, the death of a number of his former comrades during the Allied offensive on the Somme in 1916 affected him so much that he submitted a request to be posted back to his battalion and to the friends who remained there. His request was granted and he returned to the 1/4th OBLI where he gained rapid promotion and at the time of the German retreat to the Hindenburg Line in March/April 1917 he held the rank of Corporal.

On the evening of the 4th April 1917 the men of the 1/4th OBLI were, occupying a trench-line running north-south from the villages of St. Emilie and Villers-Faucon, facing the German held village of Ronssoy. As darkness fell orders were received that Ronssoy was to be attacked that night. The Battalion diarist recorded that it was a *'wild night, cold with mist.'[71]* as the men took up their positions. At 4.45 a.m. the attack was launched and by 7.00 a.m. the village had been taken with few casualties. However it was during the assault on Ronssoy on the 5th April 1917 that Harold Harris was killed. His body was never identified but it was believed at the time, that his had been one of a number of unidentified burials in the Templeux-Le-Guerard British Cemetery and today Harold is commemorated on a special memorial for sixteen soldiers from the UK who are known, or believed, to be buried there.

On the eve of his final battle Harold had written a letter home. In it he included this paragraph which, as a writer in the *Methodist Recorder*, in which publication it was later reproduced, noted '...in the light of events now seems to have been singularly prophetic'

> *"This is a curious life! Our one aim and objective day and night is to kill, or at least disable; we pursue this end, ourselves in the midst of death; death is our workmate and our playmate, he sticks to us like our shadow. If we retire from his immediate presence for a time, it is only that we make ourselves more efficient instruments of his, and on our return, court him all the more hardily. We eat in order to kill, we sleep to kill, we live to kill and be killed. When we are nurtured and cared for, we know, at the backs of our minds like Christmas ox fattening in the stall, it is to that sinister end."[72]*

---

[71] WO 95/2763

[72] Also reproduced in the *Witney Gazette*, 21st April 1917.

J. Harris
Private, John Harris, 9907,
2nd Battalion,
Oxfordshire & Buckinghamshire Light Infantry
(Younger brother of William Harris, killed in action at Loos, France, 28th
September 1915)

John Harris was born in Corn Street, Witney, at the beginning of 1895, the fourth son of Joseph, a farm labourer, and his wife Harriett (née Warner). In early 1897 John's mother died and by the end of that year his father had married again to Sarah Radburn (née Legg), a widow from Minster Lovell. Following their marriage the couple moved their families to High Cogges, where by 1911 John was working as a labourer. Around 1913 John joined the Army, volunteering for service with the Oxfordshire and Buckinghamshire Light Infantry and following his basic training he was posted to the Regiment's 2nd Battalion, part of the 2nd Division.

When the order for mobilisation was issued at the beginning of August 1914 the 2nd Division was at Aldershot. In less than a fortnight it had been fully equipped and deployed to France, one of the first British formations to do so, arriving in Boulogne on the 14th of the month. Although not directly involved in the Battle of Mons (23rd – 24th August 1914) it did go into action during the subsequent retreat. However, the first major action the Division became engaged in was on the Aisne in September, followed one month later in Belgium by what came to be known as the First Battle of Ypres (October-November 1914).

On the 21st October the 2nd Division went into action at Langemarck to the north east of Ypres. Although this element of the overall battle was to last for three days, John Harris did not live to see the end of the first day. He was killed in action on the 21st October 1914. His body was never identified and he has no known grave. Today his name is remembered on the Ypres (Menin Gate) Memorial, Ipres, Belgium.

Eleven months later, on the 28th September 1915, John's elder brother William was killed in action at Loos, France, whilst serving with the 1st Battalion, Royal Berkshire Regiment.

W. Harris
Lance-Corporal, William Harris, 7028,
1st Battalion,
Princess Charlotte of Wales's (Royal Berkshire Regiment)
(Elder brother of John Harris, killed in action at Langemarck, Belgium, 21st October 1914)

William Harris was born in Witney around 1885 the eldest son of Joseph, a farm labourer, and his wife Harriett (née Warner). At the time of the 1891 census the family were living in Corn Street. In early 1897 William's mother died and by the end of that year his father had married again to Sarah Radburn (née Legg) a widow from Minster Lovell. The couple moved their families to High Cogges where, by 1901, William was employed as a farm hand. Shortly afterwards he joined the British Army and served for several years in the Royal Berkshire Regiment. By 1911 however, he had been discharged to the Reserves and was back in Witney, working as a 'hawker' and living with his uncle and aunt, Jessie and Annie Warner, at their home in the Crofts.

On the outbreak of war, William was recalled for active service and on the 20th September 1914 deployed to France where he joined the 1st Battalion of his old Regiment, part of the 2nd Division. One month after his arrival on the Western Front the news reached him that his younger brother, John, who had been serving with the 2nd Battalion, Oxfordshire and Buckinghamshire Light Infantry, had been killed at Langemarck during the First Battle of Ypres.

By mid September 1915 William, promoted to the rank of Lance Corporal, was with his battalion to the north of the French mining town of Loos. The 2nd Division along with five other British Divisions were poised to take part in what had, up to then, been popularly referred to as the 'big push'- when the Allied armies would be given the opportunity to punch through the German lines, breaking the stalemate of trench warfare and opening up a new phase of mobile fighting. This offensive would later become known as the Battle of Loos.

During the early hours of the 28th September, several days after the opening of the battle, the 1st Royal Berks launched a night attack on the strategically important 'Fosse 8'. This was one of many mining pit-heads in the area but upon it stood a tower, known by the British soldiers as 'Tower Bridge', which

74

held commanding views over the Loos battlefield. British artillery fire had failed to destroy it and although it had been taken by the British at the start of the battle it had subsequently been retaken by the Germans. The clear moonlit night offered no protection for the attackers, they were quickly spotted and made easy targets for the Germans. Concentrated enemy rifle and machine gun fire took their toll and the attack floundered with the 1ˢᵗ Royal Berks being forced to retreat with the loss of over 300 men killed, wounded or missing.[73]

William Harris was one of the dead. His body was never identified and he has no known grave. Today his name is recorded on the Loos Memorial, France, alongside the names of over 20,000 officers and men who were killed in the area and who have no known grave.

E.R. Hawkes
Driver, Ernest Richard Hawkes, T/243109,
1ˢᵗ Auxiliary Horse Transport Company,
Army Service Corps
(Elder brother of John Hawkes, killed in action in France, 29ᵗʰ July 1918)

Ernest Hawkes was born in Witney (most likely in High Street) during the spring of 1888, the second son of Edward, a grocer's warehouseman, and his wife Phoebe (née Hemmings). During the 1890's the family moved to the Crofts where Ernest is recorded as living in the census of 1901.

Ernest volunteered for military service upon the outbreak of the war in August 1914 and was posted to the 1/4ᵗʰ Battalion of the Oxfordshire and Buckinghamshire Light Infantry. At the beginning of 1915, on the eve of his unit's deployment to active service, he was married to Bessie Viner, a domestic servant from Oxford, but the indication is that when he enlisted he had volunteered primarily for Home Service and therefore did not move to France when his unit did in March 1915. However, as the war continued and the demand for trained men increased, Ernest did join his unit on the Western Front in 1916.

---

[73] WO 95/2762

At some point within the following two years he was transferred from the infantry to the Army Service Corps. Such a move is most likely to have been due to Ernest having been injured or wounded and thereby rendered unfit for front line service. In Oxford during the spring of 1917 Bessie gave birth to the couple's only child, a daughter, Kathleen, whom Ernest would have seen when he returned home on leave that Christmas. In July 1918 Ernest's younger brother, John, serving with the 1/4th Battalion of the Cheshire Regiment was killed in action near Grand Rozoy, France.

As the war neared its end Ernest Hawkes caught influenza which developed into pneumonia. Despite receiving medical attention he died on the 15th November 1918 in a military hospital at Le Treport, France. His family were informed that he had been buried with full military honours in the nearby Mont Huon Military Cemetery, approximately one mile south of the town.

His widow, Bessie, never re married and continued to live in the Oxford area until her death in 1983.

J. Hawkes
Private, John Hawkes, 201348,
1/4th Battalion,
Cheshire Regiment
(Younger brother of Ernest Hawkes who died in France, 15th November 1918)

John Hawkes was born in Witney (most likely in High Street), in early 1890, the third son of Edward, a grocer's warehouseman and his wife Phoebe (née Hemmings). During the 1890's the family moved to the Crofts, where, by the time of the census of 1911, John was still living with his parents and working as an assistant in a local china shop. Shortly after, John left Witney to find work abroad and when, in August 1914, war broke out in Europe, he was in Argentina.

He returned to England as soon as he could and upon arrival in the U.K. volunteered for military service. He was accepted and posted to the Cheshire Regiment and following his basic training he was deployed to Egypt to reinforce his regiment's 1/4[74] Battalion[74], recently evacuated from Gallipoli. On the 31st May 1918 the 1/4th left Egypt to move to France where, on the 1st July 1918 it was attached to the newly reformed 34th Division on the Western Front.

The final German offensive of the war opened on the Marne on the 18th July 1918. In a huge diversionary attack, devised to lure Allied troops south from Belgium in preparation for a major assault in Flanders, the Germans threw 40 divisions against the French at Reims. Although initially successful the Germans were forced into retreat when the French, supported by British and Empire troops, counter attacked. On the 23rd July the 1/4th Cheshires were ordered into the attack to support the advancing French. The battalion was relieved during the night of the 27th/28th of July but within 24 hours they were back in action again near the village of Grand Rozoy.[75]

It was during this fighting on the 29th July 1918 that John Hawkes was killed. Initially he was buried in one of the many burial grounds scattered across the battlefield[76] but, following the Armistice his body was removed to the newly constructed Raparie British Cemetery, a larger 'concentration' cemetery at Villemontoire, France.

Several months later, on the 15th November 1918, John's elder brother, Ernest, who had been serving with the Army Service Corps in France, died in a military hospital of pneumonia.

---

[74] The 1/4th Bn. had been earlier transferred to Egypt from where it had taken part in the Gallipoli campaign in 1915. John Hawke's record of medal entitlement shows that he did not qualify for the 1914/15 star and must therefore have joined his battalion after they had returned to Egypt at the beginning of 1916.

[75] WO 95/4628

[76] It is likely that he was one of 16 men of the Cheshire and Herefordshire Regiments who had originally been buried in the small 'Cheshire Cemetery' at Parcy-et Tigny.

L.E.J. Hinton
Company Sergeant Major, James Edward Lewis Hinton, MM (Military Medal), 10130,
5th Battalion,
Oxfordshire & Buckinghamshire Light Infantry

James Hinton, known to all as 'Lewis', was born in the village of Cubbington, Warwickshire, during the summer of 1891. He was the eldest son of James, a baker, and his wife Elizabeth (née Daniels). Lewis was just a year old when his parents brought him to Witney when they took over the management of the Post Office at Newland. Following his education at the town's Wesleyan Day School and thereafter at the Grammar School, by 1908 Lewis was working as an assistant master at St. Mary's School. A keen and talented footballer and cricketer he continued working at St. Mary's for a further five years before moving to take up a new position in Gloucestershire in 1913.

When war broke out in August 1914 Lewis was quick to volunteer for military service. He enlisted at Nailsworth, Gloucestershire, and was duly posted to the newly formed 5th Battalion of the Oxfordshire and Buckinghamshire Light Infantry, part of the 14th (Light) Division. 'His knowledge of drill etc. soon gained him promotion'[77] and by the time his unit deployed to France, on the 20th May 1915, he was a Sergeant.

The men of the 14th Division saw action in many notable engagements during the War: on the 30th July 1915 at Hooge, when the Germans used flame throwers for the first time to attack the British lines, and on the 25th and 26th September 1915 during the Second Attack on Bellewaarde. In 1916 the Division took part in the great Somme Offensive; between the 15th July and the 3rd September at Delville Wood and between the 15th and 22nd September at Flers-Courcelette. It was during this period that Lewis was awarded the Military Medal for bravery in the field,[78] although the original citation remains elusive. Towards the end of 1916, following the horrors of the Somme, Lewis was back in England where he married his fiancée, Daisy Bruton of Stroud. However their time together was all too brief and Lewis soon returned to

---

[77] *Witney Gazette*, 19th May 1917.
[78] Announced in the *London Gazette* on the 27th October 1917.

France to rejoin his unit. He gained further promotion and by the time his unit went into action during the Arras Offensive (9th April 1917 - 16th May 1917) he was a Company Sergeant Major.

On the 3rd of May 1917 Lewis led his men in an assault on the German positions near the River Scarpe. The enemy's resistance was stubborn and fierce and British casualties began to mount. Lewis, although wounded, continued to advance until he and his men were forced to shelter in a shell crater. It was later reported that, having gained this relatively safe position, he observed a wounded man lying out on the battlefield. Without thinking of his own safety he left the crater and went to his fallen comrade. He dragged him to shelter and whilst engaged in binding the man's wounds he was shot in the head and throat, killing him instantly.

Lewis was buried on the battlefield and, following the Armistice, his grave was moved to L'Homme Mort British Cemetery, Ecoust-St. Mein, Pas De Calais, France.

His widow, Daisy, was married again in 1922 to Herbert Smith of Stroud.

G. Holland
Private, George Holland, 14398,
'B' Company,
7th Battalion,
Duke of Edinburgh's (Wiltshire Regiment)

George Holland was born in the first quarter of 1893, the youngest son of Solomon (known by his second name of 'John'), a house painter, and his wife Eliza (née Buckingham). George's mother died in 1909 and two years later his father married again to Harriett Pratley. At the time of the 1911 census the family were living on Woodgreen and George was working as a grocer's assistant. His father and step-mother later went on to manage the *Three Pigeons* public house on Woodgreen.

When war broke out George volunteered for military service and was initially posted to the Oxfordshire and Buckinghamshire Light Infantry. However, as was often the case, he was later transferred to reinforce another unit. Thus, on the 21st September 1915 George arrived in France as part of the

7th Battalion, Duke of Edinburgh's (Wiltshire Regiment). The battalion remained on the Western Front for just two months before being redeployed, at the beginning of November, along with the rest of the 26th Division, to Salonika, Greece, where it was to stay for the rest of the war.

On the night of the 24th/25th April 1917 the 7th Battalion was part of an Allied attack on the Bulgarian front line, to the south of Dorian. In what came to be known as the Battle of Dorian 'A', 'C' and 'D' Companies, with 'B' Company in reserve, advanced on heavily defended positions but failing to take their objective were forced to retire to their starting point. The substantial casualty report was compiled several hours after the failed attack and on it was George Holland's name, his fate unknown. Officially listed at the time as 'missing' his date of death was later confirmed as being the 24th April 1917. His body was never identified and he has no known grave. Today his name is remembered on the Dorian Memorial, Dorian, Northern Greece, alongside more than 2,000 of his comrades who also have no known grave.

H. Hooper
Private, James Henry Hooper, 7497,
2nd Battalion,
Oxfordshire & Buckinghamshire Light Infantry

James Hooper, known as 'Harry', was born in Witney during the third quarter of 1887, the eldest son of John, a plumber, and his wife, Harriett (née Conway). During the 1890's the family moved from their home at Hailey Fields to Lowell's Place, Corn Street. In November 1903 Harry, aged just 16, joined the Army and served for several years with the Oxfordshire Light Infantry. Following his period of regular service he was discharged to the Reserves and returned to Witney where, towards the end of 1907, he married Emily Leach. The couple lived in a house in Lowell's Place and at the beginning of 1910 their first son, Bernard, was born. At the time of the 1911 census Harry was employed as a labourer in one of the town's blanket mills. The couple's second son, Frederick, was born in the spring of 1913

As a reservist, Harry was recalled to the colours when Britain went to war with Germany in August 1914. He was posted to the 2nd Battalion of the

Oxfordshire and Buckinghamshire Light Infantry (OBLI), part of the 2nd Division, at Aldershot and, less than a fortnight later, on the 13th August he, along with his unit, left Southampton aboard the *SS Lake Michigan* bound for Boulogne, France. Upon their arrival the troops moved into a rest camp in the port area whilst the rest of the Division was assembled. On the 16th August the Battalion began its journey to the front, crossing the Belgian border on the 23rd. The following day the Battalion came under enemy fire for the first time as they covered the withdrawal of several other units. Over the following two weeks the men of the 2nd OBLI were constantly on the move as the enemy continued their advance.

On the 13th September the battalion arrived in Soupir, a French village on the northern bank of the River Aisne. At dawn on the 17th, three companies: 'B', 'C' and 'D' were deployed to relieve the 2nd Grenadier Guards in a trench line running through the grounds of La Cour-Soupir, a large farm to the north west of the village. A quiet start in the trenches was broken when the German artillery brought down a heavy barrage on the battalion's position. The shelling started on the afternoon of the 19th and continued until early evening when the enemy attempted an infantry attack which was easily repelled.

During the course of this action on the 19th September 1914, nine men of the 2nd OBLI lost their lives, all as a result of shell fire.[79] One of those killed was Harry Hooper – the first Witney man to lose his life in the war. Initially his body was buried in a battlefield cemetery near to his place of death (La Cour-De-Soupir Farm) but after the Armistice his grave, along with the sixty five other British soldiers also buried there, was moved to the specially constructed Vailly Britsh Cemetery in the town of Vailly Sur Aisne, France.

Phyllis Mary Hooper was born in Witney on the 14th May 1915, eight months after her father's death in France.

---

[79] WO 95/1348

A.C. Horne
Driver, Albert Caleb Horne, 93658,
'B' Battery,
124th Brigade,
Royal Field Artillery

Albert Horne was born in Newland, Witney, during the fourth quarter of 1897, the youngest son of Leonard, a grocer, butcher and owner of Newland Stores, and his wife Kate (née Betts).

Albert volunteered for military service shortly after the war began and following his basic training he was posted to 'B' Battery of the 124th Brigade, Royal Field Artillery[80]. This was one of Kitchener's New Army units and was originally part of the 31st Division. However following a reorganisation it became part of the Artillery Reserve before being attached to the 37th Division. This Division was concentrated on Salisbury Plain during April 1915 and three months later, following an inspection by King George V, it was deployed to France.

Albert arrived in France as part of 124th Brigade on the 30th July 1915. By the beginning of August the entire Division was concentrated near Tilques. The 124th Brigade was to remain on the Western front for the rest of the war and, as part of the 37th Division, was engaged in the following notable actions: The Somme (1916), Arras and Passchendaele (1917), The Somme, The Hindenburg Line and the Final Advance in Picardy (1918).

Towards the very end of the war Albert was taken ill with influenza. This developed into bronchial pneumonia and he was admitted to the No2 Canadian Hospital at Le Treport. It was here that he died on the 2nd November 1918. He was buried in the nearby cemetery and today his grave can be found in the Mont Huon Military Cemetery, Le Treport, France.

---

[80] Each Battery of the 124th Brigade, A, B, C and D, were equipped with four 18 pounder artillery pieces.

A.E. Horne
Private, Albert Edwin Horne, 1865,
'A' Squadron,
1/1st Queen's Own Oxfordshire Hussars

Local baker and corn merchant, Albert Horne (senior) and his wife Dorcas (née Cantell) adopted Albert shortly after his birth, around 1896. The identities of the child's natural parents are not known. Bert, as he was known, was educated at the town's Wesleyan Day School and was an active member of the 1st Witney Company of the Boys Brigade. At the time of the 1911 census the family were living in Corn Street and Bert was working as an assistant to his father. Between late 1913 and early 1914 he volunteered to serve with the local yeomanry regiment; the Queen's Own Oxfordshire Hussars (QOOH).

When war was declared in August 1914 the men of the QOOH were quickly mobilised. Moving first to Reading and from there, on the 29th August, to Churn, a remote part of the Berkshire Downs, two miles south of Blewbury, an area which since the late 19th century had been the site of numerous military summer camps. Here the regiment came under the authority of the 2nd Mounted Division.

After just one month's training the QOOH received orders from the First Lord of the Admiralty, Winston Churchill, to move to Southampton for immediate deployment to France.[81] The regiment was to join the Naval Brigade which was being sent to Flanders to prevent a German advance on the channel ports. On the 19th September 1914, Bert, alongside his comrades of the QOOH, sailed out of Southampton Water aboard the steamer *Bellerophon,* bound for France - the first territorial unit to be deployed to an active theatre of operations.

The QOOH landed at Dunkirk on the 22nd September and after a week of further training, moved inland to Hazebrouk where it was employed in various guard duties and scouting forays. On the 17th October the Regiment moved to Saint-Omer where it provided a continuous guard for the town until the 30th October when it was ordered to Neuve Église and attached to the 1st Cavalry

---

[81] Winston Churchill championed the Regiment as both a former member and older brother of Jack Churchill, who at the time was a serving officer with the QOOH.

Division as part of the operations around Ypres. As hopes for a war of movement, in which the use of mounted troops would be decisive, quickly evaporated into the stalemate of trench warfare, the men of the QOOH, like those of the other cavalry units, began to take their turn in the front line alongside the infantry.

At 6 a.m. on the morning of the 16th November 1914 the men of 'A' Squadron, QOOH, went into trenches near Wulverghem, facing the German front line on the high ground of Messines Ridge. About midday the men of 'C' Squadron were sent to dig trenches behind the line occupied by 'A' Squadron. The Germans spotted this activity and began shelling the British lines. It was during this sudden and fierce bombardment that Bert Horne was killed.[82]

A few days later Major Scott, Officer commanding 'A' Squadron QOOH, wrote a letter to Bert's father in which he said that:

> *By his* [Bert's] *death the Regiment has suffered the loss of a most efficient and steady soldier, and one upon whom I would rely absolutely under fire, and whose loss I as his Squadron Commander, deeply deplore. We buried him that evening just outside Wolverghem village, in the garden of a farm, besides several others, who had been killed in action.*[83]

Bert's final resting place became lost in the course of the war and today, with no known grave, his name is recorded on the Ypres (Menin Gate) Memorial, Ipres, Belgium.

---

[82] Keith-Falconer, A., The Oxfordshire Hussars in the Great War (1914-1918), London, John Murray, 1927. (p.88)

[83] From a letter published in the *Witney Gazette*, 12th December 1914.

A.J. Horne
Lance Corporal, Albert Job Horne, 20853,
5th Battalion,
Oxfordshire & Buckinghamshire Light Infantry

Albert Horne was born in Witney during the third quarter of 1897, the eldest son of Walter, a blanket dyer, and his wife Ellen (née Phipps). At the time of the 1901 census the family were living in Mill Lane, later moving to a house on the Burford Road where they were recorded in the census of 1911; at which time Albert was working as a grocer's assistant.

Albert volunteered for military service in November 1915, joining the Oxfordshire and Buckinghamshire Light Infantry. Following his basic training he was deployed to France in early 1916 where he was attached to his Regiment's 5th Battalion, part of the 14th (Light) Division. Albert fought with his unit on the Somme battlefields of 1916 and through the winter of 1916/17, eventually being raised to the rank of Lance Corporal.

On the 9th April 1917 the Allies launched their spring offensive near the French town of Arras. As in the earlier great offensive operations the overall plan of attack was broken down into smaller phases which would themselves come to be remembered by their own names. The offensive opened with the First Battle of the Scarpe (9th – 14th April) and Vimy Ridge (9th – 12th April), and was followed by, amongst others, the battles of Bullecourt (10th – 11th April), Lagnicourt (15th April) and Arleux (28th – 29th April). On the 3rd May the 14th Division went into action in what would come to be known as the Third Battle of the Scarpe. Within twenty four hours, following heavy casualties, the attack was called off.

One of those killed on the 3rd May 1917 was Albert Horne. His body was buried on the battlefield and following the Armistice in 1918 his grave was moved to the Tilloy British Cemetery, in the village of Tilloy-Les-Mofflaines, south-east of Arras, France.

E.A. Horne
Private, Ernest Arthur Horne, 9231,
'C' Company,
2nd Battalion,
Oxfordshire & Buckinghamshire Light Infantry

Ernest Horne was born in Witney at the beginning of 1877, the youngest son of John, a grocer, and his wife Juliana (née Tee). At the time of the census in 1891 Ernest was living with his elder brother, Thomas, and his family in Leyton, London. He later returned to Witney where he was briefly a member of the local Volunteer Battalion of the Oxfordshire Light Infantry. In the spring of 1897 he married Ethel Hughes of New Brompton, Kent and by 1901 the couple were living in Gravesend where Ernest was employed as a Butcher. During the final quarter of 1902 Ethel gave birth to the couple's first child, a son they named Wyndham[84]. By 1911 the family had moved to Leytonstone, London, where Ernest was working for a wholesale meat seller.

Upon the outbreak of war in August 1914 Ernest volunteered for military service joining the Oxfordshire and Buckinghamshire Light Infantry. Initially he was posted to the 3rd (Reserve) Battalion, based at Portsmouth and after two months of training he was deployed to France to join the Regiment's 2nd Battalion, part of the 2nd Division, on the Western Front. The 2nd Division had been landed in France within days of the declaration of war, becoming one of the first formations to do so and it was to remain on the Western Front for the rest of the conflict. By the time Ernest arrived the men of his unit had seen action in most of the opening engagements of the war.

On 15th May 1915 the 2nd Division went into action at the Battle of Festubert where the fighting was to rage for eleven days with little gain. When the offensive operations finally ended on the 26th May it was discovered that the 2nd Division had sustained over 5,000 casualties – the greatest number of the five Divisions involved. On this occasion Ernest was one of the lucky ones. He

---

[84] A second child (sex unknown) was born between 1901 and 1911 but had died in infancy before the time of the 1911 census.

survived and by August 1915 he was serving in 'C' Company as a member of a hand grenade party, or 'bombers', as they were known[85].

On the night of the 26th/27th of that month there was a minor engagement with German bomb throwers. It is likely that they had attacked the British trenches, due to the fact that the enemy casualties were all buried by the British; something which would have been very difficult to achieve had they been killed during an attack on the German lines. It was during this engagement that Ernest was killed. In the words of his Company Commander, Captain A. Ponsonby, writing to Ernest's widow on the 27th August 1915;

> "... [Ernest] *died instantly, suffering no pain, and his body is laid to rest in a military cemetery close behind the line, by the side of his friends who were killed at the same time. For you I know it will be a most terrible blow, but I hope that later on you may be able to receive some slight comfort from the thought that he died fighting most gallantly for his Country, and that every one of us in the Company feel that we have lost one of our best soldiers and most reliable comrades. Speaking personally, as Captain of the Company, I feel that I have sustained a great loss, for he was always so cheerful and ready to help in any way, and so absolutely fearless and steady when any danger was before him. Please accept the sincerest sympathy of myself and all the members of the Company in your loss of so gallant a soldier and husband...* "[86]

Today Ernest's grave can be found in the Guards Cemetery, Windy Corner, near the village of Cuinchy, Pas de Calais, France.

---

[85] His job would have been to join assault parties and be responsible for the launching, or throwing, of grenades in, or near, the enemy positions.

[86] Published in the *Witney Gazette*, 4th September 1915.

A.C. Hudson
Private, Albert Charles Hudson, 28879,
1st Battalion,
Herefordshire Regiment
(Younger brother of Mark Hudson, killed in action, France, 4th March 1917)

Albert Hudson was born in Mill Lane (now known as Mill Street), Witney, in the spring of 1891, the sixth son of Mark, an agricultural labourer, and his wife Sarah (née Goodenough). By 1911 the family had moved to Burford Road and Albert, still living with his parents, was employed as a market gardener.

On the outbreak of war in 1914 Albert enlisted in the Army and was posted to the newly formed 5th Battalion of the Oxfordshire & Buckinghamshire Light Infantry, part of the 14th (Light) Division. In May 1915 the fully trained and equipped Division was deployed to France, where it was to remain until 1918. In the spring of 1917, following the death of his older brother Mark who had been killed in action in France, Albert returned home on leave. In the brief time he had back in Witney he married his fiancée Fanny Tovey, before returning to France to re join his unit.

The men of the 14th Division continued fighting doggedly through into the spring of 1918 but during the battles of St. Quentin and the Avre, the Division suffered such heavy casualties that it was withdrawn from the line and subsequently reduced to cadre strength[87] with many of the remaining men being transferred to reinforce other units. Amongst those transferred was Albert Hudson who was posted to the 1st Battalion of the Herefordshire Regiment, part of the 34th Division.

In the closing weeks of the war, in a phase now referred to as 'the final advance', the battle scarred fields of Flanders became the scene for a series of battles between the advancing Allied forces and the retreating German Armies. It was during one of these actions, on the 16th October 1918 as the Allies fought

---

[87] Reduced to a very small unit, or cadre, of officers, NCOs and men who would be used to train other units. By mid 1918 many of the British units thus reduced in strength were used to train the newly arrived soldiers of the United States Army. These cadres would eventually receive new drafts of men and be returned to the order of battle.

their way across the River Lys at Courtrai, that Albert was killed. Today his body lies in the Dadizeele New British Cemetery, Dadizele, Belgium.

Following Albert's death his pregnant widow, Fanny, moved to Christchurch in Dorset, where, at the beginning of 1919, the couple's only child was born; a son whom Fanny named Albert Charles after his late father.

Albert's younger brother, Frederick, also served with the Oxfordshire and Buckinghamshire Light Infantry during the war. He was gassed twice and on the second occasion was so badly affected that he was initially left for dead. It was only when he was placed with a number of corpses that it was noticed he was still alive. He survived the war and returned home to Witney to marry and have children.

M. Hudson
Sergeant, Mark Hudson, 12/585,
12th Battalion,
The King's Own (Yorkshire Light Infantry)
(Elder brother of Albert C. Hudson, killed in action, Flanders, 16th October 1918)

Mark Hudson was born in Mill Lane (now known as Mill Street), Witney, around September 1883, the third son of Mark (Sen.), an agricultural labourer, and his wife Sarah (née Goodenough). On the 10th April 1902 Mark, then working as a blanket finisher in one of the town's mills, joined the local 4th Volunteer Battalion of the Oxfordshire Light Infantry (OLI) having previously failed in his attempt to join the regular army because of his poor level of fitness. However his fitness improved and military life appears to have agreed with him because on the 24th July 1902, once his basic training with the Volunteers was complete, he enlisted with the regular army and moved to Chatham on the 22nd November to join the 1st Battalion of the OLI.

On the 19th January 1905, with his period of regular service at an end, Mark transferred to the Army Reserve and returned home to Witney and once again took up employment in the town's blanket mills. By 1910 he had moved north to find work in the Yorkshire woollen industry and on the 16th May 1910, at Normanton parish church, he married local girl Mary Newton. The couple set up home together in the nearby village of Gomersal, where Mark was employed as a willyer and fettler[88] in the local textile factory. The couple's first child, Edna, was born on the 27th May 1911 and their second child, Doris, followed on the 15th June 1913 by which time the family had moved to Normanton. In March 1914 Mark wrote to the military authorities and volunteered to extend his period of reserve service, due to expire that July. His offer was accepted and he was requested to present himself at the headquarters of the King's Own Yorkshire Light Infantry (KOYLI) at Pontefract. However he failed to appear and his nine years Reserve Service duly expired on the 22nd July 1914.

Mark volunteered for military service once again around October 1914 and was posted to the newly formed 12th Battalion of the KOYLI, soon to become a pioneer battalion in the 31st Division. Perhaps due to his previous military experience Mark was quickly promoted and by December 1915, when his Division was sent to Egypt as part of the defence of the Suez Canal, he was already a Lance Sergeant. In March 1916 the 31st Division was redeployed to France and the Western Front where it was to remain for the rest of the war.

By the beginning of 1917 Mark had been promoted to full sergeant and was with his unit engaged in operations on the Ancre, near the Somme. It was here, on the 4th March 1917, that Mark was killed in action. Today his grave can be found in the Sailly-au-bois Military Cemetery, Sailly-au-Bois, France.

S. Humphris
Private, Sidney Humphris, 81229,
4th (Reserve) Battalion,
Devonshire Regiment

Sidney Humphris was born at the family home on Woodgreen, Witney, during the early summer of 1901, the youngest son of James, a blanket weaver, and his wife Eva (née Bartlett). Upon finishing his education Sidney, a former pupil of St. Mary's School, secured a job working as a shop assistant in G. Osborn Tite's, Draper's shop in the High Street. But he was keen to join the Army and

---

[88] A willeyer operated a willeying machine – used in the textile manufacturing process and a fettler cleaned the machines.

'do his bit'. As soon as he was able, at just 17 years old, he left his job and enlisted with the 4th (Reserve) Battalion of the Devonshire Regiment – a third line training battalion, which at the time of his enlistment, was stationed in Ireland. By all accounts young Sidney was not of a robust nature and whilst his unit was at Clonmany Barracks, County Donegal, in what is now the Irish Republic; he was struck down with influenza. This quickly developed into pneumonia and, despite receiving hospital treatment, he died on 3rd October 1918.

One of the letters of condolence which were sent to his father came from the Army Chaplain at Clonmany. He testified to Sidney's courage and brightness and assured him that the medical services had done all they could for his son. His body was laid to rest in the churchyard of Straid Church (Church of Ireland) in Clonmany – the only Commonwealth War burial at this site. Sadly the church has long since been abandoned and left in a ruinous state but the grave marker of Sidney Humphris remains and can be found about 7 yards north of the main gate.

In January 1920 Sidney's older brother, Walter, married Rose Langford. A little over a year later the couple had their first child – a son, they named Sidney.

W. Jackson
Sergeant, William Jackson, 201386,
2/4th Battalion,
Oxfordshire & Buckinghamshire Light Infantry

William Jackson, born in Witney towards the end of 1895, was the youngest son of John, a farrier, and his wife, Jane (née Whitlock). In 1911 the family were living in the High Street and William was working as a 'telegraph messenger'.

In early 1915 William volunteered for military service. He was posted to the 2/4th Battalion of the Oxfordshire and Buckinghamshire Light Infantry, part of the 61st (2nd South Midland) Division and by the late spring of 1916 he had been promoted to the rank of Sergeant. It was around this time that the Division was inspected by King George V at Bulford, on Salisbury Plain and deemed ready to go to war. The 2/4th was deployed to France on the 24th May 1916 and upon arrival moved to the Merville area for Divisional concentration. It was not long after, following a brief period of instruction and trench familiarisation, that the battalion received it's 'baptism of fire' in the Fauquissart sector, east of Laventie.

The men of the 2/4th were to remain on the Western Front for the remainder of the war. They fought through the Attack at Fromelles in July 1916, when the battalion suffered very heavy losses and in the following year they were involved in the Operations on the Ancre, the pursuit of the Germans to the Hindenburg Line, the Third Battle of Ypres, or "Passchendaele" as it is more commonly known, and the Battle of Cambrai.

On the night of the 18th March 1918 the 2/4th went into the line between the villages of Gricourt and Fayet, to the northwest of Saint Quentin. All appeared to be quiet in the area but a number of German prisoners, captured two days later, confirmed a widely held suspicion that the enemy was planning to launch a huge offensive operation in the area. In the early hours on the 21st the Germans unleashed a massive artillery bombardment of the Allied lines on the Somme. They targeted not only the wire and trench lines but also the transport lines, rest billets and ammunition and fuel dumps in the rear. Within hours the wire had been smashed and the trench lines were in disarray. Around 9:30 a.m. the Germans began their infantry assault. Fast moving German 'storm troops' exploited weak points in the British front line and infiltrated British positions causing chaos and confusion. The British fought desperately as they were forced to retreat in the face of the German advance.[89]

It was during this first day of the 1918 German spring offensive that William Jackson was killed in action. His body was never identified and he has no known grave. Today his name is recorded on the Pozieres Memorial, Pozieres, France. Alongside the names of over 14,600 British and Commonwealth soldiers who were killed during the German spring offensive of 1918 and who have no known graves.

---

[89] WO 95/3067

A. Johnson
Private, Albert Johnson, PLY/1794(S),
2nd Royal Marine Battalion,
Royal Marine Light Infantry

Albert Johnson was born on the 27th April 1898 in Kentish Town, London, the eldest son of Joseph, a railway porter, and his wife Matilda (née Winfield and a native of Witney). Around 1910, after having a further five children, the couple moved out of London and came to live in the town of Matilda's birth at a house in Bridge Street. It was here, at the time of the census in 1911, that the family were living and Albert's father was working as a bootmaker.

On December 29th 1916, 18 year old Albert, who had been working as a grocer's assistant, enlisted for service with the Royal Marines. On the 30th April 1917, following his basic training and having reached the age of 19 (the minimum age for active service overseas) he was posted to the British Expeditionary Force in France. Upon his arrival on the Western Front he spent several weeks at a Base Depot before being attached, on the 19th July 1917, to the 2nd Royal Marine Battalion, part of the 63rd (Royal Naval) Division. [90]

On the 6th November 1917 during the second battle for Passchendaele, Albert received gunshot wounds to his chest and right side of his body. He died on the 14th November 1917 whilst being treated at the 4th Casualty clearing station, Poperinge, Belgium.[91] Today his grave can be found in the Dozinghem Military Cemetery, Poperinge, Belgium.

---

[90] Upon the mobilisation of the Royal Navy Reserves in 1914 there was found to be a surplus of between 20,000 and 30,000 personnel who could not be utilised on the ships currently in service. The authorities recognised that this would be sufficient numbers to form a Naval Division, made up of two Naval Brigades and a Brigade of Royal Marines, who could then be used in land operations.

Following their part in the Gallipoli campaign there were very few remaining men in the Division who had served at sea, subsequently the command of the Division passed from the Admiralty to the War Office and in May 1916 the Division was landed in France for service on the Western Front.

[91] ADM 159/178/144

G.W. Jones
Private, George William Jones, 1625,
'B' Squadron,
Queen's Own Oxfordshire Hussars

George Jones was born in Corn Street, Witney, during the spring of 1893, the eldest son of Richard, a cabinet maker, and his wife Mabel (née Wright). George was educated at the town's Wesleyan Day School and by 1911 he was working for his father as a cabinet maker.

George had joined the Queen's Own Oxfordshire Hussars (QOOH)[92] around December 1910 and when Britain went to war on the 5th August 1914 he was mobilised along with the rest of his regiment. After only one month's training at a camp on the Berkshire Downs the QOOH received orders to deploy to France. Sent to support a brigade of Royal Marines the regiment landed at Dunkirk on the 22nd September - the first territorial unit to enter an active theatre of operations and the first to see action. However not all of the QOOH deployed at the same time and it was not until more than a fortnight later (12th October 1914) that George arrived in France, joining his unit at Malo-les-Bains.

During November 1914 the men of the QOOH took their turn in the trenches of Wulverghem and thereafter were temporarily withdrawn from the front line. Cavalry units were trained in a particular kind of warfare, which, it was still hoped, would be in demand once a war of movement could be resumed, and it would have been folly to waste that training in the trenches. Moreover in the poor weather conditions and with a lack of shelter, the regiment's horses had not fared well. On the 22nd November the regiment moved to billets in the Noote Boom area where it was to remain until the beginning of February 1915 when once again it returned to the front.

On the 27th April 1915 the QOOH moved to Potijze, on the eastern outskirts of Ypres, and took over a section of the trench line there. At around 3 a.m. on the morning of the 28th, having marched eight miles to their destination, the Regiment went into the reserve trenches running between Potijze and Wieltje.

---

[92] The QOOH was a locally raised yeomanry regiment. It had its headquarters' in Oxford where 'A' Squadron was based and three other composite squadrons located around the county one of which, 'B' Squadron, was based in Woodstock with drill halls in Witney and Bicester.

Because of their distance from the front line these reserve trenches were not subject to enemy rifle fire but they were vulnerable to enemy artillery fire and on the 28th a German shell exploded in one of the trenches wounding seven men of the QOOH.

One of those wounded was George Jones.[93] He was evacuated to the No.13 Stationary Hospital, at Boulogne, where he died on the 27th May 1915. Today his grave can be found in the Boulogne Eastern Cemetery, France.

C.H. Keene
Private, Charles Henry Keene, 113408,
87th General Hospital,
Royal Army Medical Corps

Charles Keene was born in Corn Street, Witney, on the 11th February 1889, the youngest son of Richard, a shoemaker, and his wife Emma (née Haines). In the census of 1911 Charles, was recorded as living with his widowed mother, his father having died in 1907, and working as a grocer's assistant at Messrs *Saltmarsh and Druce* in the Market Square.

On the 24th November 1915 Charles, still a grocer's assistant, presented himself at the Army recruitment office in the High Street, Oxford, and volunteered for military service. He was attached to the Royal Army Medical Corps and posted to a training camp near Blackpool, (most likely to have been at Weeton Camp). Charles remained at Blackpool for the next eighteen months and in the early summer of 1917 he received orders for his deployment overseas. He left Southampton on the 24th June 1917 and, after travelling through France and catching another troop ship at Marseilles, he arrived at the Egyptian port of Alexandria on the 9th July. Charles spent the rest of the war in Egypt and, on the 6th November 1918, as the conflict neared its conclusion, he was posted to the 87th General Hospital at the vast British military base at Kantara, on the eastern bank of the Suez Canal.

---

[93] The official history of the QOOH records that there were only seven casualties whilst the Regiment was at Potijze and the brief details of George's death state simply that he "D[ied of]. W[ounds]. Potijze" – taken from Keith-Falconer, A., The Oxfordshire Hussars in the Great War 1914-1918, John Murray, London, 1927. (p.350)

When the war ended in 1918 military personnel were selectively demobilised and returned to their civilian lives. It was an anxious time for many who were desperate to get back home and secure a job in what all knew would become a saturated labour market. None was more anxious than Charles Keene. His mother and his girlfriend awaited his return and he was eager to get back to them, but the weeks dragged on and by the spring of 1919 he was still at Kantara. His anxiety appears to have developed into despondency and it is possible that he may have descended into a state of depression.

At the end of April 1919 he was moved into a shared tent with a number of other soldiers from a mixture of units. He was remembered by these men as being quiet and never sharing any more than the briefest of conversations with them save only to complain about his continued stay in the Army. At around 5:45 p.m. on the afternoon of the 3rd May Charles joined one of his comrades, Driver William Cove of the Royal Engineers, for a meal. William and Charles were in the same tent together and in the few days prior to the 3rd the two had been set to work in the Sergeant's Mess. It was in the Sergeant's Mess, at around 6:30 p.m. that evening that Charles was last seen by William.

At 6:00 a.m. on the morning of the 4th May, with Charles having failed to return to the tent the previous night, William reported his absence to the Duty Sergeant. It was more than a day later before any news was heard of Charles's whereabouts. At 10:30 a.m. on the morning of the 5th May 1919 it was reported to the sentry on guard duty at the South Bridge, Kantara that a body had been seen in the Canal. The fully clothed body was soon found and recovered from the water and conveyed to the mortuary of the 44th Stationary Hospital in the camp, where an examination of the deceased's identity discs revealed the body to be that of Charles Keene. Formal identification was conducted later that afternoon by Private Lee of the RAMC, who had known Charles and had shared the same tent with him for several days.

Following a hastily arranged post mortem a Court of Enquiry was convened that same evening to ascertain the cause of Charles Keene's death. There was no medical evidence of foul play and following the testaments of a number of witnesses it was concluded that at the time of his death on the 5th May 1919, "...*he* [Keene] *was not on duty and that owing to lack of evidence as to mental condition it cannot be stated if he was to blame and that no other person was to blame.*"[94]

He was buried with full military honours in the Kantara Military Cemetery, Egypt, on the morning of the 6th May 1919, in a service which was attended by his Commanding Officer and around 200 of his comrades.

T. Keen
Private, Thomas Andrew Keen, 7496,
2nd Battalion,
Oxfordshire & Buckinghamshire Light Infantry

Thomas 'Tom' Keen, was born in Corn Street, Witney, during the spring of 1887, the son of Thomas, a builder's labourer, and his wife Elizabeth (née Woodley). In the census of 1901 Tom, like his father, was recorded as being employed as a builder's labourer. It appears that he joined the Army around 1905, serving with the Oxfordshire Light Infantry, and had been discharged to the reserves by the spring of 1911 when, in the census of that year, he was recorded as living with his parents in Corn Street and working as a jobbing gardener. In the fourth quarter of 1912 Tom married Harriett Wing at Witney and in the autumn of the following year their first child was born, a daughter they named Margaret.

Upon the declaration of war in August 1914 Tom, still a reservist, was recalled to the colours and posted to the 2nd Battalion of the Oxfordshire and Buckinghamshire Light Infantry, part of the 2nd Division. Tom landed with his Battalion at Boulogne on the 14th August 1914 as part of the 2nd Division which itself became one of the first units of the British Expeditionary Force to be deployed to France. Once on the Western Front the 2nd Division fought in most of the major engagements of the war, including the opening actions at Mons and the subsequent rearguard actions, as the Allies were pushed back towards Paris, and again in the Allied counter attack and the so called 'race to the sea'

---

[94] Taken from the official report of the court of enquiry contained within Keene's military record.

in which both sides sought to outflank each other as they moved in a north westerly direction towards the Channel ports.

On 14th October 1914, during this 'race to the sea' the British occupied the Belgian town of Ypres and despite its extremely vulnerable position within a salient, or bulge in the front line, and repeated German attempts to take it, it was to remain in British hands until the end of the war. Between mid October and mid November 1914 a bitter fight took place between the British and Germans in the first of a series of battles over control of the town. It is not known if Tom was wounded during this period of fighting or shortly after but, in a letter sent home to his family in Ducklington, Colour-Sergeant Harry Edwards described what happened:

> "...It was me who helped to bandage up Tom Keen from Witney, he was in my company and section, and I was close to him when he was hit. It was very unfortunate for him, as it was a stray shot, and we were well away from the firing line. It hit him in the back and came out of his stomach. Poor old Keen, I did feel sorry for him, and I shall never forget when he was hit. He was a very willing fellow, and would do anything."[95]

Tom Keen died from his wounds on the 30th November 1914. Today his grave can be found in the Ypres Town Cemetery Extension, just over half a mile from the town centre, Ieper, Belgium.

A.J.W. Launchbury
Private, Alfred John William Launchbury, 203217,
1/4th Battalion,
Oxfordshire & Buckinghamshire Light Infantry

Alfred Launchbury was born at Newland in the spring of 1898, the eldest son of John, an assurance agent, and his wife, Selina (née Green). At some point between 1901 and 1907 the family moved to Brize Norton where John began

---

[95] Originally printed in the *Witney Gazette*, 5th December 1914.

trading as a grocer. It is unclear exactly when the move back to Witney took place but it was before 1917, when Alfred enlisted, and by 1918 John and Selina were living at *Moor View* in the town.

It is likely that Alfred joined the Army during the first half of 1917 and around August of that year, following a period of basic training, he was posted to the 1/4th Battalion of the Oxfordshire and Buckinghamshire Light Infantry, part of the 48th (South Midland) Division, which had been on the Western Front since March 1915. In November 1917, having taken part in the Third Battle of Ypres, or "Passchendaele" as it came to be known, the 48th Division, received orders for a move to the Italian Front.

Between the 1st and 16th of March 1918 the Division held the front line sector at Montello before moving west to the relatively quiet Asiago sector. However the peace did not last. On the 15th June 1918 the Austrians launched a surprise offensive against the Allied forces in the area, managing to breach the front line and penetrate to a depth of 1,000 yards. It was during this fight that:

> *"...Pte. Launchbury, A.J., was killed in action...he was a most willing, obedient and gallant fellow. He was killed by a bullet from a machine gun while the Austrians were attacking our position and he fought bravely to the last. He is buried in a British Cemetery behind the line, and the position of it will be sent to you by myself if possible ... W. Wince, 4 O.B.L.I."*[96]

During the *Battle of Asiago,* as it came to be known, the Austrians failed to consolidate their initial gains and on the following day the Allies counter attacked, driving the Austrians back and regaining all the lost ground.

Alfred was buried, alongside a number of his comrades including fellow Witney men; Arthur Mace and William Cox, in the Boscon British Cemetery on the Asiago Plateau, Northern Italy.

---

[96] From a letter sent to Alfred's parents from his platoon officer. Published in the *Witney Gazette,* 13th July 1918.

C.E. Launchbury
Private, Charles Edwin Launchbury, 9984,
6th Battalion,
Oxfordshire & Buckinghamshire Light Infantry

Charles Launchbury was born in Witney during the last quarter of 1896, the third child and first son of Albert, a rural postman, and his wife Emily (née Haley). He was only two years old when his mother died and a year later, in 1899, his father married Elizabeth Pickett, a local girl twelve years his junior. At the time of the 1901 census the family were living on Woodgreen but by 1911 the recently widowed Elizabeth (Charles's father had died towards the end of 1910) and her children[97], were living in Gloucester Place and Charles was working as a grocer's errand boy.

When war broke out in August 1914 Charles was quick to volunteer for military service. He was accepted into the Oxfordshire and Buckinghamshire Light Infantry (OBLI) and posted to the newly formed 6th Battalion, part of the 20th (Light) Division. Following a period of training and equipping, the Division was inspected on the 24th June 1915 by King George V at Knighton Down and deemed ready to go to war. It landed in France a month later.

Once in France the 20th Division was first concentrated in the St. Omer area and then in the Fleurbaix area for trench familiarisation and further training before beginning its rotation through the trench lines of the Western Front. The Division's first major offensive operation was the attack on Mount Sorrel in the Ypres Salient[98] in June 1916. Later that year it was involved on the Somme in the Battles of Delville Wood, Guillemont, Flers-Courcelette. Morval and Le Transoy.

Upon the cessation of offensive operations on the Somme in November 1916 the units of the 20th Division remained in the area. Charles and his comrades in the 6th OBLI spent Christmas Day in billets at Meaulte, having left the trenches several days earlier on the 21st December. They returned to the front line near Bouleaux Wood, east of Guillemont on the 2nd January 1917 and rotation in and out of the line continued. On the 26th February 1917 the Battalion was once

---

[97] Three step children from Albert's previous marriage and two children from her own marriage to Albert.

[98] The bulge in the Allied front line protecting the town of Ypres.

again ordered into the line at Guillemont. There were no entries in the unit diary during this brief spell in the front line and the battalion was relieved on the 1st March to go into camp at Carnoy.[99] However it was during this period in the trenches, on the 27th February 1917, that Charles Launchbury along with two others was killed in action as a result of shell fire.

In a letter sent to Charles's step mother shortly after his death Thomas Howell, a non-conformist military chaplain wrote that *"...he lies with his other fellow comrades in the cemetery... A single cross (with inscription) will be placed shortly to mark the spot."*[100] But the site of Charles's grave was subsequently lost as the fighting continued and today, with no known grave, his name is recorded on the Thiepval Memorial to the missing of the Somme. Thiepval, France.

In 1918 Charles's eldest half-sister, Lucy Harris, died whilst in service with the Women's Royal Air Force. Lucy, who is buried in an unmarked grave in Cogges Churchyard, is not recorded on the Witney War Memorial. (see appendix i)

R. L. Leigh
Lieutenant, Reginald Lea Leigh,
No.3 Squadron,
Royal Air Force

Reginald Leigh was born in Corn Street, Witney, on Saturday 6th August 1898, the eldest son of Edmund, a prominent local ironmonger, and his wife, Kate (née Stevens). In 1905, following an acrimonious dispute, Reginald's mother, pregnant with the couple's third child, left Witney to go and live with her mother in Bournemouth. Whilst there her baby was born, a son she named Edmund. Shortly after Edmund's birth the couple formally divorced and it is believed that neither Reginald nor his younger sister Rita, born in 1902, who had both remained living in Witney with their father, ever saw their mother

---

[99] WO 95/2120
[100] Extract taken from a letter published in the *Witney Gazette*, 17th March 1917.

again. In 1908 Reginald's father married for the second time to Maud Whillans and the couple had children of their own.

On the 10th August 1916, four days after his 18th birthday, former Burford Grammar school pupil, Reginald, joined the Mechanical Transport (MT) section of the Army Service Corps (ASC) and following basic training was posted on the 25th January 1917 to 606 ASC MT Company based at Holland Park, London. Four months later he moved to the 104th Training Reserve Battalion based in Edinburgh. Later he transferred to the Royal Flying Corps (RFC) and on the 14th August 1917 he joined the Cadet Wing of the RFC to begin his initial pilot training. On 24th October, having successfully completed the first stage of his course he was officially discharged from the Army and granted a commission with the RFC.

On 25th October he moved to a Military Aeronautics school where he spent several weeks consolidating his military knowledge and learning new subjects such as aviation theory, navigation, photography and artillery and infantry co-operation. On the 20th November Reginald moved to No.3 Training Depot Station at Lopcombe Corner in Wiltshire. Here he would have completed a minimum of 25 hours of elementary flying training on an older aircraft. The following month he moved to Scotland for training, first at the No.1 School of Aerial Fighting near Ayr and then at the nearby No.2 Auxiliary School of Aerial Gunnery. Whilst in Scotland, as well as completing a further 35 hours of flying time he would have experienced a minimum of 5 hours of flying a modern 'front-line' type of aircraft. All that remained was for Reginald to proceed to the final specialist stage of his training which he began on the 10th March at the Royal Naval Air Station, Manston in Kent. Just over two weeks later, on the 27th March 1918, training completed and finally permitted to wear his Pilot's Wings, Reginald was deployed for operational service with No.3 Squadron in France.

No.3 Squadron had been one of the first squadrons deployed to France with the British Expeditionary Force (BEF) in 1914 and on the 26th March 1918, the day before Reginald Leigh's deployment, it had moved for the thirtieth time since its arrival in France to a new airfield at Valheureux, some 15 miles north of the city of Amiens. The squadron was equipped with the famous and very successful Sopwith Camel aircraft, a type originally intended solely as a fighter but due to its poorer performance in speed and altitude, when compared with other types, was by 1918 being used increasingly as a ground-attack and infantry support aircraft. This then was the unit Reginald joined in March 1918.

At 3 p.m. on the 18th June 1918, Reginald, promoted a month earlier to Lieutenant, and four of his squadron left the airfield at Valheureux to undertake an aerial patrol along the British 3rd Army Battle Front. One hour into the patrol and flying over the village of Neuville St Vaast, behind the German front line, it became necessary for the aircraft to descend from 14,000 feet to 12,000 feet to move below some local cloud cover which had obscured their view of the battlefield. Captain Arnot, the patrol leader and last man to see Reginald before he entered the cloud, later confirmed that all the aircraft of the patrol had been together as they began their dive but that when they had cleared the cloud cover two of the aircraft were missing. Major Ronald McClintock, Commanding Officer of No.3 Squadron, in a letter written a couple of days later to Reginald's father, surmised that Reginald's machine and that of his fellow pilot, Lieutenant Owen Nicholson, who it was reported had been flying close to him as they entered the cloud, must have collided as there were no reports of enemy aircraft in the vicinity and enemy anti-aircraft fire had been very slight.[101]

Despite the best efforts of the authorities, and of his father, the bodies of Reginald and his fellow pilot were never recovered. Reginald's service record does however contain two letters written in 1919 which identify two separate locations where he was thought to have been buried at the time. Neither of which have ever been substantiated, therefore he has no known grave and today his name and that of his comrade are recorded on the Flying Services Memorial in Arras, France.

---

[101] AIR 76/295/116

G.H. Long
Sapper, George Henry Long, 24286,
57th Field Company,
Royal Engineers

George Long was born in Northleach during the fourth quarter of 1894, the eldest son of Ernest, an ironmonger, and his wife Mary (née Hobbs). Around 1900 the family moved to Swindon where Ernest had found work as a gas fitter but, by the time of the 1911 census, he had brought his family to Witney, the town of his birth, where they were living in a house on the Woodstock Road. Ernest was employed as an ironmonger's assistant and George was working as an apprentice steam fitter.

When the war began in 1914 George volunteered and was initially posted to the Oxfordshire and Buckinghamshire Light Infantry. However, and no doubt due to his work experience, he was transferred to the Royal Engineers (RE) and it was with the RE that he was posted to France on 21st March 1915. On the 19th December 1915 George was serving with the 57th Field Company, part of the 49th (West Riding) Division, holding the line of the Ypres Salient between Frezenburg and Boesinghe. It was here, on that day, that the Germans first used phosgene gas against the British.

The British units in the area had been placed on a state of alert for a possible gas attack and when, at 5:00 a.m., the gas cloud began to drift over no-man's land towards their trenches they opened fire on the German positions suppressing any attempted infantry attacks. But at 6:15 a.m. a second phase of the attack began when the Germans began to fire gas shells directly into the British lines. These shells contained a new weapon – phosgene, a chemical which when inhaled causes the lungs to fill with liquid leaving the victim to literally drown. In addition to the gas, the German attackers then unleashed a heavy artillery bombardment on the same sector before an infantry assault. Ultimately the attack failed and the line held but not without the British taking considerable casualties.

One of those casualties was George Long. Wounded, he died the following day (20th December 1915). Today his grave can be found in the Lijssenthoek Military Cemetery on the site of the casualty clearing station to which he was evacuated, seven miles west of Ipres, Belgium.

In addition to his name being recorded on the Witney War Memorial, George is also remembered on his elder sister, Winifred's, headstone. She died on 1st December 1918 and is buried in the churchyard of Holy Trinity, Woodgreen.

H.C. Long
Sergeant, Howard Charles Long, 63218,
89th Field Company,
Royal Engineers
(Elder brother of Herbert E. Long, killed in action, France, 23rd July 1916)

Howard Long was born in Witney during the first quarter of 1879, the third son of Henry, an ironmonger, and his wife Mary Ann (née Hollis). As a child he attended the town's Wesleyan Day School and after leaving school he entered into a carpentry apprenticeship. By 1901 Howard had moved to Nottingham where, living in lodgings, he was working as a carpenter and joiner. In the spring of 1903 he married Annie Morley and the couple had one child who died in infancy. At the time of the 1911 census Howard was employed as a joiner and the couple were still in Nottingham. On census night itself, 2nd/3rd April, Annie was an in-patient of the city's Samaritan Hospital for Women.

At the beginning of the war Howard enlisted for military service and following basic training was posted to the 89th Field Company of the Royal Engineers. By the time of his deployment to France he had been promoted to the rank of Lance Corporal. On 22nd May 1915 his unit arrived on the Western Front as part of the 14th (Light) Division where it was to remain for the rest of the war.

On the 12th March 1916 Howard and a party of men from both his own unit and others, were engaged in the construction of earthworks near Arras when a section of the earthworks gave way burying and killing several men, among them Sergeant Howard Long. The bodies were recovered and re-buried in the small Dainville Communal Cemetery in the village of Dainville, just west of Arras, France.

H.E. Long
Herbert Edward Long, Lance Corporal, 2622,
'B' Company,
1/4th Battalion,
Oxfordshire & Buckinghamshire Light Infantry
(Younger brother of Howard C. Long, who died in France, 12th March 1916)

Herbert Long was born in Witney during the second quarter of 1886, the youngest son of Henry, an ironmonger, and his wife Mary Ann (née Hollis). He attended the town's Wesleyan Day School and was a member of the choir of St. Mary's Church, later becoming a bell ringer there. Upon leaving school he worked as an assistant in his father's shop in the High Street.

Herbert enlisted for military service on the 1st of September 1914 and was posted to the newly formed 1/4th Battalion of the Oxfordshire and Buckinghamshire Light Infantry (OBLI), part of the South Midland (later the 48th) Division. Once trained and equipped the Division was deployed to France and the Western Front, with the 1/4th OBLI landing at Boulogne on the 29th March 1915. Herbert fought with his battalion on the Western Front for the next fifteen months. In early 1916 news reached him from home that his mother had died and in March his elder brother, Howard, a Sergeant in the Royal Engineers, was killed in an accident whilst on active service. Nevertheless Herbert persevered, eventually gaining promotion to Lance Corporal and being made a Section Leader within 'B' Company.

During the evening of July 22nd 1916 the men of the 1/4th OBLI were moved into trenches, just west of Pozieres, in preparation for a night attack on the enemy. At 12:30 a.m. the attack began with 'A' Company advancing to the right of the German line and 'D' Company, supported by 'B' Company to the left. Almost immediately 'A' Company reached their objective but 'D' and 'B' met with stiff opposition and having eventually secured their objectives were then forced to repel two very determined German counter attacks. The battalion was reinforced at 4 a.m. by men from the 4th Royal Berks and their arrival helped obscure the heavy losses sustained by the 1/4th OBLI until later in the day when the full list of killed, wounded and missing was compiled.

Herbert Long was last seen leading his section into the attack on the German line. At first he was recorded as 'missing in action' and his family hoped that he had been taken prisoner but during the first week of September 1916 confirmation was received from the War Office that he had been killed on the 23rd July. His body was never identified and he has no known grave. Today his name is remembered on the Thiepval Memorial to the missing of the Somme, Thiepval, France

J. Long
2nd Lieutenant, John Long,
8th Battalion,
(Princess Charlotte of Wales's) Royal Berkshire Regiment

John Long, or 'Jack' as he was known, was born in Witney during the final quarter of 1895, the fifth child and only son of John, a carpenter and undertaker, and his wife Annie (née Wiggins). In the 1890's the family moved from the High Street to No.18 West End, where, around the turn of the century, John (senior) entered into a business partnership with master builder, Frank Berry, also of West End. Together they ran a combined building and undertakers business - *Long and Berry*, a trading name that lived on locally for many years after John Long had left Witney. In the census of 1911 Jack Long was recorded as being in employment *"learning carpentry"*, no doubt in the employ of his father.

In 1914, following the outbreak of war, an eighteen year old Jack attempted to join the Army and serve alongside his fellow townsmen. Unfortunately and for reasons now unknown he was rejected. He tried again, only to be similarly rejected. Undaunted though, he continued trying and several attempts later, in August 1915, he was finally accepted into the Army Cyclist Corps. He landed in France on the 12th March 1916 and was to serve for the next two years as a despatch rider on the Western Front. Sadly, back home in Witney during the winter of 1917/18, Jack's mother, Annie, died and shortly after her death his father left Witney and moved to Reading. It was during this period that Jack was accepted for officer training in the U.K. and on the 27th August 1918 he duly received his commission as a second lieutenant with the 8th Battalion,

Royal Berkshire Regiment. His training took place at Fleet and then at Lowestoft and once completed he was sent back to France.

Jack joined his new battalion at some point between the 2nd and the 17th October 1918, when the 8th Royal Berks, along with the rest of 53rd Brigade, were billeted in and around the village of Allonville, 3 miles north of Amiens. Held in reserve to refit, regroup and undergo further training, they were to be used in the final assault on the German positions in the Artois region. Their time in reserve ended on the 17th October when the Battalion went back into the front line in the Le Cateau area. On the 22nd October they were involved in a successful attack on the German lines which resulted in the capture of eleven field guns and more than twenty machine guns. On the 26th they went on the offensive again at a place known as 'Mount Carmel' - not so much a hill more an undulating cultivated field which rose slightly higher than the surrounding ground, the farthest edge of which was held by the Germans. Following this engagement they were pulled back into reserve for a few days to Bousies Wood, north east of Le Cateau, before returning to the front line on the 30th October.

On the evening of the 3rd November the Battalion, mustering just 15 officers (one of whom was Jack Long) and 243 other ranks, was moved into its assembly position for the final advance through the enemy held Forest of Mormal near the Franco-Belgian border. Four years earlier British soldiers of I and II Corps had been separated by the Forest's lack of passable roads as they retreated from Mons. Now the British had returned on the offensive, pursuing a retreating German Army. At 7.35 a.m. on the morning of the 4th November, with the nearby villages of Hecq and Preux au Bois having been earlier taken by the men of the Royal West Kents, the 8th Royal Berks began their final advance towards their objective – a 'red line' drawn on a map, which cut the forest in two. Enemy resistance from hidden machine gun posts was stiff and despite the creeping barrage, behind which the 8th Royal Berks were advancing, casualties were taken. However the men kept moving forward and, at around 3 p.m., they were able to join up on their right with the 10th Essex who had been fighting their way through from the south east of the forest. Having gained the 'red line' the 8th Royal Berks and the 10th Essex set about consolidating their positions whilst further advances were continued by units of the 55th Brigade, which passed through the 'red line' deeper into the forest, onwards to their own final objectives.

Unbeknown, at the time, to the men of the 8th Royal Berks their newly won positions on the 'red line' were to mark the end of their fighting career during the Great War. They were pulled back into reserve on the 5th November and news of the armistice reached the battalion whilst they were in billets at Le Cateau. There are no records to indicate at which point during the attack on the 4th November Jack Long was killed. The Battalion diary does not mention his loss until an entry written on the 11th November – the day of the ceasefire, which records him as being one of two officers lost during that month.

Today his body lies in the communal cemetery in the village of Preux-Au-Bois situated near the Western edge of the Foret de Mormal, France.

A.G. Mace
Lance Corporal, Arthur Guy Mace, 200649,
1/4th Battalion,
Oxfordshire & Buckinghamshire Light Infantry

Arthur Mace was born in Milton-Under-Wychwood during the spring of 1885, the eldest son of John, a farmer, and his wife Elizabeth (née Guy). After leaving Burford Grammar School he entered into employment with the Metropolitan Bank at their Witney branch and, at the time of the 1911 census, he was living in the town, lodging at a house on the Woodstock Road. He remained with the bank, working as a cashier, until volunteering for military service on the outbreak of war.

On Tuesday the 1st September 1914 Arthur joined a large group of local men as they marched through Witney, to the sound of cheering crowds, on their way to the railway station and the Army recruiting centre in Oxford. The following day he enlisted and was posted to the newly formed 1/4th Battalion of the Oxfordshire and Buckinghamshire Light Infantry, part of the South Midland Division. Once trained and equipped the 1/4th were moved to Folkestone from where they deployed to France and the Western Front arriving at Boulogne on the 29th March 1915.

Whilst on the Western Front the men of the 1/4th fought through the great Allied offensive on the Somme in the summer of 1916 and then through the Third Battle of Ypres, or "Passchendaele" as it is now more commonly known. In November 1917 the Division received orders for a move to Italy, and by March 1918 the Division was holding the line at the Montello in Northern Italy. Towards the end of March it was moved to the Asiago Sector where it was to remain for several months engaged in sporadic fighting with the Austrians - the most notable engagement during this period being the battle on the 15th/16th June. It was during this engagement, on the 15th June 1918, that Arthur Mace was killed in action.

Today his grave can be found in the Boscon British Cemetery, on the Asiago Plateau, Northern Italy.

G.E. Martin
Private, George Ernest Martin, 27364,
56th Company,
Machine Gun Corps (Infantry)
(Younger brother of James and John Martin, killed in action on 3rd July 1916 and 12th October 1917 respectively)

George Martin was born in at Newland, Witney, during the spring of 1895, the youngest son of John, a blanket finisher and his wife Mary (née Haley). George's mother died in 1910 and in the census of 1911 George, working in a local blanket factory as a mill hand, was recorded as living with his widowed father at the family home in Mill Street.

On the 24th November 1915 George enlisted for military service with the Oxfordshire and Buckinghamshire Light Infantry and on the 4th December 1915 he was posted to the 9th (Reserve) Battalion. He subsequently transferred to the newly formed Machine Gun Corps on the 10th March 1916 and was deployed to France on the 10th June 1916. One month later he was posted to the 11th Machine Gun Company, part of the 4th Division, on the Western Front. On the 3rd July 1916 his brother, James, serving with the Worcestershire Regiment, was killed in action on the Somme.

George's military service record indicates that on the 21st October 1916, following either wound or sickness (it doesn't specify), he was admitted, via Field Ambulance and Casualty Clearing Station, to the 8th General Hospital in Rouen. He soon recovered and, on the 22nd December 1916, after a brief spell at the Machine Gun Corps Base Depot at Camiers, he was posted to the 56th Machine Gun Company, part of the 19th Division.

After taking his first period of leave at home in the U.K. since his original deployment to the Western Front over a year earlier, George returned to France to rejoin his unit on the 15th September 1917. Five days later, on the 20th, the opening day of the Battle of the Menin Road Ridge, he was killed in action. Today his grave can be found in the Oxford Street Cemetery, near Ypres, Belgium.

One month later, on the 12th October 1917, George's brother, John, was killed in action during the battle to take Passchendaele.

J. Martin
Private, John Martin, 14923,
1st Battalion,
Grenadier Guards
(Brother of James and George Martin, killed in action on 3rd July 1916 and 20th September 1917 respectively)

John Martin was born at Newland, Witney, in the second quarter of 1893, the fifth son of John, a blanket finisher and his wife Mary (née Haley). During the late 1890's the family moved to Mill Street where they were living when John's mother died in the summer of 1910. Shortly after her death John joined the Army, volunteering to serve with the Grenadier Guards. At the time of the 1911 census he was with the 2nd Battalion at Blenheim Barracks, Aldershot.

When Britain went to war in 1914 the 2nd Battalion, part of the 2nd Division, was stationed at Chelsea in London and was one of the first units to deploy to France, arriving on the 13th August 1914. During the First Battle of Ypres (October – November 1914) the 2nd battalion suffered catastrophic casualties with all but four officers and 140 men falling in action. In September 1915, most likely during the Battle of Loos, John was seriously wounded and evacuated back to England for medical treatment. Over the following months he made a full recovery and in June 1916 he returned to France and was posted to his Regiment's 1st Battalion. One month later, on 3rd July, his elder brother, James, serving with the 10th Battalion, Worcestershire Regiment, was killed in action on the Somme. And further bad news followed when on 20th September 1917 his younger brother George, serving with the Machine Gun Corps, was killed in action in Belgium.

On the night of the 10th October 1917, midst the heavy fighting and appalling conditions of the Third Battle of Ypres, the men of the 1st Battalion, Grenadier Guards, relieved the 1st Irish Guards in the front line trenches facing the ruins of Passchendaele. Throughout the following day preparations were made for an attack on the German lines and at 5.25 am on the 12th October 1917, zero hour, the 1st Battalion went over the top. It was during the fierce fighting which followed that John Martin was killed.

His body was never identified and he has no known grave. Today his name is remembered on the Tyne Cot Memorial, Belgium, alongside the names of nearly 35,000 British and Commonwealth troops who died in the Ypres Salient and whose final resting places are unknown.

J.W. Martin
Lance-Corporal, James William Martin, 20940,
10th Battalion,
Worcestershire Regiment
(Elder brother of George and John Martin, killed in action on 20th
September 1917 and 12th October 1917, respectively)

James Martin, who as a child was known by his middle name of 'William', was born at Newland, Witney, in the second quarter of 1886, the third son of John, a blanket finisher, and his wife Mary (née Haley). At the time of the 1901 census the family were living in Mill Street and James was working as a grocer's assistant. By 1911 he had left Witney and had moved to London where, still employed as a grocer's assistant, he was recorded as being in lodgings at a house in Leytonstone. It was around this time that he married Lily (maiden name unknown).

James enlisted shortly after the commencement of the war and following basic training was posted to the 10th Battalion of the Worcestershire Regiment, part of the 19th (Western) Division. On the night of the 18th/19th July 1915, as part of a Divisional move, the men of the 10th Battalion crossed the English Channel landing at Boulogne and by the first week in August they were in the trenches facing the enemy at Neuve Chapelle. They were to remain on the Western Front for the rest of the war.

By the end of June 1916, James Martin, now promoted to the rank of Lance-Corporal, was with his battalion and the rest of the 19th Division on the Somme, in preparation for the long planned summer offensive – the Big Push to punch through the German lines, and break-out into the open countryside beyond, thereby bringing an end to the stalemate of trench warfare. On the morning of July 1st the Allied attack began and the 19th Division, although in position close to the front line, was held in reserve, ready to exploit the breakthrough whereupon its troops would push through the initial attacking force to take the enemy held town of Bapaume. This did not happen.

In the early hours of the 3rd July, almost forty eight hours into the attack, the men of the 10th Worcesters, having managed to advance under enemy fire a short distance into no-man's-land, had been forced to take cover in whatever shell holes and depressions they could find. The 19th Division had been ordered to take the smashed but heavily fortified village of La Boiselle just behind the German lines and at 3 a.m., the 10th Worcesters, as part of the first attacking wave, rose out of their shell holes and advanced on the village. The fighting that ensued was chaotic and relentless but by mid-day half of the village had been taken;

> The ruined buildings concealed fortifications, dugouts and hidden strongpoints as apparently invincible as any on the front, but the Worcesters had fought with bayonet and bomb. They had gone on fighting when the Commanding Officer, the Second-in-Command and almost every other officer had been killed or wounded and there was no longer anyone to lead the fight.[102]

---

[102] Macdonald, L., <u>Somme</u>, Macmillan, London, 1985. (p.100)

Of the Worcesters' eight hundred and ten men that had advanced on La Boiselle that morning only four hundred and forty eight came out. One of those killed was James Martin. His body was never identified and he has no known grave. Today his name is remembered on the Thiepval Memorial to the missing of the Somme.

By the end of the following year James' two younger brothers were also dead: George, killed in action near Ypres on the 20th September 1917 and one month later on the 12th October, John was killed during the fighting for Passchendaele.

A.H. Miles
Private, Albert Henry Miles, 23035,
4th Battalion,
Worcestershire Regiment

Albert Miles, known as 'Bert', was born in Oxford Road, Newland, around February 1896, the third son of Joseph, a mason's labourer, and his wife Winifred (née Trotman). After he had finished his education Bert worked as a house painter with the local firm of *Harwood and Sons,* a job he still had in February 1914 when he joined the 4th (Territorial) Battalion of the Oxfordshire and Buckinghamshire Light Infantry. However, his initial military career did not last very long. On the 8th September 1914, a little over a month after the declaration of war and the mobilisation of the Territorial Force, he was discharged from the Army as being medically unfit.

Undeterred and keen to play his part, he volunteered for military service once again and on the 22nd February 1915 he was accepted into the Worcestershire Regiment. On the 15th July that year, following his basic training he was deployed to the Dardanelles as part of a draft of reinforcements. He landed at Helles on the Gallipoli Peninsular, Turkey, and upon his arrival was attached to his Regiment's 4th Battalion, part of 88th Brigade, 29th Division.

The fighting had been raging at Gallipoli since the initial Allied landings had been made on the 25th April, but despite repeated attempts and after suffering heavy causalities the Allies had been unable to break out from the toe hold they occupied on the tip of the peninsula. A further offensive was planned for early

August when, on the evening of the 6th August, two fresh infantry Divisions were to be landed further up the peninsular at Suvla, five miles north of Anzac. The resulting combined assault of Allied troops from Suvla and Anzac would, it was hoped, punch through the Turkish lines and break out of the Anzac perimeter thereby opening up a war of movement.

As a prelude to the landings at Suvla a number of diversionary attacks were to be made at Helles and Anzac to draw Turkish troops away from the main assault. One of those attacks, on the afternoon of the 6th August was made by the men of 88th Brigade against the Turkish lines south-west of the fortified village of Krithia, in an area known as 'The Vineyard'. Facing four Turkish Divisions, supported by a further two held in reserve, the 88th Brigade, although heavily outnumbered, mounted two determined attacks and succeeded in capturing some of the enemy's trenches. However these were swiftly taken in the immediate Turkish counter-attack. Casualties were heavy on both sides with the 88th Brigade unable to hold any of the ground taken, and the battle effectively destroying it as a fighting unit.

One of those casualties that afternoon was Bert Miles. He was last seen as he went into action alongside his comrades. Initially his family were informed that he had been posted as 'missing in action', which prompted a series of appeals for further information from Bert's parents. It was not until the 24th of February 1916 that the military authorities concluded that Bert had died on the 6th August 1915. His body was never identified and he has no known grave. Today his name is remembered on the Helles Memorial, Gallipoli, Turkey.

Before the war, Bert's two older brothers, Frederick and William had emigrated to Canada. On the 19th August 1915, a fortnight after his brother was lost at Gallipoli, Frederick, then living in Toronto, enlisted with the Canadian Expeditionary Force. Deployed to France and promoted to the rank of Sergeant he was wounded in action and although he survived the war he was unable to walk for the rest of his life without the aid of crutches.

E. Miles
Private, Ernest Edwin Miles, 22773,
2/4th Battalion,
Oxfordshire & Buckinghamshire Light Infantry

Little is known about Ernest Miles but it is probable that he was born at Cogges during the first quarter of 1897 and that he was the eldest child of Edwin, a blanket finisher, and his wife Edith (née Martin). By the time of the 1911 census he was recorded as being employed as a shoemaker's apprentice.

In the absence of his military record it is not possible to say when Ernest enlisted but his record of medal entitlement indicates that it may have been around 1917. Following his basic training he was posted to France and attached to the 2/4th Battalion of the Oxfordshire and Buckinghamshire Light Infantry (OBLI), part of the 61st (2nd South Midland) Division, a formation which had been in France since May 1916 and which was to remain on the Western Front for the duration of the War.

On the night of the 18th March 1918 the 2/4th OBLI went into the front line just north of Saint Quentin. It was widely believed, through the intelligence gathered from captured German prisoners, that the enemy were about to launch a major offensive in the area and at 4.50 a.m. on the morning of the 21st March 1918 a terrific bombardment of the British lines began. Heavy casualties were sustained amongst the infantry sheltering in their trenches and artillery batteries were knocked out by long range German guns. As daylight crept over the battlefield and the barrage began to lift it was seen that much of the front line wire had been destroyed. At around 9.30 a.m. the noise of British Lewis guns firing heralded the beginning of the German assault. Captain G.K. Rose, M.C. later recalled;

> 'In the front line showers of stick bombs announced the enemy's presence. Everywhere it seemed that quick moving bodies in grey uniforms were closing in from either flank and were behind. In the mist our posts were soon over-run.'[103]

---

[103] Rose, G.K., Captain, M.C., The Story of the 2/4th Oxfordshire and Buckinghamshire Light Infantry, Blackwell, Oxford, 1920. (p. 161)

116

The 21st March 1918 marked the beginning of the Great German offensive of that year and their last of the war. It was also the day on which Ernest Miles was killed in action. His body was never identified and he has no known grave. Today his name is remembered, alongside the names of over 14,000 British soldiers, on the Pozieres Memorial at Pozieres in France. This memorial, which encircles the military cemetery at Pozieres, records all those who were similarly killed and lost during the retreat of the Fifth Army on the Somme between 21st March and 7th August 1918.

E.J. Miles
Sergeant, Edwin John Miles (formerly Wiggins), 200040,
2/4th Battalion,
Oxfordshire & Buckinghamshire Light Infantry

Edwin Wiggins was born in Brize Norton around June 1880, the eldest son of George Wiggins, an agricultural labourer, and Flora Archer. His parents married in 1890, following the birth of two more children. Over the next two decades the family moved around the local area as Edwin's father followed work. In 1901 they were living in Bampton, by 1906 in Fullbrook and by 1910 in Chimney. At the time of the 1911 census Edwin, still living with his family at Chimney, was working with his father as a carter on a farm. By 1914 the family had moved again and were living at Burwell Farm near Witney. At some point between 1911 and 1914 the family changed their surname from 'Wiggins' to 'Miles'. Exactly when or why this change took place is not known but it is clear that in August 1914 when Edwin enlisted he did so under the name of Miles.

Initially Edwin was posted to the 1/4th Battalion of the Oxfordshire and Buckinghamshire Light Infantry, part of the South Midland Division. He was promoted corporal and on the 29th March 1915 he left for France and the Western Front.

During his time on the Western Front he was promoted Sergeant before being wounded badly enough to be invalided back to the UK. He made a complete recovery and, in the spring of 1918, he returned to France and was reassigned to his Regiment's 2/4th Battalion. It was whilst serving with the

2/4th, near the French village of Robecq, on the 24th May 1918, that he was killed in action.[104] The following two letters, sent to Edwin's mother following her son's death, convey the quality of the man:

Sergeant E.J. Miles ... was my Platoon Sergeant, and though only with us for one short month, he was loved and respected by all. We were more brothers to each other than sergeant and officer, and it was a great blow to me when I heard that he had been wounded by the very first shell we had that day ... He died before I reached him, the only consolation being in the fact that he did not suffer, being unconscious from the first. He was buried with all honour beneath a big poplar tree, in an orchard behind the farm, known as 'Carvin Farm' a few hundred yards north of the village of [Robecq]. A cross has been erected to the memory of a good God-fearing man, and a fine soldier, your son; ... My Colonel and Company Commander desire me to convey to you their deep sympathy. I should like to tell you that your son, when we were not fighting, treated all the boys as his children, never tiring in his efforts to provide for their amusement and pleasure. He was the instigator of a topping little concert party, and was the life and soul of many a good laugh, from which alone we shall always remember him. Never down-hearted in the trenches, I thought at times he took rather unnecessary risks, but he always insisted, saying it was for the good for the moral of the Platoon. I do hope you are not taking it too hard. God's will be done. Believe me, in deep sympathy yours very sincerely,
Arthur C. Stowell, 2nd Lieut."

"...I write to condole with you in the sad death of your son, and to express my sympathy with you in the loss. Serg. Miles had served a great many months with me in France. When he joined this Battalion I at once recognised him as one of my old comrades of 1915. Few men wearing sergeant's stripes could have joined this Battalion with a

---

[104] At this point he became the seventh member of his mother's family to fall in the Great War.

118

better record behind him. I regret most extremely that he should have been killed; his loss to the Battalion is great.
Yours sincerely
G.K. Rose, Major, 2nd in command."[105]

It is likely, given 2nd Lieutenant Stowell's description, that Edwin was initially buried in the small cemetery known at the time as the *Carvin British Cemetery.* After the Armistice the burials contained within a number of nearby cemeteries, including those at Carvin, were brought into a larger concentration cemetery. Today Edwin's final resting place can be found in the St. Venant-Robecq Road British Cemetery, Robecq, France

In addition to his name being recorded on the Witney War Memorial Edwin is also remembered on the War Memorial in Brize Norton.

S.E.A. Miles
Private, Sidney Edward Alfred Miles, 5676,
1/4th Battalion,
Oxfordshire & Buckinghamshire Light Infantry

Sidney Miles was born in the village of Asthall at the beginning of 1896, the eldest son of Edward, a coachman, and his wife Hannah (née Brooks). At some point after 1901 the family moved to Witney, and Sidney was enrolled as a pupil in the town's Grammar School. By 1911 the family were living in Lowell's Place and Sidney, an active member of the 1st Witney Company of the Boys Brigade, was working as a boot repairer.

Around the end of November 1915 Sidney volunteered for military service with the Oxfordshire and Buckinghamshire Light Infantry (OBLI) and in early 1916, following his basic training, he was assigned to the Regiment's 1/4th Battalion, part of the 48th (South Midland) Division, and posted to France to join his unit on the Somme.

On 1st July 1916 the British launched their much anticipated summer offensive on the Somme and the men of the 48th Division, involved from the

---

[105] Both letters originally published in the *Witney Gazette*, 22nd June 1918.

outset, were destined to fight throughout the campaign: actively engaging in the Battles of Albert, Bazentin Ridge, Pozieres, Ancre Heights and Ancre itself. On the 19th November 1916, having achieved limited gains at considerable cost, and failing in its overall objective of securing the much sought breakthrough, the great offensive on the Somme was called off.

However for the men of the 1/4th OBLI, holding the front line at Le Sars, the cessation of offensive operations on the 19th meant very little. Having sustained a number of casualties during the previous nights shelling, they were left standing in mud and water filled trenches in continuous rain with practically no shelter. There was no prospect of any hot food and, as the men moved ever closer to a state of complete exhaustion, they were continuously shelled by German artillery.

It was in these arduous conditions, on the 19th November 1916 - the last day of Somme offensive, that Sidney Miles, along with four of his comrades, was killed. His body was never identified and he has no known grave. Today his name is remembered on the Thiepval Memorial, France, alongside the names of over 72,000 officers and men who were similarly lost on the Somme.

S.J. Miles
Cadet, Sydney James Miles,
4th Officer Cadet Battalion

Sydney Miles was born in Witney towards the end of 1891, the third son of Charles, a gardener, and his wife Alice (née Lloyd). Unlike his two elder brothers, who like their father worked as gardeners, when Sydney left school he found work as an assistant in a draper's shop - a job he still had at the time of the 1911 census when he was recorded as living with his family at *The Lodge* on Woodgreen.

In August 1914 Sydney, along with three others, helped to organise a rather rousing display of patriotism. Their planning culminated at 3 p.m. on Tuesday the 1st September 1914 when, amid cheering crowds, Sydney was one of forty-two local men, all intent on volunteering for military service, who marched from the Wesleyan School through the town to the railway station and onwards by train to Oxford and the recruitment office. Upon enlistment Sydney was posted to the newly formed 1/4th Battalion of the Oxfordshire and Buckinghamshire Light Infantry, part of the South Midland Division, which deployed to France on the 29th March 1915. He continued to serve with the 1/4th throughout its time on the Western Front where it was engaged in various actions including those of the great Somme offensive of 1916.

In November 1917 the Division moved to Italy, where in 1918, Sydney by now promoted a Sergeant, was given the opportunity of returning home to England to undergo officer training.

It was whilst he was at Oxford, preparing to take his final examination for his commission, that he fell ill with influenza. This developed into pneumonia and on October 25th 1918, whilst receiving treatment at the No.3 Southern General Base Hospital in the City, he passed away. His body was brought back to Witney where he was buried in the town's cemetery, his grave today being marked by a private headstone.

W.J. Miles
Private, William James Miles, 11600,
'A' Company,
6th Battalion,
Oxfordshire & Buckinghamshire Light Infantry

William Miles was born in Witney around 1893, the eldest son of Albert, a labourer, and his wife Annie (née Gardner). In the census of 1911 Will, a former pupil of St. Mary's School was recorded working as a labourer in one of the town's blanket mills. Later that same year he married Margaret Busby and the couple went on to have two daughters.

Upon the outbreak of war in 1914 Will was amongst the first to volunteer for military service, joining the newly established 6th Battalion of the Oxfordshire and Buckinghamshire Light Infantry, part of the 20th (Light) Division. Once trained and equipped this unit was deployed to France on the 22nd July 1915.

In November 1915 a letter appeared in the *Witney Gazette* from acting Lance Corporal Will Miles who, writing on behalf of the *'Witney lads'* of 'A' Company, appealed to the people of Witney for '... *a mouth organ or so, as it would help to pass many a weary hour along, and would sometimes put us in lighter spirits'.*[106] One of the signatories to the letter was Sydney Beale. Ten months later, during the Battle of the Somme, Will and Sydney were among a group of men buried alive when a German shell brought their trench wall down. Will was dug out and in the course of attempting to rescue his friend he was injured by a second shell blast and hospitalised.

Once recovered Will returned to his unit in time to take part in the pursuit of the enemy as the Germans, exhausted and robbed of many of their experienced officers and NCOs during the fighting on the Somme, retreated to a shorter, straighter defensive line of their choosing – the Hindenburg Line. By February 1917 the withdrawal had begun, with the Germans destroying virtually everything they left behind, including roads, bridges, dug-outs, building etc. With much of what they did leave being booby-trapped. The Allies followed them in a cautious advance which halted before the Hindenburg Line on the 5th April 1917.

Will Miles was killed in action approximately two months later on the 3rd June 1917. Today his grave can be found in the Noreuil Australian Cemetery, near the village of Noreuil, approximately 6 miles north east of Bapaume, France.

W.H. Miller
Private, William Hugh Miller, 288001,
2/1st (Bucks) Battalion,
Oxfordshire & Buckinghamshire Light Infantry

William Miller, known by his second name of 'Hugh', was born in Market Square, Witney during the third quarter of 1891, the eldest son of, William, a bank manager, and his wife Amy (née North). His mother died in 1895, at the age of twenty five and Hugh and his younger brother, Douglas were left in the care of their father and a governess. Educated at the Witney Grammar School, by 1911 Hugh was working in the town as a bank clerk.

During the late summer of 1914 Hugh enlisted and was posted to the recently formed 2/1st Buckinghamshire Battalion of the Oxfordshire and

---

[106] *Witney Gazette*, 6th November 1916.

Buckinghamshire Light Infantry, part of the 61st (2nd South Midland) Division. Following their training and equipping the units of the 61st Division were deployed to the Western Front, arriving in France on, or around, the 24th May 1916. Upon their arrival they were concentrated in the Merville area. However it was not long before the 61st Division was moved further south in preparation for the Allied summer offensive on the Somme.

On the 23rd July 1916, during fierce fighting at Pozieres, Hugh, was seriously wounded by shrapnel. He was safely evacuated back to England where he remained in hospital for several months, before returning to active duty in France around Christmas 1916. He fought with his unit through the remainder of the winter and into the spring of 1917 when the 61st Division was engaged in the pursuit of the Germans as they retreated to the 'Hindenburg Line'. But in the early summer Hugh fell ill and was admitted to the No.6 Stationary Hospital at Frevent. His illness developed into pneumonia and he died on the 14th July 1917. He was buried in the St. Hilaire Cemetery, Frevent, France

F.R.G. Moore
Pioneer, Frederick Reginald George Moore, 24327,
26th Labour Company,
Royal Engineers

Frederick Moore, or 'Reg' as he was known, was born in Dublin in January 1895, the eldest son of Frederick, a soldier serving with the Oxfordshire Light Infantry, and his Irish born wife, Annie (maiden name unknown). Around 1898 Frederick's battalion left Ireland and he was posted to the Regimental headquarters at Oxford where, at the time of the 1901 census, the family were living in quarters at the Cowley Barracks. Their next move was to Witney where Reg was admitted to the Witney Grammar School in 1904, staying there until 1908 when he left to become a clerk in a local law firm. In 1911 the family were recorded as living at the Fleece Hotel on Church Green where Reg's father, now retired from the Army, was the manager. Around 1912 the family moved again, this time to a house in Corn Street.

On the 8th April 1913 Reg enlisted for military service with the Royal Engineers and later that year, on the 5th November, following his basic training, he was posted to the 26th Labour Company. On the 16th August 1914, less than a fortnight after the declaration of war, Reg along with the rest of his unit, was deployed to France where he served on the Western Front for the rest of the year and into 1915. Towards the end of January he was taken ill with severe pain in his right elbow and was invalided home to England for admission to the 1/4th Northern General Hospital in Lincoln. The initial diagnosis was synovitis – a painful swelling of the joint, but this was later revised to be tuberculous synovitis. Despite medical intervention the tuberculosis spread to his lungs and his right arm had to be amputated. With his military career over he was officially discharged from the Army on the 14th June 1915 and returned home to his family.

Reg moved with his family to a house in Ducklington and, following the deliberations of a military medical board, began to receive a small pension but his health never improved. On Monday 22nd October 1917, following a long and painful illness, Reg died. He was buried in the Witney Cemetery two days later with full military honours.

His grave does not have a Commonwealth War Grave headstone and his name does not appear in their records.

H. Morris
Lance Corporal, Henry John M. Morris, 21237,
6th Battalion,
Oxfordshire & Buckinghamshire Light Infantry

Henry Morris, known to all as 'Harry', was born in the Oxfordshire village of Kiddington in the second quarter of 1896, the third son of John, a farm labourer, and his wife Sarah (née Tooley). Around 1903 the family moved to Park Farm near Witney and at the time of the 1911 census Harry was working as a farm labourer.

Harry joined the Army in February 1916 and following basic training he was posted to France to join the 6th Battalion of the Oxfordshire and Buckinghamshire Light Infantry, part of the 20th (Light) Division. In June 1916 the Division was in action near Ypres in the Battle of Mount Sorrel, following which it was moved south to take part in the great Allied summer offensive on the Somme which had begun on 1st July.

Between the 15th July and 3rd of September 1916 the 20th Division were engaged in the protracted battle for Delville Wood, or 'Devil's Wood' as it was known by the troops. It was during this battle, on the 29th August, that Harry Morris, by this time promoted to the rank of Lance Corporal, was severely wounded. He was evacuated to one of the three Casualty Clearing Stations (CCS) located near the village of Mericourt-L'Abbe, where he died the following day.

Harry was buried in a military cemetery a short distance from the CCS where he died. The cemetery later became known as the Heilly Station Cemetery, France, so-called after the local railway halt used by the CCS's. Indeed there were so many casualties buried at Heilly during the Somme offensive of 1916 that they were buried two and sometimes three deep, leaving no room for cap badges to be engraved on the headstones.

H. Painter
Lance Corporal, Henry Painter, 14498,
4th Battalion,
Grenadier Guards
(Younger brother of John Painter, killed in action on the Somme, 13th September 1916)

Henry Painter was born in Crawley during the first quarter of 1888, the second son of John, a farm labourer and his wife Ellen (née Bishop). In 1909 Henry volunteered to join the Army and was posted to the 2nd Battalion of the Grenadier Guards. At the time of the 1911 census he was with his unit at Blenheim Barracks, Aldershot.

Upon the outbreak of war in August 1914 the 2nd Grenadier Guards, as part of the 2nd Division, were mobilised, arriving in France around the 13th August. The Battalion was to remain on the Western Front for the duration of the war and was present in all the major actions which took place in that theatre of operations. In August 1915 all the various Guards battalions were withdrawn from their respective Divisions and transferred into the newly formed 'Guards

Division'. It is likely that around this time Henry was transferred to the newly arrived 4th Battalion, Grenadier Guards.[107]

Henry's elder brother, John, who had volunteered for military service in early 1915, was posted to France in early 1916 to join his brother's former unit but it is doubtful that the two ever served together as on the 14th January 1916, in hospital at St. Omer, Lance Corporal Henry Painter died as a result of wounds he received in action. How or when he received his wounds is not known.

Today Henry's grave can be found in the Longuenesse Souvenir Cemetery, St. Omer, France.

J. Painter
Private, John Painter, 22663,
2nd Battalion,
Grenadier Guards
(Elder brother of Henry Painter, who died of wounds, France, 14th
January 1916)

John Painter was born in Crawley during the third quarter of 1884, the eldest son of John, a farm labourer, and his wife Ellen (née Bishop). At the time of the 1911census John, then employed as a blanket finisher, was still living with his parents at their home in Crawley.

He volunteered for military service at the end of January 1915 and following his basic training was posted to the same battalion in which his younger brother, Henry, had served; the 2nd Battalion of the Grenadier Guards, part of the Guards Division. In early 1916 he arrived in France to join his unit, although it is extremely doubtful if the two brothers ever served together; Henry, had been wounded in action, and died in a military hospital on the 14th January 1916.

As part of the great Allied offensive on the Somme in 1916 the Guards were identified to participate in an action which would later be known as the Battle

---

[107] This unit landed in France on the 14th July 1915 and joined the Guards Division a month later on the 19th August.

of Flers-Courcelette and so it was on the 13th September 1916, during the intense build up of men and equipment in the forward area prior to the start of the attack, that John Painter was killed in action. His body was never identified and today his name is recorded on the Thiepval Memorial, France, alongside more than 73,000 other British and Commonwealth soldiers who fell on the Somme and have no known resting place.

By the time the War memorial in Witney was being planned John's parents had moved from Crawley and were living on Woodgreen which would explain why he and his brother both appear on the town's memorial rather than upon that in their native village.

W.S. Paintin
Sergeant, Walter Shayler Paintin, 9784,
1st Battalion,
Royal Scots (Lothian Regiment)

Walter Paintin, known by his second name of 'Shayler', was born in Witney on the 5th April 1885, the son of Joseph, a carpenter, and his wife Isabella (née Mann). Following his education at the town's Wesleyan School he entered into the grocery trade and by 1906 he had left Witney and was living and working in London. On 17th September 1906 Shayler joined the Army and, following his basic training, was posted to the 1st Battalion of the Royal Scots.

In 1909 his battalion deployed to India where Shayler gained a reputation as a fine sportsman, being part of the 'C' Company hockey team which won the Meay Ahmed Hockey Cup in the 1911/12 season. He was also an excellent marksman, regularly competing in the Royal Scots Rifle Meeting in which he won the Championship Medal (India) in 1912 and third prize in the same competition in 1914.

On the outbreak of war in August 1914 his unit, still in India at Allahabad, was immediately recalled to the U.K., arriving at Devonport on the 16th November where it was attached to the 27th Division at Winchester. At that time the 27th Division was being prepared for an imminent deployment to France and almost one month later, on the 19th December 1914 Shayler was with his battalion when it landed at Le Havre.

Upon its arrival on the Western Front the 27th Division was concentrated in an area between Aire and Arques, before being moved onto the Ypres Sector. In action throughout its time in France the 27th Division fought most notably at St. Eloi on the 14th and 15th March 1915, when it was used to recapture a mound which had been lost the previous day during the Battle of Neuve Chapelle. During the following month the Germans launched their only major offensive operation of the year on the Western Front. Now known as the Second Battle of Ypres, the Germans tried in vain, between the 22nd April and the 25th May, to dislodge the British from the town and surrounding area. It was during this battle, on the 12th May 1915, that Shayler Paintin, by this time promoted to the rank of Sergeant, was killed in action whilst in command of a machine gun.

He was buried in Bellewaarde Wood near the village of Hooge in Belgium but in the course of the continued fighting the site of his grave was lost. Today his name is remembered on the Ypres (Menin Gate) Memorial, Ipres, Belgium.

G.W. Painting
Private, George William Painting, 14459,
7th Battalion,
Duke of Edinburgh's (Wiltshire Regiment)

George Painting, known by his second name of 'William', was born in Hailey during the autumn of 1893, the eldest son of Charles, a stone mason, and his wife Sarah (née Buckingham). By 1901 the family had moved to the nearby village of New Yatt. In the census of 1911 William, still living with his family but now in Crawley Road, Witney, was recorded as working as a mason's labourer.

William enlisted soon after the start of the war and was initially attached to the Oxfordshire and Buckinghamshire Light Infantry but was posted soon after to the 7th Battalion of the Wiltshire Regiment, part of the 26th Division. On the 21st September 1915 the 7th Wiltshires were deployed to France along with the rest of their Division. However their time on the Western Front was only brief. In November 1915 the entire Division was despatched to Salonika, in Greece, where it would remain for the rest of the war.

At dawn on Saturday the 6th October 1917 the 7th Wiltshires, who had been occupying a section of front line trenches in the Dova Tepe Sector, Salonika, mounted a raid on the opposing Bulgarian trench line. Unfortunately the details, as recorded in the regimental diary of the raid and indeed of any subsequent action on that date, are sparse. But it was on this day that William Painting was killed in action. He was buried the following day at the site occupied by the 78th Field Ambulance at Basili.

The Brigade Chaplain, M.R. Smith, later wrote to William's mother and described the event to her:

> ...*I officiated at your son's funeral on Sunday morning last, in a beautifully situated Military Cemetery. Unfortunately my fellow Chaplain (Rev. J.R.Duvall) was also killed about the same time, and they, and another of the same Battalion, Lce-Corp. Besant, were all thus buried side by side with Military honours. The Regimental Band was present, and played three hymns, which all joined in singing. The hymns were – "Fight the good fight", "Lead kindly light," and "For ever with the Lord..."*[108]

Today his grave can be found in the Sarigol Military Cemetery, Kriston, Greece.

In addition to his name being recorded on the Witney War Memorial William's name is also remembered on the War Memorial in his native village of Hailey.

---

[108] Extract taken from a letter published in the *Witney Gazette*, 3rd November 1917.

A. Pearse
Private, Albert Pearse, 203229,
2nd Battalion,
Worcestershire Regiment

Albert Pearse was born in Witney during the third quarter of 1886, the son of Stephen, a sawyer, and his wife Ruth (née Fowler). At the time of the 1901 census Albert was recorded as working in a local blanket mill as a factory hand. At the beginning of 1909 he married Mary Mills, of Asthall Leigh, and their first child, a daughter, Daisy, was born shortly after on the 18th April 1909. By the time of the 1911 census Albert and Mary were living at Asthall Leigh and Albert was still employed as a factory hand.

In the absence of a military record it is unknown when Albert enlisted, but from his regimental number and the birth date of his son, also named Albert who was born during the first quarter of 1916, it is likely that it was sometime in either 1915 or 1916 and that he joined as a Territorial Soldier. His record of medal entitlement indicates that he was deployed overseas in the spring of 1917.

Upon his arrival in France he was attached to the 2nd Battalion of the Worcestershire Regiment, part of the 33rd Division, which had been on the Western Front since 1914. On the 23rd April 1917 the 33rd Division went into action during the Arras Offensive and subsequently in the advance to the Hindenburg Line as the Germans retreated. It was during this period, on the 21st May 1917, that Albert Pearse was killed in action. His body was never identified and today his name is recorded on the Arras Memorial, Arras, France.

He is further commemorated by a small memorial stone in the Churchyard of Holy Trinity, Woodgreen, placed there after the war by his widow in memory of *"My Dear Husband"*. Mary never married again after Albert's death but remained living in the local area until she died in the Witney district in the spring of 1966.

A. Pickett
Lance Corporal, Albert Pickett, 7769,
2nd Battalion,
Oxfordshire & Buckinghamshire Light Infantry

Albert Pickett was born in West End, Witney around 1891, one of fourteen children born to George, a painter, and his wife Mary Anne (maiden name unknown). His regimental number indicates that he joined the Army (serving with the Oxfordshire Light Infantry) in around 1907. He was only sixteen years old at the time and must have either volunteered as a boy soldier or lied about his age on enlistment. Nevertheless in the spring of 1911, a minimum term of three years with the colours having been served (possible indication that he enlisted underage) and subsequent discharge to the reserves, he was back in Witney, working as a mason's labourer.

When war was declared at the beginning of August 1914 Albert was recalled to the 2nd Battalion of the Oxfordshire and Buckinghamshire Light Infantry (OBLI). At the time his unit was in camp at Aldershot, but quickly deployed to France, landing at Boulogne on the 14th August as part of the 2nd Division, one of the first British Divisions to arrive in France. Despite initially halting the German advance near the Belgium town of Mons the British, in fear of being outflanked, were forced to withdraw towards Cambrai – the famous *retreat from Mons*. Over the following days the troops of the 2nd OBLI fought various actions as they fell back to join up with the retreating French. These included; the Affair of Landrecies, (25th August), the Rearguard Affair of Le Grand Fayt (26th August) and the Rearguard Actions of Villers Cotterets (1st September). As the German First and Second Armies advanced further into France they became separated, exposing a large gap in their line. It was at this point that the British and French launched a counter attack aimed at the German First Army. Fearing an outflanking manoeuvre the Germans were forced back to the River Aisne where they dug in on a defensive line which was to remain largely unaltered for the next four years.

So began the race for the sea, with both sides engaged in a series of offensive out-flanking manoeuvres as they attempted to move northwards to secure the Channel ports. These operations culminated in prolonged fighting (19th October – 22nd November 1914) centred upon the strategic Belgian town of Ypres, the

131

Allied possession of which barred the way for the German advance on Calais and Boulogne. It is very likely that it was during this First Battle of Ypres that Albert Pickett, having been promoted to the rank of Lance Corporal, received the wounds from which he later died on the 8th November 1914. He was but one of 54,000 British casualties to die during that month of fighting, a month which witnessed the end of the pre-war regular British Army – The Old Contemptibles, as they became known. Albert's body lies in the Messines Ridge British Cemetery approximately 5 miles south of Ieper, Belgium.

G. Pickett & J. Pickett
No information has been found in relation to either G. Pickett or J. Pickett. Although it is believed that in 1917 both men were serving with the 2nd Volunteer Battalion of the Oxfordshire and Buckinghamshire Light Infantry.

E. Pickin
Eric Pickin served as a bomber pilot with the Royal Air Force during the Second World War. He was killed on the night of 30th/31st March 1944 when his aircraft, returning from a raid on the German city of Nuremberg, collided with another aircraft and crashed in Belgium.

His name, which was not added to the Witney War memorial until 2007, is recorded on the south facing 1914-19 panel due to there being no space available on the original 1939-45 plaques.

C.W. Pimm
2nd Lieutenant, Charles William Pimm,
12th Battalion (Sheffield City),
York and Lancaster Regiment
(Elder brother of F. Pimm, killed in action, France, 16th September 1916)

Charles Pimm was born in Gloucester Place, Witney during the second quarter of 1878, the eldest son of Charles (senior), a painter and plumber, and his wife Annie (née Weaver). Shortly after the 1901 census was taken, Charles left Witney and moved to Lichfield, Staffordshire where, in the late summer of that year he married Clara Small. On the 9th June 1902 their first child was born, a son they named Charles after his father and grandfather. Two more children followed; Clara born in 1905 and Cecil in 1910. By 1911 the family were living on the Walsall Road, to the south west of the city and Charles was working as an ironmonger's assistant.

On the 1st March 1917, six months after his younger brother, Frederick, had been killed in action on the Somme in France, Charles was commissioned into the York and Lancaster Regiment. On the 15th April, following his deployment to France, he was attached to the 12th Battalion, part of the 31st Division. At the time the 12th Battalion was encamped at Hermin, a rest area some way from the front but from where the battlefield noise of the Arras offensive (9th April – 16th June 1917) could be clearly heard. On the 1st May the men of the 12th moved into trenches, near the recently captured Vimy Ridge, ready to take their part in a phase of the ongoing offensive (this phase became known as the Third Battle of the Scarpe).

Between the 9th and 14th May and again between the 18th and 20th May, the 12th Battalion was ordered to defend the recently taken village of Gavrelle and the ruins of its nearby windmill. The 'Windmill Spur', as it was known, was of great tactical value to both sides; Allied possession of it threatened any German counter attack from the east, whilst providing a vital strategic position from which to defend the recent Allied gains immediately to the south. Possession of the windmill site itself was fiercely contested and changed hands a number of times during the fighting and was subject to constant shelling. Additionally due to its exposed position it could not be reached during daylight and heavy enemy fire at night often prevented ration parties from reaching it.

On the 18th May 1917 Charles Pimm was the officer in charge of '11' Platoon, defending Gavrelle Windmill. During the day the site came under heavy enemy shell fire and it was during this intense bombardment that Charles, along with two of his men, was killed. Indeed the shelling was so heavy that when their relief finally got through to them only three of the defenders were left unwounded

Charles Pimm was buried in the nearby Bailleul Road East Cemetery, in the village of St.Laurent-Blagny, France.

In addition to his name being recorded on the Witney War Memorial, he is also recorded on the Lichfield City War Memorial.

F.P. Pimm
Lance Corporal, Frederick Percival Pimm, 26913,
6th Battalion,
Somerset Light Infantry
(Younger brother of Charles W. Pimm, killed in action, France, 18th May 1917)

Frederick Pimm, or 'Percy' as he was known, was born during the first quarter of 1894 at the family home in Gloucester Place, Witney. He was the seventh child and third son of Charles, a plumber, and his wife Annie (née Weaver). At the time of the 1911 census, Percy was employed as a clerk in a local grocer's and drapery store. When he enlisted he was resident in Gillingham, Dorset.

Percy's record of medal entitlement indicates that he was not posted to France until after January 1916 and that at the time of his deployment he was attached to a battalion of the Wiltshire Regiment. However, once on the Western Front he was transferred to the 6th Battalion of the Somerset Light Infantry, part of the 14th (Light) Division.

On the 15th September 1916 the 14th Division was brought into action as part of the great Allied offensive on the Somme. At the battle of Flers-Courcelette, the third and final phase of the offensive, the Allies again attempted to punch through the German lines using a combination of preliminary bombardment and an infantry assault supported, for the first time, by a new British weapon – the tank. The attack continued for almost a week and, in that time, the front line was extended by the Allies with some tactical gains being made, including the capture of the villages of Courcelette, Flers and Martinpuich. Overall it was deemed to have been a success although the anticipated breakthrough did not occur.

It was during the second day of the battle on the 16th September 1916 that Percy Pimm, only recently promoted to Lance Corporal, was killed in action. His body was never identified and he has no known grave. Today his name is recorded on the Thiepval Memorial to the missing of the Somme, Thiepval, France.

On the 18th May 1917 Percy's older brother, Charles, recently commissioned into the York and Lancaster Regiment, was killed in action whilst leading his platoon in the defence of the village of Gavrelle, France.

W.R. Pinfold
Private, William Robert Pinfold, 42301,
1/5th Battalion,
Prince of Wales's (North Staffordshire Regiment)

William Pinfold was born in the village of Middleton Cheney during the second quarter of 1899, the only son of Robert, a blacksmith, and his wife Ada (née Bricknell). Following the death of William's mother in 1903, Robert brought his son to Witney where, in the census of 1911, the two were recorded as lodging in the Crofts, at the home of Robert's sister, Eliza and her husband George Smith (also a blacksmith).

Very little information remains concerning William's military career. Given that he could not have legally enlisted in the Army until he was eighteen years of age it is likely that he joined after the spring of 1917. Following basic training he was posted to France where he was initially attached to the 3rd Battalion of the Worcestershire Regiment and subsequently transferred to the 1/5th Battalion of the North Staffordshire Regiment, part of the 46th (North Midland) Division.

It was whilst serving with the 1/5th North Staffordshires on the Western Front that William Pinfold was wounded in action. As a result of his wounds he died on the 16th April 1918 whilst being treated at one of a group of Casualty Clearing Stations near the village of Haringhe (known to the troops as 'Bandaghem'). He was buried in the nearby cemetery, which today is known as the Haringhe (Bandaghem) Military Cemetery, Poperinge, Belgium.

A. Pratley
Private, Archibald Pratley, TR9/21884,
44th Training Reserve Battalion

Archibald 'Archie' Pratley was born at Newland on the 18th December 1898 and baptised at the town's Wesleyan Chapel on the 21st February 1899. He was the second son of James, a blanket finisher, and his wife Eleanor (née Cantell).

At the time of his attestation on 16th December 1916 Archie was living in Cowley, Oxford and working in the city as a bus conductor. His military service began two months later on the 17th February 1917, when he reported to Cowley Barracks to begin his training. He was posted to the 44th Training Reserve Battalion, a unit which had formerly been the 11th Battalion of the Devonshire Regiment but which, in September 1916, had been converted to a training unit.[109]

However Archie was never to be transferred to an active unit. His military career ended at Warley Barracks in Essex, on the 29th October 1917 when he was he was discharged from the Army due to poor health (diagnosed at the time as chronic bronchitis). He returned home to his widowed mother in Newland[110] but unfortunately his health did not improve and he died at home on the 12th March 1918. He was buried four days later, on the 16th, at St. Mary's Church, Cogges.

E.W. Pratley
Private, Ernest Walter Pratley, 1301,
1/4th Battalion,
Oxfordshire & Buckinghamshire Light Infantry

Ernest Pratley was born at Newland, Witney, on the 31st August 1892 and baptised at the town's Wesleyan Chapel on Christmas Day that same year. He was the eldest son of Walter, a blanket tucker, and his wife Mary (née Basson). A former pupil of the town's Wesleyan Day School, he was working as a doctor's messenger and living on Woodgreen with his Grandmother, Matilda Basson, at the time of the 1911 census. It was around this time that he joined the Territorial Army, enlisting with the Witney Company of the Oxfordshire and Buckinghamshire Light Infantry (OBLI).

When the order for general mobilisation was issued, at the beginning of August 1914, Ernest was called for active duty and posted to his Regiment's 1/4th Battalion. In early 1915, prior to his unit's deployment to the Western

---

[109] These Training Battalions, and there were a considerable number of them after the end of 1916, had no affiliation to local regiments. They existed solely to train new recruits who would then subsequently be posted on to other units.
[110] His father had died a year earlier in 1916.

Front he married Margaret Viner, a domestic servant originally from Eynsham, who was, at the time, living and working in Oxford.

On the 29th March 1915 Ernest, along with his comrades in the 1/4th OBLI, landed at Boulogne, France, as part of the South Midland Division (re-designated the 48th Division in May 1915). By the 3rd April 1915 the Division had concentrated near Cassel, on the northern edge of the Western Front, before moving into the front line in the Ploegsteert sector, to the south of Ypres. In July 1915 the Division moved again, this time to the Hebuterne area, south-west of Arras, where it was to remain for the following twelve months, holding the front line before moving to the Somme in July 1916.

It was whilst the division was at Hebuterne, that on the 12th January 1916 Ernest Pratley was killed in action. Today his grave can be found in the Hebuterne Military Cemetery, in the village of Hebuterne, France.

F.J. Pratley
Private, Frederick John Pratley, 35182,
(formerly of) 2/8th Battalion,
Royal Warwickshire Regiment

Frederick Pratley was born in Corn Street, Witney, in the first quarter of 1899, the youngest son of James, a blanket spinner, and his wife Rebecca (née Hope). A former pupil of the Witney Wesleyan Day School, Frederick joined the Army around 1917. His service record has not survived but, from his record of medal entitlement, it is evident that following his basic training he was posted to France to join the 2/8th Battalion of the Royal Warwickshire Regiment, part of the 61st (2nd South Midland) Division, on the Western Front.

On the 20th February 1918, as part of a wide-scale reorganisation of the units in France, the 2/8th Battalion was broken up and the personnel were transferred to either the 2/7th Battalion of the Royal Warwickshires (also part of the 61st

Division) or the 25th Entrenching Battalion[111]. Owing to this movement of men it is difficult to say in which unit Frederick was serving at the time of his death approximately one month later but it is probable that he was one of the men who remained with the Warwickshires and the 61st Division.

At dawn on the 21st March 1918 the Germans launched their huge spring offensive aimed at smashing the British Third and Fifth Armies on the Somme. Throughout the opening day of the attack, and into the second, the men of the 61st Division, occupying the front line and forward area to the north west of St. Quentin, were able to hold three German Divisions at bay. It was only during the afternoon of the 22nd that they were ordered to begin to retire because of the enemy's progress at other parts of the line. Over the next ten days the Division fought a successful, if chaotic, withdrawal over the Somme crossings.

It was during this fighting retreat, on the 30th March 1918, that Frederick Pratley was killed. His body was never identified and he has no known grave. Today his name is remembered on the Pozieres Memorial, Pozieres, France, alongside the names of over 14,500 British and Commonwealth soldiers who were killed during the German offensive and have no known graves.

T. Purbrick
Private, Thomas Purbrick, 6850,
2nd Battalion,
Oxfordshire & Buckinghamshire Light Infantry

Thomas Purbrick was born in the Gloucestershire village of Almondsbury on the 3rd July 1882, the eldest son of Joseph, an agricultural labourer, and his wife Annie (née Smith). By 1901 the family were living in Castle Combe and Thomas was working as an agricultural labourer. Around 1903 he joined the Army and served with the Oxfordshire Light Infantry. When his seven years of regular service was completed he was discharged to the Reserves and came to Witney in search of work.

---

[111] Entrenching Battalions were temporary units used as pools of men from which conventional infantry battalions could draw trained men as and when shortages of manpower demanded. They ceased to exist after April 1918 when they were used to make good the losses incurred during the German Spring Offensive of a month earlier.

At the time of the 1911 census Thomas was working at a local blanket mill and lodging with the widow, Emily Basson and her four daughters at their home in Church Lane, Cogges. In the autumn of 1911 Thomas was married to Edith Basson, Emily's eldest daughter; the couple's first child, Phyllis, was born soon after in the spring of 1912. In the autumn of 1913 the couple celebrated the birth of their second child, another girl, who they named Lillian.

As a Reservist, Thomas was mobilised on the outbreak of the war and deployed to France on the 13th September 1914 to join the 2nd Battalion of the Oxfordshire and Buckinghamshire Light Infantry, part of the 2nd Division. Initially he held the rank of Lance Corporal, but his record of medal entitlement suggests that he was reduced to a private during his time in France. In the spring of 1915 the 2nd Division was chosen to participate in an operation to draw German forces away from the planned French offensive near Arras. Thus, on the 15th/16th May 1915, the British launched their first night attack of the war, along a three mile front from Neuve Chapelle in the north to Festubert in the south. Although preceded by a 60 hour long artillery bombardment the German defences remained largely intact when the assault went in and despite some limited success casualties were high.[112]

It was during this battle on the 16th May 1915 that Thomas Purbrick is presumed to have been killed, his body lost on the battlefield. With no known grave his name is today commemorated on Le Touret Memorial, near the village of Festubert, France.

On the 2nd July 1916 Thomas's younger brother, Frederick, whilst serving with the 2nd Battalion the Wiltshire Regiment, was killed in action on the Somme. His body, like that of his brother, was never identified and his name is today remembered on the Thiepval Memorial, Thiepval, France.

---

[112] See also T. Broom, A. Haggitt and A.W. Englefield, who were all killed in the same action.

139

H. Richards
Private, Harry Richards, 27446,
14th Battalion,
Gloucestershire Regiment

Harry Richards was born in the High Street, Witney during the first quarter of 1893, the youngest child and only son of Charles, a local carpenter and wheelwright, and his wife Elizabeth (née Busby). Upon leaving school he entered into an apprenticeship with a carpenter, working for a local builder.

Harry volunteered for military service in 1915 and was posted to a 'bantam' battalion, the 14th, Gloucestershire Regiment – these bantam battalions, championed by the press and public, were formed from under-height recruits, those shorter than the minimum regulation height of 5 feet 3 inches. So popular were the bantams that they were able to form two complete Divisions; the 35th, to which the 14th Gloucester's were attached, and the 40th.

The 14th Gloucester's had landed in France on the 30th January 1916 but it was not until the July of that year that Harry arrived on the Western Front. He took his place amongst the ranks prior to his battalion's deployment on the Somme where he and his comrades saw action in a number of battles in that protracted and bloody offensive. They remained on the Western Front throughout the winter of 1916/17 and played an active part in the pursuit of the Germans in their retreat to the Hindenburg Line in the spring of 1917. Later that year they were in the Third Battle of Ypres, or "Passchendaele" as it was known. But Harry never got to Passchendaele. He died on the 16th June 1917, probably at the 35th Casualty Clearing Station where he was being treated, having been fatally wounded six days earlier on the 10th. His body lies in La Chapelette British and Indian Cemetery, just south of Peronne, France.

1. The dedication of the Witney War Memorial, 12ᵗʰ September 1920.
It was estimated that around two thousand people attended the ceremony.
(From a contemporary postcard)

2. The War Memorial today.
(J. Clements)

3. *Following the end of the Great War the people of Cogges and Newland erected their own memorial. Standing in a tiny square garden on Oxford Road the memorial is dedicated simply 'to all who served'.*

(J. Clements)

THE "CHURCH LEYS"
WAS PURCHASED IN 1920 AS
A PUBLIC RECREATION GROUND
OUT OF FUNDS SUBSCRIBED BY
THE INHABITANTS OF WITNEY
IN MEMORY OF
THOSE WHO GAVE THEIR LIVES
IN THE GREAT WAR
1914 - 1918

4. *With the abandonment of the Cottage Hospital scheme funds became available to purchase the 'Church Leys' for the people of Witney.*

(J. Clements)

5. Members of the 'Witney Company' – a group of forty local men who marched through Witney to the railway station on the 1st September 1914 en- route to Oxford to volunteer for military service. Back row l – r: Claude Druce, William Clarke, Bert Long, Syd Miles, Albert Broome, unknown, Harold Simms. Middle row: Mr Ballard, Harold Early, Mr Mundy, Mr Gibbons, Mr Burrell, unknown, Arthur Mace, Reg Viner, unknown, Mr Baston, Oswald Dring. Front row: unknown, Mr Marshall, Harold Mace, Ernest Tarrant, Sydney Smith, Harold Abraham, Mr Picket, Cyril Higgs. Front row sitting: "Champ" Hailey.

(Witney Gazette 1914)

6. Sydney Beale. Killed
in action on the
Somme, September
1916.

(R. Kearsey)

7. Sydney Beale, front row, left. Picture
probably taken during basic training.

(K. Cass)

Dear Friend
            Just a few lines hoping you
are keeping well as it leaves me pretty
rough Dear Friend I am sorry to be the
sender of bad news but I must tell
you that poor old Sid was killed
on the 17th he was buried with a
shell while we were in the trenches
there were seven of us buried with the
same shell and only 2 of us were dug
out alive me and another chap from
Yaxton and I assure you we think
ourselves very lucky indeed. I can assure
you I did all I could for him I was
dug out myself and then I helped to
dig Sid out and I had just got his
face clear and he was unconscious
then as another big bastard came
and finished it then I got sent out
of the trenches into hospital it was
hard times just as he had been made
full corporal and all and I assure you
we shall all miss him very much. P.S.
                    W. Miles
Sid was gis dug out afterwards and
buried as respectable as the circumstance
                    would allow —

8. The letter sent to Sydney's parents, by W. Miles,
explaining the circumstances of their son's death.

(K. Cass)

9. Frank Bennett served with the Canadian Infantry. He was killed in action on the Somme, September 1916.
(Toronto Star 1916)

10. Walter 'Blackie' Bridgman in 1908 aged about 16. He was killed at Gallipoli in August 1915.
(H. Beale)

11. The grave of Harry Churchill, Witney Cemetery.
(J. Clements)

12. The grave of James Brice, Holy Trinity Church, Witney.
(J. Clements)

13. & 14. *Detail of George Clanfield's parents' headstone in the churchyard of St. Mary's, Cogges. Although stating he was 'killed in action' he actually died after falling from a train within hours of arriving in France.*

(J. Clements)

15. *Sidney Cooper, posted as 'missing in action' near Arras, France, on the 29th March 1918.*

(W. Townsend)

16. The Royal Navy destroyer HMS Hydra, the last ship George Dix was to serve upon.

(www.clydesite.co.uk)

17. The grave of George Eaton. Tyne Cot Cemetery, Belgium.

(A.J.C. Williams)

18. The grave of James Cox, Witney Cemetery.

(J. Clements)

19. *Bert Evans, formerly of the Queen's Own Oxfordshire Hussars, died on the Somme just one week after arriving at the front.*

(W. Townsend)

20. *Arch Grant Served in Egypt, Salonika and Gallipoli before finally arriving on the Western Front.*
He was killed in action at Cambrai in 1917.

(S.C. Jenkins)

21. As a pre-war reservist Percy Gunter was recalled to the colours in August 1914.
Fatally wounded at the Battle of Arras, he died in May 1917.

(S.C. Jenkins)

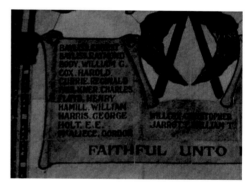

22 & 23. George Harris served with the Australian Imperial Force. He is also remembered on the Honour Roll at Trinity Cathedral in Wangaratta, Victoria, Australia.

(Wangaratta Family History Soc.)

24. Harry Hooper became the first Witney man to lose his life in the Great War. He fell victim to enemy artillery fire on the 19th September 1914.

(A. Leach)

25. Albert Hudson pictured in 1910.

(C. Powell)

26. Albert's grave in the 'Dadizeele New British Cemetery', Dadizele, Belgium.

(www.ancestry.co.uk)

26. *The grave of Mark Hudson, Sailly-au-Bois, France.*

(www.ancestry.co.uk)

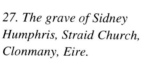

27. *The grave of Sidney Humphris, Straid Church, Clonmany, Eire.*

('D. McL')

28. *Where space was at a premium. The 'shared' grave of Tom Keen (and Pte.Sydney Taylor) Ypres Town Cemetery extension, Ipres, Belgium.*

(A.J.C. Williams)

29. Reginald Leigh in the uniform of the Royal Flying Corps, 1917.
(J. Leigh)

30 & 31. Reginald Leigh is remembered on the Flying Services Memorial, Arras, France (right). (A.J.C. Williams) As well as on the Burford School Roll of Honour, directly above fellow Witney man, Arthur Mace.
(J. Clements)

32 & 33. The headstone and detail on Winifred Long's grave at Holy Trinity, Witney.
Her brother, George Long, died in Flanders in 1915.

(J. Clements)

34. John Martin. Killed in action at Passchendaele in October 1917.
(K. Price Behrman)

35. John (Snr.) and Mary Martin's headstone in Cogges Churchyard also commemorates their three sons: James, John and George, who were all lost during WWI.
(J. Clements)

36. Albert Miles with his parents at the family home on Oxford Road, Witney, c. 1901. From l-r, unknown, elder brother Frederick, younger brother Ernest, father Joseph, mother Winifred, Albert and eldest brother William.

(B. Franklin)

37& 38. Albert Miles in 1914, just prior to his enlistment, alongside the letter informing his family he was 'missing in action' at Gallipoli.

(B. Franklin)

39. A private headstone at the grave of Sydney Miles. Witney Cemetery.

(J. Clements)

In Loving Memory
of
CADET SYDNEY J. MILES,
Nº 4 OFFICER'S CADET BATTALION.
THE BELOVED THIRD SON OF
CHARLES WILLIAM AND ALICE MILES,
OF THIS TOWN.
WHO DIED IN HOSPITAL ON
OCTOBER 25TH 1918,
AGED 27 YEARS.

"IN LIFE – LOYAL,
IN DEATH – FEARLESS,
IN FAITH – CERTAIN,
IN HOPE – SECURE."

40. Edwin Miles, killed in action in France, May 1918.

(D. Betts)

41. Shayler Paintin, a pre-war regular soldier, was killed in action at Ypres in 1915.

(www.ancestry.co.uk)

42. The small
memorial stone to
Albert Pearse. Holy
Trinity Church,
Woodgreen, Witney.
(J. Clements)

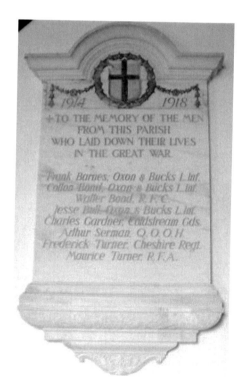

43. The War Memorial, sited
in St. Mary Magdalene,
Adelstrop, Gloucestershire,
upon which Arthur Serman is
also remembered.

(A. Beard)

44. The grave of William 'Spot' Smith in the Hyde Park Corner (Royal Berks) Cemetery, Belgium.

(A.J.C. Williams)

45. Florence Cornock with her daughter Nora in 1917. Nora's father, Arthur Titcombe, had been killed in action in December 1914.

(A. Taylor)

*46. Alfred Townsend's CWGC
headstone, Witney Cemetery.*
(J. Clements)

*47. The grave of James Turner,
Tyne Cot Cemetery, Belgium.*
(A.J.C. Williams)

48. Frank Wiltshire served with the New Zealand Engineers. He was killed in action on the Western Front in June 1917.
(Auckland War Memorial Museum)

49. Frank's name appears last on the memorial to the staff of the Bank of New Zealand who lost their lives in WWI.
(Auckland War Memorial Museum)

*50. The Crawley
War Memorial.
(J. Clements)*

*51. The grave of Harry Souch, Crawley
Churchyard.
(The CWGC headstone behind belongs to
F.J. Hunt (O.B.L.I.) who died whilst home
on leave during the Second World War).
(J. Clements)*

52. The Hailey War Memorial.
(J. Clements)

53. The headstone marking the grave of Isaac Clements, Hailey churchyard.
(J. Clements)

54. The grave of Cecil Harris, Hailey churchyard.
(J. Clements)

55. Frank Brooks in the uniform of the Canadian Engineers.

(V. Burton)

56. The letter received by Frank's father informing him of his son's death.

(V. Burton)

R.L.4-0-26 R2A.10818

...YING, PLEASE QUOTE ABOVE NUMBER.

To   Mr. T. W. Brooks,

Hailey, Witney,

OXON.

please return to ab Bragg Chipping...

CANADIAN RECORD OFFICE.

GREEN ARBOUR HOUSE.

OLD BAILEY, LONDON, E.C.4.

Sir   10th August,   191 8

It is my painful duty to inform you that a report has this day been received notifying the death of No. 506120

Rank Sapper   Name FRANK WILLIAM BROOKS

Regiment HQ 1st Bde.Can.Engrs which occurred at

on the   8th August, 1918   , and I am to express to you the sympathy and regret of the Militia Council at your loss. The cause of death was Shell Gas.

Further information regarding the personal effects and any balance of pay due to the military estate of the soldier will be communicated to you in due course by the Estates Branch, Canadian Contingents, Pembroke House, 133 Oxford St. London W.1. but some time must necessarily elapse before these questions can be dealt with. If you do not receive further communication in six weeks' time, please write to Estates Branch, quoting Reference No. above, also Regimental No.,Name and Unit of the deceased soldier.

I am, Sir,

Your obedient Servant

J.P.B.Carter

A5. R107.10M.   for Lieut. Colonel   Lieut.
5731-1-2-18.   i/c Records.
                                                         OMFC.

W.T. Richards
Private, William Thomas Richards, 57511,
10th Battalion,
Worcestershire Regiment

William Richards, who was known to all by his second name of 'Tom', was born in the Crofts, Witney, at the beginning of 1899, the youngest son of James, a brass finisher working for a mechanical engineer, and his wife Ann (née Milroy). By the time of the census in 1911 the family had moved to Church Lane, Cogges.

Tom joined the Army in March 1917 and following his basic training he was posted to France where he was attached to a battalion of the Hampshire Regiment. However, it was often the case that newly arrived men were redeployed to reinforce under strength units; so it was that Tom was posted to the 10th Battalion of the Worcestershire Regiment, part of the 19th (Western) Division. It is likely that Tom was serving with the Worcesters during their time in the Ypres sector during the Third Battle of Ypres, or "Passchendaele", in the late summer and autumn of 1917. His unit was also later involved in the initial engagements of the German spring offensive which began on 21st March 1918.

After successive phases of an initially successful offensive, by early summer the German advance had ground to a halt on the Marne. It was during the ensuing fighting, as the Germans began to be pushed back, that on the 18th June 1918 Tom Richards was killed in action. Several days after his death his father, who already had a son recovering in hospital from wounds received in action, received a letter from 2nd Lieut. Ridgeway, Tom's former platoon commander. He wrote:

> *'...I was close by when he and others lost their lives, and I am proud to say they served their country to the end, thereby enabling their comrades to hold a most important position. My brother officer also lost his life with them. It may comfort you somewhat to know that I personally supervised your son's burial, and saw it carried out in a*

141

most respectful manner, and a cross erected bearing his number, rank, name, etc...[113]

It must be assumed that Tom's original resting place was in a small battlefield cemetery or one for which future maintenance by the Commonwealth War Graves Commission could not be assured as his grave was later moved to the Terlincthun British Cemetery at Wimille, near Bolougne, France.

Tom's wounded brother, George, survived the war and returned home to Witney. He died in Oxford in 1973 aged 76.

E.J. Rose
Private, Ernest John Rose, 201967,
2/4th Battalion,
Oxfordshire & Buckinghamshire Light Infantry

Ernest Rose was born in Woodstock in the autumn of 1884, the youngest son of Amos, a carpenter, and his wife, Emma (née Warner). His father died when Ernest was just 9 years old leaving his widowed mother to continue raising their large family alone. Upon leaving school Ernest successfully completed a carpentry apprenticeship – following his elder brother, Herbert, and his late father into the trade. However, it was a trade he chose not to continue and, by the time of the 1911 census, he had found alternative employment as a porter in Woodstock Union Workhouse. On the 13th July 1912 Ernest married Eva Hosier, a blanket weaver from Witney, and their first child, a daughter they named Dorothy, was born in early 1914.

In the absence of a full military record it is not known when Ernest first volunteered for military service. However, from his record of medal entitlement, it is clear that he enlisted in the Territorial Force before the end of 1916 and was deployed to the Western Front in 1917 to serve with the 2/4th Oxford and Buckinghamshire Light Infantry (OBLI), part of the 61st (2nd South Midland) Division.

---

[113] From the *Witney Gazette*, 27th July 1918.

On the night of the 21st/22nd August 1917 the 2/4th OBLI were in the front line trenches near the village of St. Julien, to the north-east of Ypres, where they, along with other elements of the 61st Division, had been deployed to attack the German front line at dawn. At 5 a.m. on the 22nd, advancing behind a creeping barrage, the British troops began their assault. Initially the attack went well, with many of the objectives reached, but concentrated enemy rifle and machine gun fire from, in some cases, several directions took their toll and the whole of the 22nd and into the 23rd was spent trying to consolidate a hopeless position. The battalion were relieved on the night of the 23rd/24th but, almost at once, their successors gave up the ground, which had been so hard fought for, and retired to the original front line.

It was during the fighting on the 22nd August 1917 that Ernest Rose was killed. He was initially buried on or near the battlefield but after the war his grave, like so many others, was moved into a larger, concentration cemetery. Today his grave can be found in the British New Irish Farm Cemetery, to the north-east of Ipres, Belgium.

Ernest's widow, Eva, never re married. She died in Witney towards the end of 1968.

J. Soanes
Lance Corporal, John Scanes,[114] **413088,**
21st Battalion,
Canadian Infantry (Eastern Ontario Regiment)

John Scanes was born in Witney on the 2nd April 1876 the eldest son of John, a school teacher at the town's Wesleyan School, and his wife Louisa (née Leigh). By the time of the 1891 census the family were living in Gloucester Place and John, whose father had died in 1889, was employed as a builder's apprentice (carpenter). Around the mid 1890's John, who was known for his sporting success, volunteered for part-time military service with the local volunteer force[115]. In 1900 he and fellow Witney man, Leo Whitcher, answered their

---

[114] Wrongly inscribed on the Memorial as Soanes.
[115] In total he served for approximately 8½ years with the Volunteers

143

country's call for trained militia men to assist in the war in South Africa and for twelve months the two fought the Boers as part of the Oxfordshire Light Infantry. Upon their return to Witney in May 1901 they were hailed as heroes, presented with engraved pocket watches and treated to a lavish reception hosted by their fellow townsmen.

On the 5th August 1905, John was married to Mary Ellen James in Fulham, West London. Eighteen months later, in early1907, the couple left England to start a new life in Canada, following Alfred J., or 'Jimmie' as he was known, John's younger brother, who had emigrated a year earlier. They settled in Toronto Ontario where, on 20th July 1910, their second child was born, a daughter they named Dora. Their first child, a son, had been still-born in August 1908.

On 24th March 1915 John presented himself at the Army recruiting centre in Lindsay, Ontario and, declaring himself to be one year younger than he actually was, volunteered for overseas service with the Canadian Expeditionary Force (CEF). He was duly assigned to the 39th Battalion[116] and commenced his training. The 39th Battalion, CEF, landed in Plymouth on the 3rd July 1915, and moved to Shorncliffe Camp in Kent where, in August 1915 John was detailed to work in the camp cook house, for which he received an extra 50 cents a day in pay[117]. In April 1916, still in the kitchens at Shorncliffe, he was promoted to the rank of 'Sergeant Cook' but it appears that he may have abused his position because in July 1916 he was charged with '... fraudulently misapplying public goods' and 'neglect to the prejudice of good order and military discipline.' He was found guilty and sentenced to 49 days No2 Field Punishment and reduced to the rank of Private. His time at Shorncliffe was over and on the 28th August 1916, his sentence served, he was transferred to the 21st Infantry Battalion CEF in France.

John was seriously wounded on the Western Front when, on the 9th April 1917, the 21st Battalion went into action at Vimy Ridge (the *Witney Gazette* later reported that he had been recommended for the Military Medal as a result of his actions that day, but to date evidence for this claim remains elusive). Within a fortnight he was evacuated back to England for medical treatment at

---

[116] The 39th Battalion was a depot battalion and not intended to deploy directly to France itself but to reinforce other front line units.

[117] Pay was calculated in Canadian currency.

the East Leeds War Hospital and then onto a convalescent centre at Woodcote Park, Epsom, where he stayed until August 1917. Upon his hospital discharge he was transferred to the 6th Reserve Battalion at Seaford, East Sussex, where he took up a post as a bombing instructor. In October 1917 he was promoted to the rank of acting Lance Corporal and he appeared to be destined to see the rest of the war out in England.

However, in Eastbourne around 6 p.m. on Sunday the 5th May 1918, John was involved in a road traffic accident. He had been travelling as a passenger in a motorcycle side-car driven by another Canadian soldier, Robert Symington. A second passenger was also being carried on the bike behind the driver. Eyewitnesses reported that as the motor cycle turned into the road it was swaying and the three men were heard to be laughing. The road was wet from recent rain and the motorcycle skidded. As it turned over the three men were thrown from the vehicle, with one hitting a lamp post. Robert Symington, fully conscious, suffered a fracture to his right thigh and John Scanes, with a fractured skull, was left lying unconscious in the road. The third man, apparently unhurt, fled the scene.

Both the injured men were taken to the Upperton Red Cross Hospital in the town but John's condition worsened and he was removed by ambulance to the nearby Central Military Hospital. He never regained consciousness and at 3:10 a.m. on Monday 6th May 1918 John Scanes died[118]. He was buried at the Ocklynge Cemetery in Eastbourne.

At the time of his death Mary, John's widow, was living in Chatham, Kent. She, along with many other British wives of Canadian soldiers, had been assisted to travel home to her family in the U.K. through the work of the Canadian Patriotic Fund[119]. She was unable to travel immediately John was sent abroad, due to the recent birth of their son, also named John, but as soon as she was able she and the two children left Canada, arriving in the U.K. in mid November, 1915. Initially Mary and the children lived near the camp where John was based and in the spring of 1916, a third child was born, a daughter they named Grace. Following John's posting to France the family moved to Chatham.

---

[118] *Eastbourne Chronicle*, 8th & 11th May 1918.

[119] A policy which was reversed once there was a food shortage in the U.K.

Mary remained in the U.K. until May 1930 when she returned to Canada accompanied by her three children and her son-in-law, Dora's husband. Mary was still living in Toronto in 1935.

W. Seary
Lance Corporal, William Seary, 20784,
5th Battalion,
Oxfordshire & Buckinghamshire Light Infantry

William Seary was born in Witney, most likely in Lowell's Yard (later Lowell's Place), during the third quarter of 1876, the second son of Frederick, a farm labourer, and his wife Jane (née Partlett). By the time of the census in 1891 William was working in a local mop factory and his mother, who had been widowed in 1884, was employed as a 'feeder to a blanket weaver'. In 1894, just two years after her marriage to James Hickman, William's mother died and around this time William volunteered for military service, joining the Oxfordshire Light Infantry. In 1908, discharged from the Army and in employment as a mason's labourer, William was married to Rhoda Woodley (née Dix), a widow twenty-two years his senior and a former neighbour of his family in Lowell Place. The couple moved to Ducklington taking with them Rhoda's youngest son, Harry.

On the 2nd October 1914 William volunteered for twelve months military service with the National Reserves and was posted to No.1 Supernumerary Company of the 4th (Reserve) Battalion of the Oxfordshire and Buckinghamshire Light Infantry[120]. However, on the 20th October 1915, at Southampton Docks, he was discharged from the National Reserves in order to re enlist for '...*Imperial Service*' i.e. the regular Army. This he did and on the 22nd December 1915 he was deployed to France for active service on the Western Front as part of a draft of reinforcements for the Regiment's 5th Battalion.

---

[120] As part of their duties, National Reservists were deployed across the UK to guard important installations such as ports, dockyards and major rail heads.

At Courcelette, on the 15th September 1916, the British launched what was to be their third and final large scale offensive operation of the summer campaign on the Somme. As on many occasions previously, the overall aim of the attack was to break through the German lines and bring an end to the deadlock of trench warfare. The battle lasted for a week and did achieve some notable results, although the cost in casualties was high. William Seary, recently promoted to the rank of Lance Corporal, was killed in action on the opening day of the battle. His body was never identified and today he is remembered on the Thiepval Memorial on the Somme, France.

In addition to being remembered on the Witney War Memorial, William's name also appears on the War Memorial in Ducklington.

A.A. Serman
Private, Arthur Albert William Serman,
1/4th Battalion,
Oxfordshire & Buckinghamshire Light Infantry

Arthur Serman was born in Stourbridge, Worcestershire, during the fourth quarter of 1887, the eldest son of Arthur, a coachman and groom, and his wife Mary (née Mort). By 1890 the family had moved to Adelstrop, Gloucestershire, where they were to remain for many years.

There is very little further information regarding Arthur after the 1901 census. He appears to be absent from the 1911 census but he was living in Witney at the time of his enlistment around 1915. Although he had initially served with the Queen's Own Oxfordshire Hussars, by the time of his deployment to France in 1916 he had been transferred to the 1/4th Battalion of the Oxfordshire and Buckinghamshire Light Infantry (OBLI).

At 4 am on the morning of the 16th August 1917 the men of the 1/4th OBLI were in position in the front line trenches along the Steenbeeck, in the north east of the Ypres Salient. A dawn attack on the German lines had been planned, but the expected support of two tanks did not materialise due to the wet weather conditions. Nevertheless, At 4:45 a.m. the men went 'over the top', advancing behind a heavy artillery barrage. Initially the attack was met with slight rifle fire but 200 yards out from the British front line the German machine gunners, who had been hiding in their concrete strong points, opened fire. The attack faltered with many casualties being taken, but the men of the 1/4th OBLI didn't retire. They managed to occupy a row of shell holes to form a temporary trench line and stubbornly held on. They were eventually relieved by the 1/7th Worcestershire's on the night of the 17th/18th August.

Arthur Serman was killed on the 16th August 1917. Today his grave can be found in the New Irish Cemetery, Ipres, Belgium.

In addition to his name being on the Witney War Memorial he is also remembered on a war memorial inside the parish church of his native Adelstrop, Gloucestershire.

F. Sherbourne
Private, Frederick Sherbourne, 3683,
'B' Company,
1/4th Battalion,
Oxfordshire & Buckinghamshire Light Infantry

Frederick Sherbourne, or 'Fred' as he was known, was born at Woodgreen, Witney, in the first quarter of 1896, the youngest son of Edwin, a fellmonger's labourer[121], and his wife Phylis (née Drewett). At the time of the 1911 census Fred was working as an ironmonger's errand boy.

Fred volunteered for military service on the 30th November 1914 and was posted to the Oxfordshire and Buckinghamshire Light Infantry (OBLI). Following his basic training he remained in the UK, most likely as part of a Reserve Battalion, until his deployment to France in the early part of 1916. Upon his arrival he joined his regiment's 1/4th Battalion, part of the 48th (South Midland) Division, which had been in France since March 1915.

On the 1st July 1916, the Allies on the Western Front launched their summer offensive against the German forces on the Somme. For the men of the 1/4th OBLI, and the rest of the 48th Division, this was to be their first major engagement and they were involved from the outset. On the night of the 16th July 1916, after more than two weeks spent in and out of the trenches near

---

[121] A fellmonger traded in skins and hides.

Hebuterne, the 1/4th OBLI were moved to a different sector of the battlefield in preparation for an attack on the German held high ground near the village of Pozieres.

Orders for the attack were received by the 1/4th OBLI at 7:10 p.m., on the 18th July. Over the following few hours the men collected their equipment and moved up the Albert-Bapaume road to take their positions in what was known as 'Sickle Trench', which straddled the aforementioned road between Ovillers and Pozieres. At 1:30 a.m., on the 19th July, the attack began. The Germans defiantly resisted the first attack, and Allied casualties were high. A second attack, which had been planned for around 3:00 a.m., had to be cancelled because of the confusion and congestion in the British trenches. By 4:15 a.m., with the second attack still not having taken place, the 1/4th OBLI was ordered to withdraw from the front line, which it did amidst much confusion.

Fred Sherbourne was seriously wounded during the attack on the 19th July and had to be evacuated to a field ambulance at Warloy-Baillon, to the west of Albert. He died the following day (20th July 1916) and was buried in the nearby military cemetery. Today his grave can be found in the Warloy-Baillon Communal Cemetery, Warloy-Baillon, France.

H. Sherbourne
Lance Corporal, Harold Sherbourne, 8713,
19th (Queen Alexandra's Own Royal) Hussars

Harold Sherbourne was born in West End, Witney, during the fourth quarter of 1894, the third son of George, a wool blender, and his wife Mercy (née Broom). In the census of 1911 Harold was recorded as working as a general labourer. In 1913 he joined the Army and following his basic training he was posted to the 19th (Queen Alexandra's Own Royal) Hussars.

Upon the outbreak of war in August 1914 the 19th Hussars was broken up to provide cavalry units for other Divisions: 'A' and 'B' Squadrons being sent to France with the 4th and 5th Divisions, respectively, whilst 'C' Squadron, with whom Harold was serving, landed in France on the 10th September as part of the 6th Division. The three squadrons were brought back together in April 1915 when the Regiment was reformed and placed under the command of the 1st Cavalry Division.

Throughout the war the men of the 1st Cavalry Division took part in most of the major battles where a mobile mounted force was used. Additionally, and significantly more frequently, they fought dismounted alongside the regular infantry, seeing action at Mons and in the first Battle of Ypres (1914); the Second Battle of Ypres (1915); Flers-Courcelette an element of the Somme offensive (1916); phases of the Arras Offensive and operations at Cambrai (1917).

From 21st December 1917 through to 21st January 1918 the 1st Cavalry Division was based behind the lines at Le Mesnil-Bruntel. Although officially 'out of the line' it was required to supply a dismounted brigade with each Regiment of the Division effectively providing a rifle company to fight as infantry. Additionally the Division also had to provide pioneer companies. It is unknown whether Harold Sherbourne, by now promoted to the rank of Lance Corporal, was serving in one of the pioneer companies or as part of the rifle company on the 15th January 1918, but it was on that day that he is recorded as being killed in action.

Today his grave can be found in the Vadencourt British Military Cemetery, Maissemy, France.

C.J. Sherwood
Private, Caleb John Sherwood, M/225119,
904th Mechanical Transport Company,
Army Service Corps[122]

Caleb Sherwood was born in Eynsham, around August 1879, the son of George, a stone mason, and his wife Julia (née Turner). In the census of 1881 the family were recorded as living in a cottage at *Barnard Gate Farm*. When he left school Caleb trained as a coachsmith[123] and by 1901 he had left home and

---

[122] The Commonwealth War Graves Commission has erroneously recorded his rank as Sergeant. He was in fact a Private.
[123] A coachsmith was a smith who worked the metal used in the building and maintenance of railway coaches, carts etc.

was living and working in Bicester. In August 1902 he married Louisa Bourton at the town's Independent Chapel and the couple's first child, a daughter they named Doris, was born in the July of the following year. The family were still in Bicester in 1911, moving thereafter to Windsor in Berkshire.

On the 5th June 1916 Caleb joined the Army Reserve and was mobilised six months later, on the 21st December, at Grove Park, London (an Army Service Corps mobilisation and training centre). Here he underwent training on the maintenance of various military vehicles and on the 27th March 1917, upon completion of his course, he was posted to the 904th Mechanical Transport Company and at the beginning of April Caleb left the UK, aboard the troop transport *HMT Arcadian*, bound for Alexandria via Salonika.

Once in the Mediterranean the *Arcadian* fell under the protection of two Japanese destroyers, one of which put in at Malta and left the remaining destroyer to shepherd the *Arcadian* on the remainder of her voyage. However, marauding German submarines operating in the area caused a slight delay to the journey and the *Arcadian* was forced to seek shelter for several days in the mouth of a river on the African coast before proceeding onwards with her Japanese escort. She reached Salonika unscathed and discharged the troops who were destined for that theatre of operations before starting out on the next leg of her voyage to Alexandria.

On the evening of Sunday the 15th April, as the *Arcadian* was steaming south through the Aegean, she was spotted by the crew of a German U Boat. The submarine discharged a single torpedo which struck the *Arcadian* inflicting enough damage to cause her to sink within six minutes with the loss of over 270 personnel. Despite the rapidity with which the vessel sank, over 1300 lives were saved and one of the survivors was Caleb Sherwood.

However, he subsequently died from pneumonia on the 27th April 1917. Initially buried at the Suda Bay Consular Cemetery on the island of Crete, his grave, along with 18 other First World War burials, was moved in 1963 to the larger Suda Bay War Cemetery on the island.

In addition to Caleb being recorded on the Witney War Memorial[124] he is also remembered on the war memorial in Eynsham.

---

[124] His parents had, by 1911, moved from Barnard Gate to Newland, Witney.

151

C.W. Shurmer
Private, Cyril Walter Shurmer, 32248,
8th Battalion,
South Lancashire Regiment

Cyril Shurmer was born in Fairford, Gloucestershire, in December 1897, the only child of Harry, a local baker and confectioner, and his wife Sarah (née Titcombe). After leaving school Cyril worked for his father as a baker's assistant until he enlisted in June 1916. Being only 18 at the time of volunteering he was initially placed into the Army Reserve but upon reaching his 19th birthday in December 1916 he was mobilised and transferred to the Territorial Reserves, being posted to the Western Front on the 26th April 1917.

On May 19th 1917, after having spent a little over two weeks at the 46th Infantry Brigade Depot in France, Cyril was posted as part of a draft of reinforcements to the 8th Battalion South Lancashire Regiment, an element of the 25th Division. The Division had been selected to take part in the assault on the German held Messines Ridge – the taking of which was to be the opening action of the Third Battle of Ypres, or "Passchendaele". In the days leading up to the attack the Division was moved into the front line between the Wulverghem to Messines and the Wulverghem to Wytschaete roads. The preliminary artillery bombardment of the German positions began on 21st May involving 2,300 guns and 300 heavy mortars and did not cease until 2:50 a.m. on the 7th June at which time the German defenders rushed back to their battered positions and prepared to defend themselves against the attack which they assumed to be imminent.

At 3:10 a.m. the order was given to detonate twenty one mines which had been carefully prepared in advance by British tunnellers working deep under the German positions. In the ensuing simultaneous explosions the crest of the Messines to Wytschaete ridge was blown to pieces with the resultant sound being heard as far away as London and Dublin - up to this point the loudest man-made explosion ever produced. It was estimated that around 10,000 men were killed, many simply vaporised, by the blast. Upon this signal nine Divisions of Allied infantry advanced behind a creeping barrage up the ridge taking all their objectives within three hours. It was during this attack that Cyril

Shurmer was killed. His body was never identified and today his name is recorded on the Ypres (Menin Gate) Memorial in Ieper, Belgium.

In addition to his name being recorded on the Witney War Memorial he is also remembered on the war memorial in his native Fairford, from where his parents had moved, in the latter part of 1916, to take up residence in Witney.

F. Smith
Private, Frederick Smith, 41782,
1st Battalion,
Royal Irish Fusiliers

Frederick, 'Fred', Smith was born in Poffley End, Hailey, around 1896, the youngest son of Thomas, a carter on a local farm, and his wife Mary Jane (née Townsend). In 1911 Fred, still living in Poffley End, was working as a baker's assistant. By 1915 the family had moved into a house on the New Yatt Road Witney.

In September 1915 Fred enlisted in the Army Service Corps as a baker and within three weeks he had left England for Mesopotamia (now Iraq), arriving in the Middle East on the 15th October 1915. He spent a brief time there before being transferred, in March 1916, to France and the Western Front. In January 1918 he transferred from the Army Service Corps to the Infantry and, following a short period of training, he was posted to the 1st Battalion of the Irish Fusiliers, part of the 36th (Ulster) Division.

On the morning of the 21st March 1918 the Germans launched what was to be their final major offensive campaign of the war. Seventy-two Divisions from three Armies punched a sixty mile wide hole through the British front line on the Somme. At the time of the attack the 36th Division was on the Somme, holding a sector of the British front line and Forward Zone south west of St. Quentin. The Division fought the Germans determinedly in what became known as the 'Actions at the Somme Crossing' and the 'Battle of Rosieres' but casualties were high. The 36th Division sustained over 7,000 casualties during the opening phase of the German offensive and was effectively destroyed. It was removed from the order of battle and rebuilt.

By the 10th April the 36th Division was back in action at the Battle of Messines, a phase of the Fourth Battle of Ypres and it was during this engagement, on the 11th April 1918, that Fred Smith was killed. His body was never identified and he has no known grave. Today his name is remembered on the Tyne Cot Memorial, Zonnebeke, Belgium.

S.W. Smith
Private/Bugler, Stephen William Smith, 655,
'B' Company,
1/4th Battalion,
Oxfordshire & Buckinghamshire Light Infantry

Stephen Smith, who was known by his middle name 'William', was born at Newland around 1884, the only son of Stephen, a housepainter and decorator, and his wife Sarah (née Davis). In the census of 1901 William was recorded as working with his father as a housepainter's apprentice. In the spring of 1907 he married Gertrude Horne, who was known by her middle name, 'Alice'. Their first child, a daughter, Lilian, was born in early 1908 and a second daughter, Kathleen, known by her middle name 'Louisa', was born in 1909. By the spring of 1911 the family were living at Park Terrace on Tower Hill and William was recorded as being in employment as a house decorator.

William joined the local Territorial (4th) Battalion of the Oxfordshire and Buckinghamshire Light Infantry (OBLI) towards the end of 1908 and was still serving on the outbreak of war in August 1914. Upon mobilisation the Territorial's were called up and William was transferred to the newly formed 1/4th Battalion where he was posted to 'B' Company as a bugler. The 1/4th OBLI deployed to France on the 29th March 1915, as part of the South Midland Division (later designated the 48th) and by the 3rd of April it was encamped near the town of Cassel. Following a brief period of training and trench familiarisation the 1/4th OBLI began to take its turn in the front line. But it was to be a short lived experience for William. He was killed on the morning of the 17th June 1915 in Ploegsteert Wood, in the southern sector of the Ypres Salient.

The story of his demise is told in the words of one of his comrades, Harold Harris, a fellow Witney man who was himself later to become another of the war's fatalities. In a letter sent from the front to the Editor of the Witney Gazette Harris described how:

'... "Spot" Smith, as he was familiarly known in the Company was killed yesterday morning, adding another to the list of Newlander's who have fallen. He was back in the subsidiary line (support trenches is the more familiar title) sitting down, when a bullet passed through a hole, about the size of a penny, in the parapet and entered his heart. He died immediately. The subsidiary line is well protected, but the probability is that the death messenger was a "stray" bullet.... "Spot" was always bright and cheerful and very popular in the Company. "Spot" was buried back in the wood the same night; he lies in a pretty nook, close to the late Lieut. Poulton-Palmer. We shall regret his death and sympathise deeply with his widow... '[125]

As Harris stated, William was buried near to the grave of Lieutenant Ronald Poulton-Palmer, heir to the Huntley and Palmer biscuit factory in Reading and former captain of the 1914 England Rugby Team, who had been killed just one month earlier. The two men rest just a few yards apart in the Hyde Park Corner (Royal Berks) Cemetery, Comines-Warneton, Hainaut, Belgium.

N.H. Souch
Private, Norman Harold Souch, 22182,
2/4th Battalion,
Oxfordshire & Buckinghamshire Light Infantry

Norman Souch was born in Cogges during the second quarter of 1896, the fifth son of James, a baker, and his wife Mary Ann (née Langford). At the time of the 1911 census the family were living in a house on Bridge Street and Norman was employed as a draper's assistant.

In the absence of a military record it is unclear when Norman enlisted for military service. However his regimental number indicates that it is likely to

---

[125] *Witney Gazette*, 26th June 1915.

have been after the beginning of 1916. Following his basic training he was posted to the 2/4th Battalion of the Oxfordshire and Buckinghamshire Light Infantry (OBLI), part of the 61st (2nd South Midland) Division. This formation was deployed to France on the 24th May 1916 in preparation for the Allied summer offensive on the Somme.

The Division's first major action at Fromelles on the 19th July 1916 was a disaster and resulted in the Division taking heavy casualties. With its reputation severely damaged the Division was not used for anything other than defending existing trench lines until January 1917 when it was back in action during the Operations on the Ancre. Following this series of battles the Division was engaged in the pursuit of the Germans as they withdrew from the Somme area to their pre-prepared and heavily defended Hindenburg Line. Subsequently the Division was used at the battles of Langemarck (August 1917), and Cambrai (November 1917).

At the end of March 1918 the men of the 61st Division were on the Somme engaged in covering a huge British withdrawal of the area as the Germans launched their final offensive of the war. During the Battles of the Lys (9th – 29th April) the Division once again suffered heavy casualties, but the German advance had ground to a halt and the enemy were forced to retreat. By the middle of October the 61st Division was in action again during the final Allied advance in Picardy throughout which the German rearguard relentlessly protected its centre and flanks and fiercely resisted possession of every village and hamlet.

On the 24th October 1918 the men of the 2/4th OBLI were ordered to take an area of high ground to the east of Bermerain. They advanced on the Germans from the direction of Haussy and soon succeeded in occupying and securing the position. At some point during this engagement Norman Souch was killed in action.

Originally buried on the battlefield his grave was moved, following the Armistice, to the Romeries Communal Cemetery Extension, near the village of Romeries, France.[126]

---

[126] Also buried here is fellow Witney man, Ernest Brotheron of the 2/4th OBLI, killed on the 24th October during the same action.

G. Stanley
Driver, George Stanley, 826675,
'D' Battery,
298th Brigade, Royal Field Artillery

Very little information has been discovered concerning this man but, from the records of the Commonwealth War Graves Commission, it appears that George Stanley was born in Witney around 1898, the son of George and his wife Emma. In 1916, at the time of his enlistment, George was recorded as living in Oxford.

Upon joining the army George was drafted into the Territorial element of the Royal Field Artillery (RFA) and in 1917 he was deployed to France. Once on the Western Front he was attached to 'D' Battery of 298th Brigade RFA.

It is not known where or when he was wounded but it is clear that he died on the 22nd September 1917 at a military field hospital several miles west of Ypres and was buried in the nearby Brandhoek New Military Cemetery, Belgium, which served the field hospital.

In the early 1920's, when information on the war dead was begun to be collected by the Imperial, later Commonwealth, War Graves Commission, George's parents were recorded as living in Manchester.

E. Stephens
Sergeant, Ernest Stephens, 6755,
1st Battalion,
Oxfordshire & Buckinghamshire Light Infantry

Ernest Stephens was born at the beginning of 1882, in the Cornish village of Lostwithiel, the fifth son of William, a stone mason, and his wife Elizabeth (née Clarke). During the 1890's the family moved to Battersea in London where Ernest's father had found work as a bricklayer. Around 1900 Ernest enlisted in the army and at the time of the census of 1901 he was a Private in the Oxfordshire Light Infantry and stationed at Cowley Barracks in Oxford.

In the summer of 1904 Ernest married Jessie Warnock, the daughter of Mary, the landlady of the *Original Swan* Public house in Cowley. At around this time

Mary Warnock moved to Witney and Ernest was posted to his regiment's 2nd battalion which was at Chatham. It is likely that Jessie moved to be with her husband although at the beginning of 1907, heavily pregnant with the couple's first child, she was in Witney, staying with her mother, and their son, William, was born in the town.

At the time of the 1911 census Ernest, his wife and their son, were all living together in a single room in a house in Elham, Kent, near to Shorncliffe Camp, where Ernest's unit had been moved. The following year it is likely that Ernest, having completed twelve years regular service, was discharged from the Army to the reserves.

When the order for full mobilisation came, in August 1914, Ernest was recalled to his regiment and on the 5th December 1914 he arrived in Mesopotamia (now Iraq) to join the 1st Battalion of the Oxfordshire and Buckinghamshire Light Infantry (OBLI), part of the 6th (Poona) Division, which had recently arrived from India. The campaign in Mesopotamia, an often forgotten theatre of operations, involved British and Indian troops fighting the forces of the Ottoman Empire for control of the region. Death as result of enemy action was just one peril facing the British and their colonial forces. Many troops succumbed to sickness, disease and, during the long summer months, the relentless heat.

On the morning of the 15th July 1915 the name of Sergeant Ernest Stephens was added to the list of casualties. His death, most probably as a result of sickness, was recorded by the battalion diarist who wrote that he was buried around lunchtime on the same day.[127] Today his grave can be found in the Amara Military Cemetery, in the town of Amarah, about two hundred miles south-east of Baghdad, Iraq.

In the months following Ernest's death his comrades in the 1st OBLI helped take the town of Kut and then participated in the pursuit of the Ottoman forces as they retreated towards Baghdad. Failing in their attempt to take the city, the British and Indian troops were forced to fall back on Kut where the garrison of ten thousand were besieged by the advancing Ottomans. On the 29th April, 1916, following a series of aborted attempts to relieve the town and in the face

---

[127] WO 95/5122

of mounting casualties and shortages of supplies, the garrison, including 300 men of the 1st OBLI, were forced to surrender.

C.J. Stratford
Gunner, Clement John Stratford, 291838,
132nd (Oxford) Heavy Battery,
Royal Garrison Artillery

Clement Stratford, known by his second name, John, was born on the Charterville Estate, Minster Lovell, at the end of 1891, the eldest son of John, a general labourer, and his wife Elizabeth (née Cook). By the time of 1911 census the family were still living on 'the estate', as it was known, and nineteen-year-old John was recorded as being employed by the General Post Office as a letter carrier.

On the 5th May 1915 John, who had by then left his job with the Post Office and was working as a mill hand, enlisted for military service. He joined the Royal Garrison Artillery and was posted to the locally raised 132nd (Oxford) Heavy Battery. On Saturday the 4th December 1915 John married Lillian Gardner, of Crawley Road, Witney. Their time together was brief. In the early spring of 1916 John's Battery received orders to deploy to France and the Western Front, landing on the 21st March at Le Havre. John was to spend the next seventeen months with his unit in France before he was granted his first period of ten days leave. After which, having spent time at home with his wife, John returned to France, rejoining his unit on the 6th September 1917.

On the 21st March 1918 the Germans launched a massive offensive operation on the Western Front in an attempt to deliver a knock-out blow to the Allied forces before the great weight of American assistance could be deployed effectively. In a break from the traditional tactics of full frontal assaults, using large numbers of troops, the Germans planned to use small units of 'stormtroopers' to by-pass defending front line units and destroy enemy headquarters, supply depots and artillery positions in the rear. The attack started at 4.40 am on the morning of the 21st with the biggest artillery barrage of the war - over one million shells were fired in an hour into an area of 150 square miles. By the end of the day the British were in retreat having suffered more than 55,000 casualties killed or wounded. John Stratford's family were informed that John had been posted as missing in action.

Initially there was no other news from France regarding John's situation. The family wrote asking for further information but there was none. John's only child, a boy named Frederick John, was born in West End, Witney on the 5th May 1918, and still no news had been received. On the 15th July his wife wrote to the authorities again asking if there was any information. By this stage it was assumed that he had indeed been killed on the 21st March and a pension for his widow began to be arranged although, given the fact that a child was now involved in the calculations, the authorities required confirmation of the dates of John's last home leave. On the 25th November 1918 his wife received confirmation that, for the loss of her husband, she was to receive a weekly pension of 20 shillings and 5 pence.

John Stratford's body was never identified and he has no known grave. Today he is remembered on the Pozieres Memorial, in the village of Pozieres, four miles north east of Albert, France.

In addition to his name being commemorated on the Witney War Memorial John Stratford's name also appears on the War Memorial in Minster Lovell, alongside that of his younger brother Henry who, whilst serving with the 10th Battalion of the Gloucestershire Regiment, was killed in action on the opening day of the Battle of Loos, 25th September 1915.

W.G. Stroud
Private, William George Stroud, 23197,
6th Battalion,
Oxfordshire & Buckinghamshire Light Infantry

William Stroud was born in Woodstock during the second quarter of 1888, the eldest son of Frederick, a bricklayer, and his wife Sarah (née Smith). He grew up in the town of his birth but by 1911 he had moved to Witney where, in the census of that year he was recorded as working as a hairdresser and living with his aunt and uncle at their home on Bridge Street. Towards the end of 1915 he married Mabel Pearson of Crawley and the couple took a house in West End.

William joined the Army within the first couple of months of conscription - introduced in January 1916 to satisfy the growing demand for fighting men. Once trained, he was sent to France where he was assigned to the 6th Battalion of the Oxfordshire and Buckinghamshire Light Infantry, part of the 20th (Light) Division. During the summer of 1917 the 20th Division were used in the opening phases of the Third Battle of Ypres or "Passchendaele" as it is more commonly known. It was during the fighting at Langemarck in mid-August 1917, that William was seriously wounded by shrapnel.

He was brought home to England to be treated at the Beaufort Military Hospital in Bristol. However, on Tuesday 2nd October 1917, after six weeks of medical care he died. His body was brought back to Witney on the night of 4th October where it was met at the railway station by a contingent of the Witney Platoon, Oxfordshire Volunteer Reserves (OVR) who bore his coffin back to his home on West End.

The funeral took place on the following Sunday afternoon at Holy Trinity Church on Woodgreen. William's coffin, draped with the Union Jack, was carried from his home to the church by men of the Witney Platoon, OVR and he was laid to rest in the leafy churchyard. Amongst the mourners that day in the Church was William's younger brother, Frederick. He was, at the time, a serving soldier with the 7th Battalion, Norfolk Regiment. A little over a year later he too was dead; killed in action in France during the last month of the war.

In addition to being recorded on the Witney War Memorial William is also remembered on the War Memorial in Woodstock.

A.S. Tallett
Private, Alfred Samuel Tallett, 3685,
'B' Company,
1/4th Battalion,
Oxfordshire & Buckinghamshire Light Infantry

Alfred Tallett was born in Witney, around June 1897, the son of Samuel, a whitesmith, and his second wife, Millicent (maiden name unknown). As a child he attended the town's Wesleyan Day School.

Alfred enlisted in the Army on the 30th November 1914 and was posted to the recently formed 1/4th Battalion of the Oxfordshire and Buckinghamshire Light Infantry (OBLI), part of the South Midland (later the 48th) Division. However, at only eighteen years of age and therefore one year younger than the minimum age required for overseas deployment on active service, he was not allowed to join his comrades when the battalion sailed for France on the 30th March 1915. He eventually arrived on the Western front on the 28th June 1915 and rejoined his unit.

On the 1st July 1916 the long awaited Allied offensive began, the 'big push' which was widely hoped to end the war by sheer weight of numbers. For the men of the 1/4th OBLI this was to be their first major engagement. Three weeks into the offensive they, along with the rest of the 48th Division, were assigned to support Australian troops from the 1st Australian and New Zealand Army Corps (ANZAC) in an attempt to take the high ground near the village of Pozieres. Despite the initial phases of the attack being deemed a success, the German defenders refused to be moved from the ridge and there was a further two weeks of bitter fighting before the ground was finally taken.

Alfred Tallett never saw the top of the ridge he was fighting to take. During the early stages of the battle, on the 23rd July 1916, he was killed in action. Today his body lies in the Pozieres British Cemetery, at Ovillers – La Boisselle, France.

O.E. Tarrant
Lance Corporal, Oswald Edward Tarrant, 2641,
1/4th Battalion,
Oxfordshire & Buckinghamshire Light Infantry
(Elder brother of Ernest Tarrant who died of wounds, 1st August 1916 and of Norman Tarrant who died of wounds, 14th August 1916)

Oswald Tarrant was born in Witney during the second quarter of 1884, the eldest son of William, a grocer, and his wife Mary Jane (née Abraham). Following his education at Bourne College,[128] in Quinton, Worcestershire, he returned to Witney and began working for his father who owned three shops in the town. During the summer of 1912 he married Annie Smith, the daughter of Samuel Smith, a local blanket manufacturer.

On the afternoon of Thursday 1st September 1914 Oswald, a former member of the Boys Brigade, and his younger brothers, Ernest and Norman, joined a party of around forty local men as they marched, midst a cheering crowd from the Wesleyan School to the town's railway station. There the 'Witney Company', as they came to be known, boarded the train for Oxford where they volunteered for military service. The following day a number of the men failed to pass the medical examination and were sent home but Oswald and his brothers were accepted and posted to the newly formed 1/4th Battalion of the Oxfordshire and Buckinghamshire Light Infantry (OBLI), part of the South Midland Division (later redesignated the 48th Division). In the spring of 1915, following training and equipping, the Division was deployed to France. Oswald, who had been promoted to the rank of Lance Corporal, landed with his unit at Boulogne on the 30th March.

On 1st July 1916 the great Allied offensive on the Somme began and units of the 48th Division were involved from the outset. The 1/4th OBLI received orders to attack the German lines during the late afternoon of the 2nd July, but these orders were later cancelled and the battalion was withdrawn from the front line. On the 4th July it moved back into the line near Hebuterne, relieving a battalion of the Warwickshires. The weather conditions were extremely poor and the

---

[128] Bourne College, which opened in 1882, was one of only two boarding schools in the country for the sons of primitive Methodists, although entry was later opened to boys of other denominations. It closed in 1928.

men were put to work draining their trenches. On the 8th July the Battalion was relieved and retired to an area between Sailly-u-Bois and Coigneux, from where, during the evening of the 10th July 1916, it moved back towards the front line as a working party to dig and consolidate the trench line. It was during this operation that Oswald Tarrant was mortally wounded by shrapnel. He never regained consciousness and died that night. Today his grave can be found in the Hebuterne Military Cemetery, near the village of Hebuterne, France.

Within days of Oswald's death both his younger brothers, Ernest and Norman, had also suffered fatal wounds on the battlefield. Ernest died on the 1st August 1916 and Norman, a fortnight later on the 14th August 1916.

As well as being remembered on the War Memorial in Witney, Oswald and his brothers were recorded on a marble war memorial at Bourne College. When the college closed in 1928 the memorial was moved to the College Road Methodist Chapel but was subsequently lost when the chapel was demolished to make way for the M5 motorway in 1967. In early 2001 the Quinton Local History Society began a successful campaign to raise funds to reinstate the memorial and later that year a new carved oak memorial was unveiled at the Quinbourne Centre in Quinton.

Oswald's widow, Annie, never re married and remained living in the Witney area until her death in early 1948.

E.W. Tarrant
Lance Corporal, Ernest William Tarrant, 2624,
'B' Company,
1/4th Battalion,
Oxfordshire & Buckinghamshire Light Infantry
(Younger brother of Oswald Tarrant who died of wounds, 10th July 1916 and older brother of Norman Tarrant who died of wounds, 14th August 1916)

Ernest Tarrant was born in Witney at the beginning of 1890, the second son of William, a grocer, and his wife, Mary Jane (nee Abraham). Educated at Bourne

College, in Quinton Worcestershire,[129] by 1911 Ernest was lodging in London where he was working as a counting house clerk for a wholesale draper.

On 1st September 1914 as a member of the 'Witney Company', Ernest travelled to Oxford with his two brothers, Oswald and Norman, to volunteer for military service. He and his brothers were accepted and posted to the newly formed 1/4th Battalion of the Oxfordshire and Buckinghamshire Light Infantry (OBLI), part of the South Midland (later redesignated the 48th) Division. In March 1915, following a period of training and equipping, the Division was deployed for service in France. Ernest arrived with his unit in Boulogne on the 30th of the month.

The first major offensive operation that involved the 48th Division was the great Allied summer offensive of 1916. On the 10th July 1916, ten days into the offensive, Ernest's older brother, Oswald, was killed by shrapnel as he toiled as part of a working party near the front. Ernest, who had been promoted to the rank of Lance Corporal, was with his brother at the time of his death and assumed the responsibility of writing home to inform their parents of the sad news.

On the 18th July the 1/4th OBLI, whilst in the front line trenches, received orders to attack the German lines between Ovillers and Pozieres. The first wave of troops began their attack at around 1:30 a.m. on the morning of the 19th but confusion and congestion in the British trenches prevented a second wave and the assault was halted and the battalion withdrawn. On the 22nd July the men of the 1/4th OBLI were ordered back into the line to resume the offensive – this time from a position just to the west of Pozieres. At 12:30 a.m. on the morning of the 23rd July the battalion rose out of their trenches and advanced across the battlefield towards the enemy. In this, as in the previous action on the 19th, the battalion suffered heavy casualties.

One of those wounded at Pozieres was Ernest Tarrant. He was evacuated to a military hospital on the outskirts of Rouen but died several days later on the 1st August 1916. He was buried in the St. Sever Cemetery, Rouen, France.

---

[129] Ernest's name also appears on the Witney Grammar School's Roll of Honour although no records exist for his ever having been a student there. See Cavell (p.94)

His younger brother, Norman, who had been seriously wounded in the same action, died two weeks later on the 14th August 1916 at a military hospital near Etaples, France.

F.N. Tarrant
Private, Frederick Norman Tarrant,
'B' Company,
1/4th Battalion,
Oxfordshire & Buckinghamshire Light Infantry
(Younger brother of Oswald Tarrant who died of wounds, 10th July 1916 and of Ernest Tarrant who died of wounds, 1st August 1916)

Frederick Tarrant, who was known by his second name of 'Norman', was born in Witney at the beginning of 1890, the third and youngest son of William, a grocer, and his wife Mary (nee Abraham). Like his two older brothers before him, he studied at Bourne College, in Quinton, Worcestershire and by 1911 he was working as a clerk in an insurance company in London. By the summer of 1914 he had returned to Witney.

On the 1st September 1914, as a member of the 'Witney Company', he travelled to Oxford alongside his two older brothers, Oswald and Ernest, to volunteer for military service. He was accepted and, with his brothers, was posted to the newly formed 1/4th Battalion of the Oxfordshire and Buckinghamshire Light Infantry (OBLI), part of the South Midland (later redesignated the 48th) Division. In the spring of 1915, following a period of training and equipping, the Division was deployed for service in France with Norman and the rest of his unit, landing in Boulogne on the 30th March.

Identified for offensive operations on the Somme in the summer of 1916 the 48th Division was engaged from the outset. Ten days into the battle on the 10th July, whilst their battalion was being used as a working party near the front line at Hebuterne, Norman's elder brother, Oswald, was killed by shrapnel. Just over a week later the battalion went into action during the early hours of the 19th July when it was ordered to attack the German lines between Ovillers and Pozieres. The initial attack faltered and a second attack was cancelled because of confusion and congestion in the British trenches. The 1/4th OBLI was

166

temporarily withdrawn from the line but on the 22nd July it resumed the attack from a position to the west of Pozieres. At 12:30 a.m. on the morning of the 23rd July the 1/4th went 'over the top' again and advanced towards the German lines. The fighting was intense and protracted. It was several hours before it became clear that the battalion had suffered a large number of casualties.

Norman and his brother Ernest were amongst the wounded and both were evacuated from the battlefield for medical treatment. Ernest was taken to a hospital at Rouen where, on the 1st August 1916, he died from his wounds and Norman, whose condition remained serious, was moved to a hospital near Etaples. When the terrible news of Ernest's death, following so soon after that of Oswald's, reached William and Mary Tarrant they obtained permission from the military authorities to cross the Channel to visit their only surviving, but seriously wounded, son. On the 14th August 1916, just days after his parents had arrived in France, Norman Tarrant died in hospital. He was buried in the Etaples Military Cemetery, France.

Norman's parents returned to Witney where William Tarrant, a prominent businessman and civic official, continued, amongst other things, to occupy a seat on the local Military Service Tribunal - a body which deliberated on individual appeals against conscription. Following the end of the war William was appointed to a Council subcommittee set up to establish a fitting memorial for the fallen of the town. At the same time the family personally donated a new organ to St. Mary's Church and dedicated it to the memory of the three brothers.

In the early 1920's William and Mary Tarrant left Witney and moved to Bournemouth. It was said that they both found it too painful to gaze upon the memorial which bore the names of their three sons.

A. Titcombe
Lance Corporal, Arthur Titcombe, 6792,
1st Battalion,
East Surrey Regiment

Arthur Titcombe was born in Witney on the 3rd September 1881, the third son of Albert, a brewer's clerk, and his wife Charlotte (née Jackson). During the

1890's the family left Witney and moved to Bristol from where, in August 1897, Arthur moved to High Wycombe to undertake a three year apprenticeship at *'Gale Bros, Drapers and Outfitters'*. Perhaps work was hard to find or maybe he sought adventure but, for whatever reason, in November 1900, just three months after completing his apprenticeship, he joined the Army. Initially Arthur enlisted for three years service with the East Surrey Regiment, to be followed by nine years service as a reservist, but he volunteered to increase his length of service and at the time of the census in 1911 he was recorded as being in Southampton on board the troopship *Rewa*. By early 1914 Arthur had begun a relationship with eighteen year old Florence Cornock, a domestic servant from Falfield in Gloucestershire and when he was deployed to France on the 11th September 1914 it was a pregnant Florence who was left to wait for his return.

On the 10th December 1914 the 1st Battalion, East Surrey Regiment, left their temporary billets in Neuve Eglise and moved into the front line trenches near Wulverghem, south of Ypres. It was dark and the weather was wet and foggy and the battalion found the trenches they were required to defend and from which they may be expected to launch an attack, to be very muddy and in a generally poor condition. For the next few days the men of the battalion managed to consolidate their position, whilst being intermittently shelled and sniped at. On the 14th, described by the battalion diarist as being *"the busiest day so far in the trenches"*[130], the battalion helped support an attack by the 3rd Division and French Corps on their left flank. The weather hadn't improved, it continued to rain and the situation was exasperated by difficulties in communications throughout the day.

It was whilst in the trenches at Wulverghem, on the 14th December 1914, that Arthur Titcombe, along with two of his comrades, was killed in action. He has no known grave and today his name is recorded on the Ypres (Menin Gate) Memorial, Ieper, Belgium.

In the spring of 1915 Florence gave birth to a daughter. She was a young unmarried mother and, not uncommonly in such circumstances; the baby, whom she called Nora, was taken and raised by her grandmother, Emma

---

[130] WO 95/1563

Cornock. Nora was brought up to believe that she was Florence's younger sister.

Florence married in 1921 to Sidney Wilton. She died in 1969.

A. Townsend
Private, Alfred Townsend, 33885,
24th Protection Company,
Royal Defence Corps

Alfred Townsend was born in Corn Street, Witney, around June 1865, the fourth son of William, a stone mason, and his wife Sarah (née Clarke). At the time of the 1881 census Alfred was working as a carpenter. On the 8th January 1890 he married Florence Clarke of Woodstock. The couple settled in Witney, initially in Corn Street, and their first child, Mabel, was born the following year. By the spring of 1901 the family had grown – Mabel was now one of four children and they had all moved to a house in the Crofts, although at the time of the census that year Alfred was working in Weston-Super-Mare and lodging with his elder sister, Lizzie, and her family. The records suggest that Florence and the children later joined Alfred and, in 1903, the couple's fifth child, Dorothy, was born in Weston. It is unclear if Alfred stayed in Weston after this date but we do know that Florence had returned to the Woodstock area by April 1906 where the couple's youngest child, Jack, was born. By the time of the 1911 census the family were back in Witney and living in the Crofts.

He volunteered for military service on the 6th May 1915 and was posted to the Army Veterinary Corps.[131] On the 22nd May, barely three weeks after he had enlisted, he was deployed to France and the Western Front but it was not long before he was back in the UK. At the time of his enlistment Alfred had been almost fifty years old and on the 15th August 1915 he was admitted to a military hospital in Brockenhurst, Hampshire, to be treated for rheumatism in his hands and feet. He remained in hospital for three months until being allowed to leave on the 13th November. As a result of his condition he was referred to a medical board who considered him no longer fit for active service

---

[131] Interestingly his trade at the time of his attestation was given as 'groom' and not 'carpenter'.

and on the 1st January 1916 he was transferred to the Royal Defence Corps (RDC). [132]

On Wednesday the 27th December 1916 Alfred, serving as part of the 24th Protection Company, RDC, was guarding a railway bridge near Cardiff, in South Wales, when he slipped and fell onto the line. Before he could rise he was hit by an engine travelling from Cardiff to Porthcawl. First aid was administered at the scene by railway officials before Alfred was conveyed by train to Cardiff. When he arrived at the city's station he was attended by Dr de Vere Hunt who accompanied him in an ambulance to the 3rd Western General Hospital where, upon closer examination, he was found to have suffered serious injuries to his right arm and leg. [133] But his injuries were far more severe than first thought and he died in hospital the following day (28th December 1916).

His body was conveyed to Witney and on Tuesday 2nd January 1917 he was buried in the town's cemetery. No firing party was present, due to the short notice of his interment, but the local recruiting officer, Mr Hayter, representing the military authorities, was able to cover the coffin with a Union Jack. [134]

Today Alfred's grave is marked by a Commonwealth War Graves headstone.

H. Townsend
Private, Herbert Townsend, 202404,
'B' Company,
1/4th Battalion,
Oxfordshire & Buckinghamshire Light Infantry

Herbert Townsend was born in Witney around 1879, the seventh son of James, a railway labourer, and his wife Emma (née Holland). At the time of the 1901 census Herbert was living in Eastbourne, Sussex where he was working, as a 'liftman', at the *Queen's Hotel*. He remained employed there for a number of years and by 1911 he was one of the hotel's porters.

---

[132] The RDC had been formed during the war to protect a variety of strategic points in the UK, such as ports, rail junctions and certain roads and drew its manpower from men who were generally either too old or not fit enough for active service. It was a national resource and as such the men could be posted anywhere in the UK.

[133] From an account of the incident reported in the *Western Mail*, 28th December 1916.

[134] As reported in the *Witney Gazette*, 6th January 1917.

Herbert joined the Army in March 1916 and following basic training was deployed to France where he was attached to the 1/4th Battalion of the Oxfordshire and Buckinghamshire Light Infantry (OBLI), part of the 48th (South Midland) Division. This formation took part in the huge Allied offensive on the Somme in the summer of 1916 and was used in the battles of; Bazentin Ridge; Pozieres Ridge; the Ancre Heights and the Ancre.

In the spring of 1917, during the German Army's strategic withdrawal to their pre-prepared positions on the Hindenburg line, the Division occupied the French town of Peronne before being moved northwards to the Ypres Salient for the Third battle of Ypres (31st July 1917 – 6th November 1917), or "Passchendaele" as it is often referred to.

On the evening of the 5th August 1917 the 1/4th OBLI moved into front-line trenches following the line of the Steenbeek, north east of Ypres. Many casualties were sustained during the 6th as a result of enemy shelling and on the night of the 7th/8th the battalion was relieved by the 1/4th Royal Berkshires allowing the 1/4th OBLI to move into reserve, before coming out of the line completely the following night and returning to Dambre Camp[135]. It was during the evening of the 8th August 1917, as the battalion prepared to leave the battlefield, that Herbert Townsend and several of his comrades became victims of a German high explosive shell which burst amongst them, killing them instantly.

On the 13th August Herbert's Company Commander, Captain Andrew Wotherspoon, wrote to Mr Townsend informing him of his son's death:

"Your son ... never hesitated, and always did his duty. We, his comrades, miss him much, but our loss cannot compare with yours. I trust you and yours will obtain some comfort in your grief. We buried your son's body, with other comrades, in a shell-stricken area, and I marked the spot ... so that in due course, when that area can be reached, your son's grave will be attended to. Some private things found in his pockets will be sent through their proper channels."[136]

---

[135] A rest camp near Vlamertinge, several miles west of Ypres.

[136] From a letter originally published in the *Witney Gazette*, 1st September 1917. Three days after writing his letter Captain Wotherspoon was also dead, killed in action on the 16th August 1917.

Although originally buried on the battlefield, Herbert's grave was one of many in the immediate area to be removed to a number of larger 'concentration' cemeteries after the Armistice. Today his grave can be found in the New Irish Farm Cemetery, north-east of Ieper, Belgium.

F. Turner
Private, Frederick Turner, 17851,
5th Battalion,
Oxfordshire & Buckinghamshire Light Infantry

Frederick Turner was born in Witney in the second quarter of 1888, the son of Frederick, a grocer's porter, and his wife Ann (née Cox). In the census of 1911 Frederick was recorded as living with his widowed mother, his father having died in 1907, at a cottage in High Cogges. At the time he was working as a labourer at Marriott's blanket factory in Witney.

Frederick volunteered for military service around February 1915 and was posted to the Oxfordshire and Buckinghamshire Light Infantry. On the 10th June 1915, following his basic training, he was deployed to France to join his Regiment's 5th Battalion, part of the 14th (Light) Division. In 1915 the units of the 14th Division saw action at Hooge (July), when the Germans used flamethrowers for the first time and the Second Attack on Bellewaarde (September).

In August 1916, during the Allied summer offensive on the Somme, the 14th Division were in action at Delville Wood. The wood had been first assaulted on the 15th July by the South African Regiment and after four days of bitter hand to hand fighting they had succeeded in clearing the enemy from the southern edge of the wood but the rest of the ground remained in German hands. It took several more weeks of determined fighting by various units before, on 25th August, troops of the 14th Division finally overcame the last of the enemy resistance and took the ground.

It was during this final phase of the fight for Delville Wood that Frederick Turner was mortally wounded. He was evacuated from the battlefield and taken to one of the Casualty Clearing Stations at Dernancourt, just south of Albert. It was here, on the 25th August 1916, that Frederick succumbed to his wounds. He was buried in the local military cemetery, now known as Dernancourt Communal Cemetery Extension, France, where his grave can be found today.

J. Turner
Gunner, Henry James Turner, 213349,
'A' Battery,
84th Brigade,
Royal Field Artillery

Henry Turner, known by his second name, 'James', was born in Witney during the second quarter of 1878, the son of James (senior), a carter on a farm, and his wife Elizabeth (née Barrett). Towards the end of 1904 James, who had left Witney some years previously, was married to Ellen Hogg of Manchester. The couple's first child, John, was born a year later in 1905 and at the time of the 1911 census James was living with his family in the Gorton area of Manchester, where he was working as a messenger in a bank.

In the absence of his service record it is not known when James first enlisted for military service. However his service number and record of medal entitlement, indicate that it was before late 1916 and that he was deployed to France at some point after the beginning of 1917. Joining 'A' Battery of the 84th Brigade, Royal Field Artillery (RFA), which up to the 21st February 1917, was part of the 18th Division.

At the beginning of 1917 a new artillery unit was created which was designed to plug the gaps in the provision of artillery in whichever division, corps or army needed reinforcing. This new unit was made up of artillery brigades drawn from existing divisions, with one of those selected being the 84th Brigade. Between the 22nd February 1917 and the end of the war in 1918 the 84th Army Brigade RFA served with twenty two different divisions and fought in the Battles of Vimy Ridge, Messines, Flanders, the German offensive on the Somme in March 1918 and the Allied counter offensive in August 1918.

It was on the 12th November 1917, during the Third Battle of Ypres, or "Passchendaele" as it is more commonly known, that James Turner was killed in action. Today his grave can be found in the Tyne Cot Cemetery, the largest

Commonwealth War Grave cemetery on the Western Front, near Zonnebeke, Belgium.

A.E. Walker
Private, Albert Edward Walker, 33319,
6th Battalion,
Oxfordshire & Buckinghamshire Light Infantry

Albert Walker was born in Cogges on the 11th September 1892, the eldest child of William, a gardener, and his wife Elizabeth (née Keen). At the time of the 1911 census Albert was employed in a weaving shed at one of the town's blanket mills. He married Flossie Godfrey, of West End, on the 25th May 1914 and their first child, a daughter they named Edna, was born on the 6th November the following year.

When Albert enlisted is not known but his record of medal entitlement shows that he was posted to France, most likely during 1916 after transferring from the 83rd Provisional Battalion[137] to the 6th Battalion of the Oxfordshire and Buckinghamshire Light Infantry (OBLI), part of the 20th (Light) Division. The 6th OBLI had fought through the Allied summer offensive on the Somme in 1916 and was to remain on the Somme throughout the winter of 1916/17.

The official record of Albert Walker's death shows that he died of wounds on the 13th January 1917 although it is not clear where, or when, these wounds were received. Today his grave can be found in the Grove Town Cemetery, Méaulte, just south of Albert, France.

---

[137] In 1915 a number of Provisional Battalions were formed which comprised of those Territorial soldiers who were medically unfit for overseas service or who had declined to take the Imperial Service Obligation (their agreement to serve overseas). By the beginning of 1917 all the Provisional Battalion's had been either disbanded, or redesignated as Home Service Territorial Battalions.

G. Walker
Private, George Walker, 41782,
10th Battalion,
Worcestershire Regiment

George Walker was born at Newland in the autumn of 1880, the third son of Frederick, a road contractor, and his wife Esther (née Goodlake). George was just eight years old when his father passed away in 1888 and his mother was forced to support her family of nine working first as a glove maker and later as a blanket machinist. By 1901 George and his elder brother Harry had also entered the mills and were both employed as blanket finishers. In the autumn of 1908 George was married to Emily Haggitt and the couple set up home on Oxford Road, Newland. The couple's first child, a daughter they named Vera, was born the following year and their second daughter, Margaret, arrived at the beginning of 1911 when George was still working as a blanket finisher.

George joined the Army in September 1917 and following basic training was deployed to France around November 1917 to join a battalion of the Cambridgeshire Regiment. However, newly arrived men were often redeployed to reinforce under strength units and so it was that George was posted to the 10th Battalion, Worcestershire Regiment, part of the 19th (Western) Division. His unit fought through the initial engagements in response to the German spring offensive, which had begun on 21st March 1918.

By 6th June the German advance had ground to a halt on the Marne but the fighting continued. It was here, on the 18th June 1918, that George Walker was killed in action. Today his grave can be found in the Marfaux British Cemetery, near the village of Marfaux, France.

I. Walker
Private, Isaac Jesse Walker, 51243,
37th Field Ambulance,
Royal Army Medical Corps

Isaac Walker was born in Corn Street, at the beginning of 1884, the second son of Isaac (senior), a butcher, and his wife Elizabeth (née Brown). After leaving school he entered into an apprenticeship with a local printer and was to remain in that trade until the time of his enlistment in 1914.

Isaac volunteered for military service during the early stages of the war and, whether through personal choice or a demand for new recruits in particular units, he was assigned to the Royal Army Medical Corps. He landed in France on the 22nd May 1915 and by 1918 he was serving with the 37th Field Ambulance, part of the 12th Division.

In the late summer and early autumn of 1918 the British forces on the Western Front were engaged in a series of actions against the retreating Germans, who were forced further and further back towards the Hindenburg Line. On the 18th September the 12th Division was ordered to attack the German defences at Epehy. In the ensuing battle, which lasted for over a week, the British took heavy casualties. On the 29th September the Division was in action again attacking the formidable German defences in front of Ossus Wood which, once taken, allowed for an advance on the small town of Vendhuile. This battle, on what was deemed to be the most successful day of the final offensive, allowed for Allied troops, fighting to the right of the 12th Division that day, to break through the Hindenburg Line.

Officially it is recorded that Isaac Walker was killed in action on the 29th September 1918 however the *Witney Gazette,* recording his death several months later, reported that he had died from wounds received.

Today his grave can be found in the Templeux-Le-Guerard British Cemetery, in the village of Templeux-Le-Guerard, France.

E.A. Weaver
Private, Ernest Archer Weaver, 266673,
'D' Company,
2/1st (Bucks) Battalion,
Oxfordshire & Buckinghamshire Light Infantry

Ernest Weaver, known as 'Arch', was born in Gloucester Place, Witney, on the 18th January 1894, the third son of George, a mill worker, and his wife Leah (née Batts Merry). By the time of the 1911 census Arch had entered into an apprenticeship with a local printer.

176

On the 1st September 1914, Arch Weaver joined a gallant group of local men as they marched through Witney, midst cheering crowds, to the train station where they boarded the train for Oxford and military service. However the selection process during these early stages of mass recruitment was far more stringent than it was to become later on and as a result Arch was declared to be medically unfit for service due to his *'poor physique and chest'*. Nevertheless, undeterred by initial rejection, he tried again and in 1915 was drafted into the Oxfordshire and Buckinghamshire Light Infantry (OBLI). Having completed his basic training Arch was deployed to France where he was posted to the Regiment's 2/1st (Bucks) Battalion, part of the 48th (South Midland) Division.

Through the summer and autumn of 1917 the men of the 48th Division were engaged in the Third Battle of Ypres, or "Passchendaele" as it is more commonly referred to. On the morning of the 22nd August 1917, as the 2/1st OBLI launched an attack against German positions...

> *'...poor Arch got hit by a sniper in the head and was killed .... By Archie getting killed the company has lost one of the very best of men. He was always steady under fire, and on more than one occasion has shown great bravery.... I have known Archie right from the very first day we joined the army, and we have always been the very best of chums, in fact he was liked by all officers and men in our company. ... Sincerely, W.J. Saunders, Sergt.*'[138]

Despite the best of intentions the continued fighting made it impossible for the British to recover all of the bodies of the fallen on the battlefield. Arch's body was never identified and he has no known grave. Today his name is remembered on the Tyne Cot Memorial, Zonnebeke, Belgium.

In 1919, Lillian, Arch's older sister who had married Alic Ridge in 1911, gave birth to a son. The couple named him Archer.

---

[138] Quoted from a letter sent to Arch's mother and subsequently published in the *Witney Gazette*, 15th September, 1917.

G. West
Private, Gordon West, 25812,
5th Battalion,
Oxfordshire & Buckinghamshire Light Infantry

Gordon West was born in the town of Newbury, Berkshire during the spring of 1885, the fifth son of Samuel, a grocer's assistant, and his wife, Emily (née Sayer). Upon leaving school Gordon entered the workplace and, by 1901, was employed as a junior corn merchant's clerk. According to the 1911 census, Gordon was a lodger in the home of Mr and Mrs Baker of Corn Street, Witney, and he was still employed as a corn merchant's clerk.

From his service number it appears that Gordon joined the army at some point during the late summer of 1916 at which point he was still living in Witney. After completing his basic training he was posted to France and the 5th Battalion Oxfordshire and Buckinghamshire Light Infantry (OBLI), part of the 14th (Light) Division. Between late March and early April 1917, the 5th OBLI were on the Somme, in action against the Germans retreating to the fortified Hindenburg Line. Then, on the 9th April they were deployed in the First Battle of the Scarpe, part of the Arras Offensive – an Anglo/French operation which, like many plans before and after, was designed to end the stalemate on the Western Front and end the war in 48 hours – where it was planned that British and Empire forces would attack the German lines to the East of Arras and draw enemy forces away from the site of a larger French assault further south.

The achievements of the initial phases of the battle encouraged further Allied advances and on the 3rd May the 5th OBLI went into action again in the Third Battle of the Scarpe. This time the British were unable to repeat their earlier success and the following day, having taken heavy casualties, the attack was called off. The order came too late for Gordon West who had been killed in the opening hours of the Battle. His body, like so many of his comrades, was never identified and he has no known grave. Today his name is recorded on the Arras Memorial, Arras, France.

L. Whitcher
Private, Leopold Whitcher, 11732,
1st (Cape of Good Hope) South African Infantry Regiment

Leopold 'Leo' Whitcher, was born in Witney during the final quarter of 1878, the fourth son of William, a hair dresser, and his wife, Mary Jane (née Brewer). The family had moved to Witney approximately one year earlier from Hertford where they had lived briefly after leaving their native Hampshire.

In 1896 the young Leo joined 'F' Company of the local Volunteer Battalion of the Oxfordshire Light Infantry. He quickly proved himself to be an excellent shot with the rifle, representing his battalion in numerous shooting competitions including those which took place during Queen Victoria's Diamond Jubilee celebrations in 1897. In 1899 the British went to war in South Africa against a significantly smaller force of Boer farmers and settlers and, despite the large numbers of troops sent there, the protracted nature of the conflict soon necessitated an increase in the size of the British forces deployed. Volunteer Battalions at home were called upon to form Active Service Companies to reinforce the regular battalions of their county regiments already serving. Answering the call to arms Leo and fellow townsman John Scanes (also to become a casualty of WWI) both volunteered for active service. Upon their return in May 1901 they were feted, as returning heroes, by the people of Witney, being presented with inscribed silver pocket watches, and a concert was held in their honour at the *Cross Keys Hotel*.

Perhaps having recognised the opportunities that presented themselves to an enterprising young man in South Africa, Leo didn't stay at home very long before deciding to emigrate. Before the year was out he had left his family and Witney, bound for Cape Town. By 1905 he had joined the local Cape Town Volunteers, a part-time unit similar to the volunteer unit he had been part of back in the UK, and he continued to shoot competitively, representing his unit in numerous competitions across the Colony. He married a local girl, Adeline Johanna (maiden name unknown), and the couple set up home together in Cape Town.

When the declaration of war with Germany was announced in 1914 Leo immediately volunteered to serve. Initially he joined the Colonial forces in German West Africa but soon found himself transferred to German East Africa where he served under General Smuts. In December 1916 he was struck down with fever and, being discharged from military service, was sent back to South Africa to convalesce. Following his recovery at the beginning of 1917 he again volunteered for military service. This time though it was to join the South African forces being assembled and trained to go to Europe to fight on the Western Front. Just prior to his departure in February 1917 the troop ship *Tyndareus,* carrying his younger brother, Victor, along with his unit, the 25th Middlesex Rifle Regiment, hit a German mine off the South African coast and almost sank. The survivors and the stricken ship were brought in at Simonstown Naval Base and whilst in camp there Victor was delighted to be 'found' by his older brother, Leo, who he believed to be still in German East Africa, and the two spent a full day together.

Following his training in South Africa Leo and his fellow volunteers moved to the UK, where further training took place, before they were deployed to France in May 1917 as part of a reinforcement draft, Leo himself being posted to the 1st South African Infantry Regiment, part of the South African Brigade, 9th (Scottish) Division. From the date of his arrival in France his unit was engaged in the Battle of Arras (9th April – 16th June 1917) and the Third Battle of Ypres, or "Passchendaele" (31st July – 6th November 1917). In March 1918 the South African Brigade fought impressively against overwhelming German forces during the initial enemy attacks of 'Operation Michael'. After which they were moved to Flanders, just in time to meet the second major German offensive aimed at the Ypres salient. In this, the Fourth Battle of Ypres, or Battle of the Lys, the Germans attacked the Allied forces to the south of Ypres. During the success of their initial assault on the 9th April they overran the Messines Ridge which the South Africans were immediately ordered to counter attack and retake.

Leo Whitcher, along with many of his comrades, was killed in action on the 10th April 1918 during the unsuccessful South African counter attack on Messines Ridge. Indeed such were the level of casualties sustained by the South Africans during those following few days that the original South African Brigade was effectively destroyed and the 1st, 2nd and 4th Regiments were temporarily merged to form one battalion. Leo's body was never identified and, having no known grave, his name is today recorded on the Ypres (Menin Gate) Memorial, Ieper, Belgium.

F. Wiltshire
Sapper, Frank William Wiltshire, 12687,
Divisional Signal Company,
New Zealand Engineers,
New Zealand Expeditionary Force

Frank Wiltshire was born in Egham, Surrey, on the 17th March 1894, the eldest child of Alfred, a post office clerk, and his wife Alice (née Duntze). By 1911 Frank was employed as a clerk in a local bank and the following year his parents left Surrey and moved to Witney, where his father had been appointed manager of the town's main Post Office. Frank served briefly with the Territorial Army and in 1913 emigrated to New Zealand. By 1915 he was working for a branch of the Bank of New Zealand and living in the town of Thames, about 120 miles south east of Auckland.

On the 11th January 1916, Frank volunteered for military service with the New Zealand Expeditionary Force and following basic training was posted to the Signalling Corps of the New Zealand Engineers (NZE). On the 6th May 1916, as part of a draft of reinforcements, he left his adoptive country and, after a brief stop in Egypt, he arrived in Southampton on the 7th August. Within a month he was moved to France and the Western Front.

After three weeks at the huge Allied military base of Etaples he was attached to the Divisional Signalling Company of the NZE with which unit he remained throughout his time in France. The information in Frank's military record, concerning his service on the Western Front, is brief. It is noted that on the 6th December 1916 he was evacuated from the battle front to the 1st Australian Casualty Clearing Station at Rouen, suffering with tonsillitis and that he rejoined his unit on the 18th December. Thereafter there is nothing except an entry recording his death in the field on the 10th June 1917, during the Battle of Messines (7th–14th June 1917).

Today his grave can be found in La Plus Douve Farm Cemetery, about 1¾ miles south west of Messines, Belgium. As well as being recorded on the Witney War memorial his name is also remembered on a plaque in the Bank of New Zealand Arcade, Wellington, which commemorates all the officers of the bank who laid down their lives during the Great War.

Perhaps it was due to the grief of his eldest son's death but on the 30th July 1919, Frank's father, aged just fifty two, died. Frank's mother, with no more reason to stay in Witney, left the town and returned to Surrey.

W.D. Winterbourne
Private, Walter Dix Winterbourne, 200167,
'B' Company,
1/4th Battalion,
Oxfordshire & Buckinghamshire Light Infantry

Walter Dix was born in Witney around 1894, the illegitimate son of Daisy. In late 1896 his mother married Henry Winterbourne, an agricultural worker from Childrey in Berkshire. The couple had two children of their own and at the time of the 1901 census they were living in Lowell's Place, off Corn Street. However at this point Walter was not living with them. He was residing at his grandparent's home, also in Lowell's Place. Whether or not this arrangement was temporary is unclear but a decade later in 1911 the census reveals that the whole family had moved to Newland and Walter, now employed as a factory hand in a local blanket mill, was recorded as being Henry's son. He had also taken his step-father's surname as his own. At some point during the next few years the family moved to a house in the Crofts.

Walter's military career began in 1910 when he joined the ranks of the Territorial Force, serving with a volunteer battalion of the Oxfordshire and Buckinghamshire Light Infantry (OBLI), part of the South Midland Division. During the first week of August 1914 the composite units of the Division had only just begun their annual summer camp when the order for full mobilisation came. Returning to Oxford Barracks, Walter was drafted into the 1/4th OBLI and moved with his comrades to the battalion's wartime divisional concentration point of Chelmsford where, by mid August, they had been joined by the rest of their division. Training and equipping the Division for war became the priority and on the 13th March 1915 advance warning was given to the troops that they were soon to leave for overseas service. One week later the 1/4th were moved by train to Folkestone bound for the Western Front.

Walter and his Battalion landed in France at the port of Boulogne on the 29th March 1915 and by the 3rd April they, along with entire South Midland Division, were encamped near the town of Cassel. It was here, in France and Flanders that the Division was to remain until late 1917 when it was transferred to Italy. During its time on the Western Front the 1/4th, as part of the re-designated 48th (South Midland) Division, were engaged in a number of significant battles. These included participation in various phases of the massive Allied offensive on the Somme in the summer of 1916 and later, in 1917, it took part in the pursuit of the German forces as they retreated to the Hindenburg Line. By the summer of 1917 the 1/4th was in the Ypres sector in preparation for the Third Battle of Ypres, or "Passchendaele" as it is more commonly known. This offensive lasted from July to November of 1917 and involved a series of operations with the single aim of breaking out of the salient and capturing the village of Passchendaele from the Germans. Having done so, it was planned that the Allies would drive north and east to push the Germans away from the Belgian channel ports, denying them to the enemy for continued U Boat operations.

On the 16th August, as part of the overall Third Ypres offensive, the Allies launched an attack against the Germans at Langemarck. During the opening stages of the attack Walter was wounded whilst leading a section of his unit against the enemy. He didn't consider his wound to be serious and was observed by his comrades making his way back to the British front line unaided. However his wounds were serious and after several days of medical attention, he lapsed into unconsciousness and died at 6:30 p.m. on the evening of the 20th August 1917. Following his death he was, his family were reassuringly told, placed in a local chapel for the night and buried the following morning at 11 a.m. in the Brandhoeck New Military Cemetery No.3, near Ypres, Belgium – a site which had been freshly prepared in anticipation of the offensive and where Walter lies to this day.

A. Woodcock
Private, Andrew Woodcock, 32979,
15th Battalion,
Royal Warwickshire Regiment

Andrew Woodcock was born at Cogges around April 1883, the third son of Henry, a blanket weaver, and his wife Elizabeth (née Walker). As a young man Andrew was employed as a blanket finisher and in his spare time he served with the local 2nd Volunteer Battalion of the Oxfordshire Light Infantry. On the 23rd February 1903 he enlisted for full time service with his regiment, and was posted to the 1st Battalion. But within a year he had submitted a successful request to transfer to the 12th Royal Lancers, with whom his elder brother Herbert was serving. For almost all of his remaining service he served with his unit in India only returning to the UK in late 1910 for his discharge and transfer to the Army Reserve on the 8th January 1911. It had been his wish to find employment as a groom once he left the Army but, having returned home to Witney, he was soon working as a labourer in a blanket mill.

On the 10th June 1914 Andrew was married to Lucy Ivey in the district of Woodstock but their happiness was cut short when, less than two months later, on the 5th August, a telegram arrived with orders for Andrew to report to his barracks for mobilisation. On the 15th August 1914 the 12th Royal Lancers sailed for France, where they were to remain for the rest of the war. On the 20th March 1916 Andrew, having completed the terms of both his regular and reserve service, was discharged from the army and returned home.

However, with his country still at war, Andrew wasn't ready to return to civilian life. He re-enlisted and returned to France. Failing in a bid to rejoin his old unit, he was initially posted to the Middlesex Regiment and then subsequently to 15th Battalion of the Royal Warwickshire Regiment. He was killed on the 26th October 1917, during the opening day of the Second Battle of Passchendaele. His body was never identified and today his name can be found on the Tyne Cot Memorial to the Missing, Tyne Cot Cemetery, Zonnebeke, Belgium.

G.W. Woodcock
Private, George William Woodcock, G/40595,
11th Battalion,
Middlesex Regiment

George Woodcock, known by his second name of 'William', was born at Woodgreen, Witney in the early part of 1889, the illegitimate son and only child of Annie, a blanket weaver. In the census of 1891 he was recorded as being the son of Thomas and Eliza Woodcock who were in fact his grandparents and in whose house on Woodgreen, he was to spend his childhood.

On 1st September 1914, amidst crowds of cheering people, William joined a party of fellow Witney men as they marched through the town to the train station. They were bound for Oxford where they hoped to enlist and fight for their country. Of the forty-two men who went that day ten failed to pass the Army medical, William Woodcock amongst them. Undeterred William tried again and eventually, possibly towards the end of 1915 or the beginning of 1916, he successfully joined the 11th Battalion of The Middlesex Regiment. His battalion was already in France, having been deployed in June 1915, but due to the fact that William did not qualify for the 1914-1915 campaign medal[139] and that he was originally given a four digit Territorial Army number – a practice discontinued at the start of 1917, it is highly probable that he arrived on the Western Front as a reinforcement at some point during 1916.

In 1916 the 11th Middlesex saw action on the Somme and remained with their Division, the 12th, in the front line until December of that year. In January 1917 William's unit arrived in the Arras sector in preparation for the spring offensive. On the 4th April 1917 the Allied bombardment opened on the German lines to the east of Arras and on the 9th April the attack began. Advancing behind a creeping barrage the British troops quickly overcame German resistance and, over the following few days, significant gains were made. On the night of 11th/12th April, William's Battalion moved up into the front line east of Monchy, relieving units of the 8th Cavalry Brigade. They were

---

[139] This medal was awarded to those individuals who served in France and Flanders between 23rd November 1914 and 31st December 1915, or for service in any other active theatre of operations between 5th August 1914 and 31st December 1915.

relieved themselves the following day, going back into reserve but it was during this brief period in the front line in what became known as the First Battle of the Scarpe that William was killed (11th April 1917). His body was never identified and he has no known grave. Today his name is recorded on the Arras Memorial, Arras, France.

M.R. Woodcock
Mark Robert Woodcock, Rifleman, 8818,
3rd Battalion,
Rifle Brigade (Prince Consort's Own)

Mark Woodcock, known by his second name 'Robert', was born in West End, Witney, around 1882 the son of Robert, a blacksmith and his wife Elizabeth (née Jennings). By 1891 the family had moved to Newland, Cogges. After leaving school Robert found employment and in the census of 1901 was recorded as being a baker's journeyman, but adventure beckoned and on 3rd December 1901 nineteen year old Robert, describing himself now as a labourer, enlisted in the British Army for a term of twelve years – seven years with the colours and the remaining five years as a reservist. He joined his unit, the 3rd Battalion Rifle Brigade, in Ireland where he remained until July 1902 at which point his battalion returned to England. In September 1902 the battalion moved to Egypt and from there to India in November 1905. Robert, having served one year longer than his original term of engagement, was back in the UK in December 1909 preparing for his discharge from the regular Army, which took place on the 3rd January 1910.

Thus at the start of a fresh decade Robert was transferred to the Army Reserves. It would appear that he was unable to settle back into civilian life in Witney and on the 26th July 1913, several months before his time as a reservist was due to expire; he left his job as a mason's labourer and re-enlisted for a further period of four years with his original unit.

At the beginning of August 1914 the 3rd Battalion Rifle Brigade was in Cork, Ireland as part of 17th Brigade, 6th Division but when the order came to mobilise they quickly moved back to England. Initially to Cambridge, and then on to Newmarket and finally to Southampton where, on the 8th September

1914, they boarded the *SS Lake Michigan* bound for France. Although the troop ship arrived at St. Nazaire on the 10th September it was forced to remain outside the harbour until the rest of the 6th Division had disembarked and it was not until the morning of the 12th September that Robert and his Battalion landed in France. A short but tedious train journey took them just east of Paris to join the rest of their division. On the 13th the Division began their march towards the River Aisne, arriving several days later and on the 20th, in an area known as the Chemin des Dames, the division went into the trenches for the first time. It was here, on the 27th September 1914, that Robert Woodcock was killed in action. His body was never identified and he has no known grave. Today he is commemorated on La Ferte-sous-Jouarre Memorial which stands near the village of La Ferte-sous-Jouarre on the south bank of the River Marne, France.

Before the war Robert's younger brother, George, had followed him into the Army – in the census of 1911 he was recorded as being in India with the 2nd Battalion Royal Berkshire Regiment. When War came in 1914 he went to France and served with his Battalion throughout the conflict, ending his military career with the rank of Corporal. After the war he returned to his home in Witney where he lived for many years until his death in 1958.

F. Young
Private, Frank Young, 23158,
5th Battalion,
Oxfordshire & Buckinghamshire Light Infantry

Frank Young was born in Newland, Witney, during the last quarter of 1897, the youngest son of Charles, a leather grounder who was known by his second name of 'Ernest', and his wife Catherine (née Winfield). Frank's father died in 1909 and by the time of the 1911 census his mother, still with two children at school, had begun to take in lodgers, most likely to supplement the small income she derived from stitching leather gloves. Frank himself was working as an errand boy.

It is not possible to specify when Frank joined the Army however, his regimental number indicates that it was at some point during the first half of 1916. Following his basic training he was posted to France where he joined the

5th Battalion of the Oxfordshire and Buckinghamshire Light Infantry, part of the 14th (Light) Division. In 1916 the 5th Battalion was involved in two significant actions on the Somme: The Battles of Delville Wood and Flers-Courcelette.

In March 1917 the 14th Division formed part of the pursuing Allied force as the Germans retreated to the heavily defended 'Hindenburg Line'. One month later it was back in action at the start of the Arras Offensive which had initially been devised as a diversionary operation to draw German troops north towards the British front line at Arras and away from the ground chosen for a huge French attack fifty miles to the south. At 5:25 a.m. on the morning of Easter Monday 9th April 1917 the British unleashed a hurricane five minute artillery bombardment of the enemy trenches. Five minutes later the attacking troops began their assault. It had been snowing heavily and the advance was hindered by drifts but through a combination of surprise and poor visibility the attack was a success. The Battle of Arras was to continue for over a month, until the 16th May, when offensive operations were finally ceased. Significant gains were made during the operation at the cost of nearly 160,000 British and Commonwealth casualties, but the much hoped for breakthrough remained elusive.

Frank Young never saw the end of the battle. He was killed in action on the first day of the fighting, 9th April 1917. His body was never identified and he has no known grave. Today he is remembered on the Arras Memorial, Arras, France.

H.W. Young
Private, Harold William Young, 16399,
8th Battalion,
Oxfordshire & Buckinghamshire Light Infantry

Harold Young was born in Witney during the spring of 1894, the eldest child of Harold, a glover, and his wife Mary Anne (née Smith). When he was around four years of age his parents took Harold and his younger brother, Sidney, to Bolton in Lancashire where, it is likely, their father had better prospects of employment. Around 1907 the growing family returned to Witney, taking up residence on Narrow Hill. By the time of the 1911 census Harold, still living at home with his parents, was working as a farm servant.

Volunteering for service in the Army around November 1914, Harold was posted to the newly formed 8th Battalion of the Oxfordshire and Buckinghamshire Light Infantry, part of the 26th Division. Having undergone basic training on Salisbury Plain the 26th Division was deployed to France in September 1915 but within two months orders had been issued for them to move to the port of Marseilles for embarkation to Salonika in northern Greece, where they were to assist in an Anglo-French military expedition (the 'Salonika Force') in support of Serbian forces in the region. But by the time the Salonika Force had arrived the Serbs had been beaten. Nevertheless with the stability of the region under threat and, following Bulgaria's entry into the war on the side of Austria and Germany, it was decided to leave the Salonika Force in place for future operations.

Considered by many contemporary observers to have been something of a sideshow, the campaign in Salonika was not unproblematic, and conditions were tough for the troops posted there. For every casualty of battle three died of malaria, influenza and other diseases and this unfortunately was the fate of Harold Young. Admitted to the 21st Stationary Hospital in March 1918 suffering with pneumonia, he died on the 13th of that month and was buried in the Sarigol military cemetery, which lies near the village of Kristoni, just north of Thessaloniki (formerly Salonika).

H.B. Young
Driver, Hariph Bernard Young, DM2/154316,
Mechanical Transport,
Royal Army Service Corps

Hariph Young was born at the family home next door to the Carpenter's Arms, Newland in the first quarter of 1890, the youngest son of Charles, a leather glover, and his wife Mary (née Castle). He was an active member of the 1st Witney Company of the Boys Brigade, rising to the position of Staff Sergeant. Before the war he worked as a gardener and driver to prominent local Methodist and blanket manufacturer, James Early of 'Springfield', Woodgreen.

On 1st September 1914 Hariph was among a group of over forty local men, who marched through the town midst cheering crowds to the railway station and onwards by train to the Army recruiting centre at Oxford, all eager to serve their King and country on the battlefield. Unfortunately Hariph's application was rejected after his medical examination revealed that he had defective eyesight and he was sent home. Undeterred he continued to apply and in February 1916, several months after his marriage to Ellen Horne, he was at last successful, being accepted into Army Service Corps as a driver.

For a while he served as an ambulance driver in North Wales but in April 1917, around the time that his only child, Barbara was born, he was transferred to France as a driver in the Ammunition Column attached to 290 Siege Battery, Royal Garrison Artillery. Exact dates are unknown but whilst at Cambrais, Hariph fell victim to a German gas attack. He was taken the No.3 Australian General Hospital in Abbeville where, whilst being treated, he developed pneumonia and died on 3rd November 1918.

His grave can today be found in the Abbeville Communal Cemetery Extension, Abbeville, France.

The Crawley War Memorial

At a public meeting, held in Crawley during the first week of January 1919, it had been decided to erect a monument to the memory of the six local men who had given their lives in the Great War. The necessary funds were duly raised by public subscription and on 7th November 1920 the village War Memorial was finally unveiled. The event being duly reported in the local press:

'Last Sunday was a memorable day in the history of Crawley, for it was the day on which the War Memorial Cross was unveiled accompanied by an impressive service of great power and simplicity in which 500 persons joined. They came from all points of the compass on that beautiful Sunday afternoon and wended their way to the centre of the village, and reverently ranged themselves around the beautiful Cross that memorialises the sacrifice of six men of Crawley who fought to the death for us in the great war. It was an inspiring sight the great crowd of worshippers in this pretty secluded valley of the Windrush where nature seemed to join in honouring the dead, for the trees and hedges were shedding the last of their leaves kissed into glorious colours by the setting sun on this lovely Autumn afternoon, and all around, as silent sentinels, were the everlasting hills.

The Cross, which stands upon a base of local stone, is of Ancaster stone and bears the following inscription: "Erected by the parishioners of Crawley in memory of the glorious dead who fell in the Great War 1914-1918. Their memory liveth for evermore." The names inscribed on the Cross are Reginald Hicks, John Hunt, Harry Souch, Matthew Strong, William Ward, Frederick Weaver.

The Service was conducted by the Rev. Corden Nash, Vicar of Hailey-cum-Crawley, assisted by the Rev. F. Ellis, Wesleyan Minister of Witney. The opening words were read by the Vicar followed by the reading of the 23rd

Psalm. The lesson was read by the Rev. F. Ellis. The dedicatory prayer was read by the vicar, after which "O God our help in ages past" was sung.

The Rev. F. Ellis gave the address. He said the greatest Englishman God ever gave to us Shakespeare found it difficult to forgive the sin of ingratitude. The Old Testament referred frequently to ingratitude, and they would remember these words – "Thou shalt remember all the way the Lord thy God hath led thee. Beware lest thou forget, for if thou dost forget I call heaven and earth to witness that thou shalt surely die." It was also a modern sin, and they were in danger of forgetting the great mercy of God which has been with us. These noble men, whose names were inscribed on this Cross, if they could speak, would say to us that they did not care about those present being here today, even speaking in reverence of them, if that was all they were going to do. These men who laid down their lives called upon them to be patriots. Patriots, the saviours of a nation, were men and women who feared God. There was no nation like their own, no country half so free or half so sweet. He was a lover of England, as they were, and he wanted to appeal to them. Were they showing their gratitude to God for the great victory and national deliverance which had come to them? How had they been spending their Sunday today? The Germans in 1871 celebrated their victory over France by desecrating their Sunday. That was the beginning of her downfall. He believed everyone present had a strong desire that they should retain their place as a nation, and that the great sacrifices that had been made should not be made in vain. They could all do something greater than erect this monument here today. If every man and woman would say "Now by God's grace I will fear Him, and love Him, and keep His commandments," then he was sure God's blessing would be upon our nation, and the sacrifices of its sons will not have been in vain. "The nation that forgets God shall perish." There was not a single example in history otherwise. This country that was so dear to them, and to the lads who died for it, would surely go down if we forget God. He beseeched them in this great hour of their country's history to fear God and keep His day. If they forgot God their brethren would have died in vain, and today as they met there to dedicate this Cross to the memory of their fallen sons let them do something that we know would please them best. If those lads could speak to them today they would say "Fear God". That was what would help them to be true to the great ideals for which these lads died. If they did that then this Cross would be a great blessing to this village and every wayfarer who passed through it.

The Vicar read further prayers, and the hymn "They whose course on earth is o'er" was sung. The "Last Post" was sounded by two soldiers of the Oxon & Bucks Light Infantry and the service closed with the blessing and placing of wreaths on the Cross.

At the close the Vicar thanked the Witney Band, who led the singing, for having kindly come over and given their services that afternoon.'[140]

These then are the men of Crawley as commemorated on the village memorial:

---

[140] *Witney Gazette*, 13th November 1920.

Reginald Hicks
Private, Reginald Thomas Hicks, 2774,
No.3 Section,
No.5 Platoon,
'B' Company,
1/4th Battalion, Oxfordshire & Buckinghamshire Light Infantry

Reginald Hicks was born in Crawley during the third quarter of 1893, son of Thomas, a farmer, and his wife Lydia (née Venwell). As a child he attended the Wesleyan Day School in Witney and by 1911 he was working as an apprentice to a local grocer. In his spare time he was active within the local Methodist movement and eventually became a preacher in the Witney circuit.

When the war came in August 1914 Reginald was quick to volunteer for military service and was posted to the newly formed 1/4th Battalion of the Oxford and Buckinghamshire Light Infantry (OBLI). Once fully trained and equipped the Battalion was despatched to France, landing at Boulogne on the 30th March 1915. Several months later Reginald sustained a head wound, but upon making a full recovery he returned to join his unit at the front.

During the evening of Tuesday the 18th July 1916 the 1/4th OBLI moved into the front line trenches between Ovillers and Pozieres and prepared to attack the German lines. The attack was launched at 1:30 a.m. on the 19th and Reginald Hicks, his section being led by another Witney man, Lance Corporal Herbert E. Long, went over the top. Unfortunately the attack foundered quite quickly and the men of the 1/4th were forced to retire to their own trenches which then became targets for retaliatory German artillery fire. It was during the ensuing barrage, around 2.30 a.m., that Reginald was killed. His body was never identified and today his name is remembered on the Thiepval Memorial to the missing of the Somme, Thiepval, France.

Herbert Long wrote to Reginald's mother on the day of Reginald's death. He ended his letter with the following words which were sadly to prove very prophetic:

> *"..It will be a great blow to you, but you must think of him as dying a glorious death fighting for his country with his face to the enemy and*

now [he] *is at rest with all the other brave fellows, where we hope to meet him at some future date...*"[141]

Herbert Long was killed in action four days later near Pozieres, France.

John Hunt
Private, Edward John Hunt, 16260,
1st Battalion,
Princess Charlotte of Wales's (Royal Berkshire Regiment)
(Father of Private Frederick Hunt of Crawley, died 23rd October 1941)

Edward Hunt, known by his second name of 'John', was born in Leafield during the first quarter of 1883, the eldest son of Robert, an agricultural labourer, and his wife Harriett (née Pillinger). Upon leaving school he followed his father into work on the land and at the time of the 1901 census he was still living at home with his parents and was employed as an agricultural labourer. In early 1908 he married Mary Panting of Ramsden and the following year their first child, Florence, was born. Second daughter Sarah followed in 1911, at which time the family were living at Hailey, where John had work as a carter on a farm. The couple's only son, Frederick, was born a year later in the spring of 1912.

John volunteered for military service within the first weeks of the war and was deployed to France on the 26th May 1915 to join the 1st Battalion of the Royal Berkshire Regiment, 2nd Division. For the next thirteen months he fought alongside the men of his unit on the Western Front.

On the night of 25th/26th June 1916 the 1st Royal Berks, holding the line at Carency near Arras, mounted an attack against the opposing enemy trenches. At 11.30 p.m., under the cover of darkness, the attack began. But the Germans, alerted by the earlier cutting of their barbed wire defences, opened fire on the attackers as the signal for the British advance was heard. Faced with heavy trench mortar, bombing and machine gun fire the attack was halted before any of the planned objectives could be reached. Total casualties from the attack

---

[141] From a letter published in the *Witney Gazette*, 29th July 1916.

195

were; 2 officers and 43 other ranks either killed, wounded or missing. John Hunt was among the dead. His body was never identified and today his name is recorded on the Arras Memorial in Arras.

In addition to being remembered on the Crawley War Memorial John Hunt is also recorded on the war memorial in his native Leafield where he is listed alongside his younger brother, William, who was killed in action on the 16th August 1917 during the Third Battle of Ypres, or "Passchendaele" as it is more commonly known.

In early 1918 John's widow, Mary, married Charles Jones of Crawley.

In October 1941 Frederick Hunt, John's son, then serving with the 6th Battalion of the Oxfordshire and Buckinghamshire Light Infantry, was in Crawley on seven days leave. On the morning of the 23rd October he left his mother's home and came to Witney where he met up with Leslie Smith, a friend who lived at Cannon Pool. At around 4 p.m., following several hours of drinking in the town, Frederick became unwell and, with the assistance of two soldiers, Leslie took him back to his house where his condition worsened. A local doctor, who was summoned to Cannon Pool at around 6:15 p.m., arrived to find Frederick already dead. The subsequent Coroner's Inquiry recorded that the death had been due to asphyxia caused by vomiting.[142]

Frederick was buried in St. Peter's Churchyard in Crawley. Today his grave, marked by a Commonwealth War Graves headstone, can be found in the cemetery adjacent to the former church, now converted to a residential property. Intriguingly, he is not remembered on the village's War Memorial.

---

[142] From the *Witney Gazette,* 31st October 1941.

Henry Souch
Private, Henry Richard Souch, 6909,
'D' Company,
5th Battalion,
Oxfordshire & Buckinghamshire Light Infantry

Henry Souch, known as 'Harry', was born in Crawley during the first quarter of 1886, the third son of George, a farm labourer, and his wife Elizabeth (née Bishop). At the time of the 1901 census the family were living at Razor Hill in Witney where Harry, two of his brothers and his father were all employed as road labourers. By 1911the family had returned to Crawley and Harry, still living with his parents, was working as a farm labourer.

Harry volunteered for military service during the first weeks of the war and was posted to the newly formed 5th Battalion of the Oxford and Buckinghamshire Light Infantry, part of the 14th (Light) Division. Following a period of training and equipping the battalion were deployed to France, landing at Boulogne on the 21st May 1915.

No record exists as to how, when or where Harry received the wounds that brought him back to the U.K. for treatment at a military hospital in Oxford. However his condition was to prove fatal. He died in the city on the 20th March 1918 and his body was returned home to Crawley for burial.

Today Harry's grave, marked by a Commonwealth War Grave headstone, can be found in the village cemetery, adjacent to the former church of St. Peter – now converted to a private residence.

Matthew Strong
Private, Matthew Strong, 3107,
'B' Company,
1/4th Battalion,
Oxfordshire & Buckinghamshire Light Infantry

Matthew Strong was born in Crawley during the fourth quarter of 1887, the third son of James, a mill foreman, and his wife Harriett (née Siford). In 1895 Matthew was admitted to the Bluecoat School in Holloway, Witney and afterwards studied at the town's Grammar School. At the time of the 1911 census he was working in the town as an assistant in a grocer's shop.

Matthew and his younger brother Frederick both volunteered for military service on the outbreak of the war and both were assigned to the newly formed 1/4th Battalion, Oxfordshire and Buckinghamshire Light Infantry (OBLI), part of the South Midland Division. Following a period of six months spent training and equipping, the Division was deemed ready for active service and deployed to France at the end of March 1915.

Between April and June 1915 the Division held the line at Ploegsteert, or 'Plug Street' as it was known to the British soldiers, on the southern shoulder of the Ypres salient. It was here, on the 27th April 1915, less than a month after arriving on the Western Front, that Matthew Strong was killed.

Fellow Witney man, Harold Florey, serving with the 2nd OBLI, recounted Matthew's demise in a letter sent home to his own parents:

> *"... We have lost poor Matt Strong. A sniper shot him clean through the head. He had just washed and shaved and was putting his coat on, but, being rather tall, his head came up above the parapet. We are all very sorry to lose him, you never heard him grumbling about anything, and he was liked by all."*[143]

A couple of weeks after his death a letter, sent to Mrs Strong from Matthew's company commanding officer, was reproduced in the *Witney Gazette*. In it Captain Ernest Dashwood, who was himself later killed in action on the 12th May 1915, said that he believed Matthew had not suffered at all, having been unconscious from the time he was shot until he died about an hour later. He said that his brother had been with him '...*at the end and saw him decently buried in a piece of ground which will be honoured*'.[144] Unfortunately the site of his grave was lost and today Matthew's name is remembered on the Ploegsteert Memorial, which stands in the Berks Cemetery Extension, eight miles south of Ipres, Belgium.

---

[143] From a letter published in the *Witney Gazette*, 8th May 1915.
[144] Cavell, J., (p.94)

William Ward
Gunner, William Alfred Ward, 109571,
'B' Battery,
152nd (Nottingham) Brigade,
Royal Field Artillery

William Ward was born at White Oak Green, Crawley, during the third quarter of 1895, the second son of William, a farm labourer, and his wife Edith May (née Partridge). Following William's birth the family moved to Rowsley in Worcestershire where his father had found work as a labourer on the railway. His parents separated around 1903. His mother, taking the children with her, went to live with a younger man, George Bayliss in Halesowen whilst William's father returned to White Oak Green. By the time of the 1911 census William was living with his father at White Oak Green and working as a stable boy. He married Emily Messer of Woodeaton during the first quarter of 1916 and the couple's first and only child, Dorothy, was born on the 15th October that same year.

In the absence of his service record it is unclear when William first volunteered for military service. However, from his record of medal entitlement and service number it is apparent that he was deployed to France on active service during 1917, where he was posted to 'B' Battery, 152nd Brigade of the Royal Field Artillery, part of the 32nd Division.

On the 31st December 1917 William Ward was killed in action. Today his grave can be found in the Bucquoy Road Cemetery, Ficheux, France.

F. Weaver
Private, Frederick William Weaver, 16258,
1st Battalion,
Princess Charlotte of Wales's (Royal Berkshire Regiment)

Frederick Weaver was born in Witney during the first quarter of 1896, the third son of Stephen, a former farm labourer, and his wife Sarah (née Rowles). At the time of 1901 census the family were living near Dod's Row, Crawley where

Stephen was employed at the mill as a blanket finisher. In 1911 the family were still resident in Crawley and Frederick was employed as a grocer's apprentice.

Frederick volunteered for military service within the first months of the war and on the 18th May 1915, following his basic training, he was deployed to France to join the 1st Battalion of the Royal Berkshire Regiment - a unit which had been on the Western Front since August 1914, part of the 2nd Division. During the late summer of 1915 Frederick's unit was based in a sector of the British front line near the town of Bethune and it was whilst there that he was wounded. It is likely that he was taken to the No.1 Casualty Clearing Station in the nearby village of Chocques, where he died on Wednesday 22nd September 1915.

Today his grave can be found in the Chocques Military Cemetery, Pas De Calais, France.

The Hailey War Memorial

On the evening of the 20th December 1918 the people of Hailey attended a public meeting in the village schoolroom to discuss a suitable scheme of remembrance for those local men who had given their lives during the Great War. Messrs Habgood and Knight, representatives of the Witney War Memorial Committee, who had been invited to explain the proposed Witney and District Hospital Scheme, addressed the meeting and optimistically explained '... *that the hospital scheme was not intended to interfere in any way with the memorial the village would like to raise, but that it was thought that owing to the exceptional circumstances people would give so generously that there would be an ample surplus from these village memorial funds to be used towards the Hospital scheme.*' The two were then called upon to answer a number of questions concerning the scheme, after which a committee was appointed for the purpose of canvassing local opinion.[145]

It is not possible to say how much money, if any, was pledged by Hailey for the doomed Witney and District Hospital scheme. However it is clear that sufficient funds were raised for the village to erect its own memorial which was duly unveiled on the 12th December 1920.[146] The occasion being reported by the Witney Gazette the following week:

'On Sunday last the War Memorial Cross was unveiled and dedicated in the presence of a large number of parishioners and friends from Witney and surrounding villages. The Cross, which is of grey granite, the work of Messrs

---

[145] *Witney Gazette*, 28th December 1918.

[146] It should be noted that a separate, privately funded peace memorial was commissioned around the same time at Delly End – this simple domed memorial stands on the green and is believed to have been erected by Julia Phipps of The Manor in grateful thanks for the safe return of the male members of her family.

Knowles of Oxford, stands just outside the Churchyard, on the side of the highway, facing the road. It contains the following inscription: - "To the glory of God and to the honoured memory of the following Hailey men who gave their lives in the great war, 1914-1918 – Frank W Brooks, Ellis Buckingham, A.S.G. Buckingham, Ernest C. Buckingham, A. Victor Busby, Isaac Clements, Cecil L. Harris, James Hill, Herbert Morton, William Painting, Frederick W. Pratley, Wilfred G. Smith; erected by the Parishioners." After the opening sentences, read by the Vicar, the memorial was unveiled by Lieut. Col. F.W. Schofield, C.M.G., who said he was there to unveil that memorial to their glorious dead, through no-merit of his own, but by the kindness of their Vicar and the Committee, who had asked him to come there to perform that ceremony. He accepted that invitation at once because he considered it a great privilege to be allowed to partake, in however small a degree, in anything that perpetuated the memory of the gallant dead, and at the same time they did that let them not forget the not less gallant living, who happily had survived the terrible was that lasted so long, and desolated the homes of so many of our fellow subjects throughout the Empire.

One could not but be proud when one thought of the marvellous way in which the manhood of this grand Empire rallied to the flag at the call of duty when it came. Young men, middle-aged men, and old men, all were animated by the one thought of "doing their bit," and how well they did it was testified by the result. It had been his lot to have had something to do with the dedication of many memorials of this kind, and they could not wonder if his heart ached at the grief which had been caused by this war to so many homes, and that he, in common with many others, hated and detested war, and that they should pray earnestly to Almighty God that their Empire might be spared ever having to go through such another ordeal but at the same time let them thank God that if in his inscrutable providence they should have to undergo another such trial, that they were sure the manhood of this country would display similar courage, and a like sense of duty. And whilst testifying to the courage of their men let them not forget the magnificent way in which the women of this country took their place in discharging their duty in that time of need. In nursing, motor driving, land work, munitions work, and in many other ways they stepped into their appointed places, and in no case did they fall short of what was expected of them. No unworthy plaints ever soiled the roll of honour, whether at first or later when the losses became distributed over all classes of the people. The women of the home country and of the Empire, displayed unexampled courage, and in hundreds of thousands of stricken homes, and in this and every other sacrifice demanded by the war, were perfectly splendid.

Nothing could exceed the steadiness in which they took good and evil news alike, or the tenacity with which they set themselves to suffer anything rather than lose the war.

And now perhaps some of them were asking "what had been the good of it all." Well if they reckoned in pounds, shillings and pence they had got nothing out of it but loss, but was that all they had to consider? Was there no such thing as freedom, liberty, righteousness, justice? They had got these things out of the war. Let them think what England would have been had they lost the war – no liberty, no freedom, no righteousness, no justice. They fought for those things, and by God's help they won the battle, and having won they must set to work to make a better England.

Was there anyone there who wanted to see Witney or Oxford desolated with blood? God forbid. Yet there were people in this country who said that if they could not get what they wanted there would be a bloody revolution; men should think before they talked like that, they must get what they wanted by constitutional methods. It might be slower but it was the most righteous way, and one of the principle ways of improving this country at the present time was for all of them in their respective spheres to give an honest day's work when they were paid for it; not to listen to the voice of those who told them to get all they could, and give as little in return as possible. If they followed such evil counsels they lost sight of what had helped this country to become as mighty as she was, and thatw as fair dealing between man and man, and being strictly honest in all their ways. He congratulated Hailey people on their Cross and he trusted it would stand for many years to point the way to duty to many generations of Hailey people as well as being being their testimonial to those of their own generation who fulfilled their duty in so noble a manner in having laid down their lives for the good of others.

A number of beautiful wreaths were placed at the foot of the Cross, and the dedicatory prayer was said by the Vicar.

The address was delivered by the Rev. Ernest D. Green, who said it was a great privilege to take any part in that service. The Cross had been unveiled, and it had been dedicated, and the names of those who went forth at the time of their country's need, and gave their lives that those of them who were present that day might live, were engraved upon it. What was this Cross to be in the future to that village. Was it simply to remind them of those who had died upon the battlefield. It would serve to help them see that those whose names ought always to be in their memories were not forgotten. Was it going to be anything more than that. It stood in that village to remind them that there were those who lived in their midst who did not hesitate to give their very utmost for their fellows, and, as they had been reminded already that afternoon,   by their sacrifice they had purchased freedom for others. When they thought of the enthusiasm that swept over the land at the beginning of the war, the ideals that were held out before them, and the talk about the brotherhood of man and then think of England during the last two years, he did not think they could pass the Cross without a feeling that it reproved them. Those men, who had laid down their lives with true unselfishness, reproved the selfishness of the present day.

The Cross stood to urge them to realise that life offered something better than to live for their own ends. It stood to remind them that self sacrifice was the highest form of service. If they would serve one another then assuredly it was essential that they should take up their Cross and follow Him. They would never have erected a Cross in memory of their dead if Jesus Christ had not died on the Cross, and it was because the Cross was associated with Him that a Cross had been erected there today. It was not only a memorial of the dead but a reminder of life immortality. They thought of those who gave their lives not as dead, but as alive for evermore in the presence of the King.

This Cross should urge every one of them as they looked upon it to determine to be better than they had ever been. By the Cross of God let them take a step forward to preparing themselves to enter into that fuller and better life Christ had offered to those who put their trust in Him.

The Last Post having been sounded, the company adjourned to the Church where the remainder of the service was conducted by the Rev. F. Corden Nash. The service concluded with the National Anthem played by the Witney Town Band (conducted by Mr A. Davis), and was followed by Dr Elgar's beautiful composition "Land of Hope & Glory", which was much appreciated.

Before dispersing, the Vicar on behalf of the parishioners thanked Lieut. Col. Schofield for unveiling the Cross, the Rev. Ernest D. Green for his address, and the Band for their great help in the service. '[147]

These then are the men of Hailey as commemorated on the village memorial:

---

[147] *Witney Gazette*, 18th December 1920.

Frank W. Brooks
Sapper, Frank William Brooks, 506120,
'C' Company,
1st Brigade Headquarters,
Canadian Engineers

Frank Brooks was born in Witney on the 5th November 1889, the eldest son of Thomas, a butcher who was known by his second name, 'William', and his wife Clara (née Green). Around the turn of the century the family moved to Hailey when Frank's father, continuing to trade from his shop in Witney, took on a farm in the village. At the time of the 1911 census the family were living in Poffley End and Frank, a part time soldier in the Territorial Army, was working as a brewer's assistant. In 1912 Frank, along with his younger brother Sidney and their elder sister Edith's fiancé, Charles Pratley, emigrated to Canada.

By the time Britain went to war with Germany in 1914, Charles had died and Sidney soon returned home to enlist for military service. Frank chose to remain in Canada and by 1916 he was working as locomotive engineer and engaged to be married to his Canadian fiancée, Alys Martlew. However the war continued, as did the demand for men to fight it, and in the summer of 1916 Frank volunteered for military service with the Canadian Expeditionary Force (CEF), joining the 6th Field Company of the Canadian Engineers (CE) on the 14th August to begin his training.

Frank arrived in England aboard the *SS Grampian* on 6th February 1917 and, following several months of further training at a Canadian military camp near Crowborough, East Sussex, he was one of 107 Engineers deployed to France on 9th May 1917[148]. Soon after his arrival on the Western Front he was attached to the 1st Field Company, CE and for the next twelve months he served with this unit.

On the afternoon of Sunday, 3rd March 1918, Frank, having been granted a period of leave from the front, arrived in Hailey. Over the next ten days he visited family and friends, and, from the information he wrote in his diary, he

---

[148] See www.collectionscanada.gc.ca Ref: War diaries - Canadian Engineers Training Depot

appears to have spent some time with a local girl known only as 'Nellie'.[149] On the morning of 14th March he left Hailey for London to begin his journey back to France. He stayed in London for the next two nights, taking in a couple of shows whilst he was there, including the very popular 'Lilac Domino' which had only recently opened and was to go on to become one the great hits of the war.

Taking the 11 a.m. crossing from Dover to Boulogne on Saturday 16th March, Frank rejoined his unit at midday on the 18th. His diary entries show that his duties required him to travel between the various camps and depots behind the front line collecting and moving equipment. They also show that he always found time to write to his family and friends and that he was in regular receipt of letters and parcels from both England and Canada. On the 18th May he wrote in his diary that he had received a letter from Alys. The two had not seen each other since Frank had left Canada a year earlier and the strain of separation must have been too great for Alys and she had decided to break off the engagement. Frank responded the following day, writing her '... a straight letter' but he appears to have been consoled by his continued correspondence with Nellie, the girl he had begun a friendship with whilst on leave.

On the 28th May 1918 the 1st, 2nd and 3rd Field Companies, less a small detachment of men including Frank (which was sent to join Brigade Headquarters), were reorganised into the nuclei of three new Engineer Battalions of the 1st CE Brigade. The changes do not seem to have affected Frank's duties too much and he continued to move around the front. On 13th July, near Arras, Frank wrote that he was going 'up the line', a slang term for going into the trenches and for the next two weeks, as part of 'C' Company, he worked in the front line assisting in the construction of dugouts – shelters built into the trench line offering a degree of protection to the troops stationed there.

Frank's last entry in his diary was dated the 24th July 1918. He wrote simply 'Nice day. Wrote to Nellie'. Two days later, on Friday 26th July, the positions occupied by 'C' Company near Arras, came under heavy fire from the Germans using gas shells. Casualties were heavy with one man killed and forty eight wounded, one of whom was Frank Brooks. He was evacuated to the 14th

---

[149] Most likely to have been 'Nellie [Ellen] Jennings', a girl referred to in the last letter sent to Frank whilst he was in hospital in France from his elder sister, Edith who, incidentally, was also known as' Nell'.

Canadian Field Ambulance suffering from the effects of gas. On the 30th July he was transferred to the 7th Casualty Clearing Station before being admitted on the 2nd August to the No.2 Canadian Stationary Hospital at Outreau, Boulogne, Here his condition continued to worsen and at 9.30 p.m. on the evening of the 8th August 1918 he died.

Today Frank's grave can be found in the Terlincthun British Cemetery, Wimille, on the outskirts of Boulogne, France.

A. Stanley Buckingham
Private, Albert Stanley Buckingham, 54891,
3rd Infantry Labour Company,
Devonshire Regiment

Albert Buckingham, known by his second name of 'Stanley', was born in Hailey, during the second quarter of 1896, the eldest son of Albert, a stone mason, and his wife Annie (née Dore). At the time of the 1911 census the family were living in Whitings Lane, Delly End, and Stanley was working as a printer's apprentice.

He volunteered for military service on the 22nd May 1915, and was initially posted to the 3/4th Battalion of the Oxfordshire and Buckinghamshire Light Infantry. On the 13th February 1917 he was transferred to the 3rd Infantry Labour Company of the Devonshire Regiment at Exeter - one of twelve Devonshire Labour Companies deployed to France a month later. Upon their arrival on the Western Front each Labour Company was transferred to the Labour Corps with Stanley's unit becoming the 168th Labour Company, Labour Corps.

The exact movements of the 168th Labour Company during 1917 are unknown. However it is likely that the unit was in Flanders in July/August, involved in the Third Battle of Ypres (or "Passchendaele"), as it was here, at a Casualty Clearing Station near Poperinge, that Stanley Buckingham died of wounds received on the 1st August 1917.

Today his grave can be found in the Mendinghem Military Cemetery,[150] Poperinge, Belgium.

---

[150] The cemetery is adjacent to the site of one of three groups of Casualty Clearing Stations – popularly known to the troops as 'Mendinghem', 'Dozinghem' and 'Bandaghem'.

Ellis Buckingham
Private, Ellis Gerald Buckingham, 183712,
10th Battalion,
Canadian Infantry (Alberta Regiment)

Ellis Buckingham was born in Middletown, Hailey, on Friday the 2nd December 1887, the youngest son of George, a stone mason, and his wife Anne (née Millin). By the time of the census of 1911 Ellis was working as a bricklayer and was living in Whitings Lane, Delly End, with his older brother Joseph (also a bricklayer) and their recently widowed mother.[151] In early 1913, the two brothers, along with their friend, Walter Stone, emigrated to Canada. Sailing from Liverpool aboard the *S.S. Arabic* they arrived in Halifax, Nova Scotia on the 9th April 1913 en-route to the town of Red Deer, near Calgary, Alberta, where, despite their background as tradesmen (Walter was an electrician), they planned to farm.

In August 1914 Canada, then part of the British Empire, was drawn into a European conflict when Britain declared war on Germany and expatriates, eager to 'do their bit' began to return to the U.K. Joseph was the first of the trio to arrive back, landing in Liverpool at the end of the year. Walter followed him in May 1915 but Ellis chose to remain in Canada where, as originally planned, he was engaged in farming near Red Deer. However the war continued and, on the 27th November 1915, he too volunteered for military service joining the 89th (Alberta) Battalion of the Canadian Expeditionary Force (CEF)[152].

Following their basic training the men of the 89th Battalion left Canada aboard the *S.S. Olympic* on the 2nd June 1916. Arriving in Liverpool on the 8th June the unit was moved to Westenhanger Camp in Kent where it was to remain for some time, initially as a 'reinforcing battalion', sending men to strengthen other Canadian units already in France. Although at Westenhanger for only a short time it was whilst there that on the 28th July 1916, Ellis married Rose Harris, who, at the time of her marriage was living in Ealing, Middlesex. However, the couple's time together was brief and at the end of August Ellis received orders for his deployment to the Western Front.

---

[151] George Buckingham died in the autumn of 1910.
[152] Formed on 1st November 1915.

Once in France Ellis was assigned to the 10th Battalion CEF[153] but before joining his new unit he was first required to spend several days with the 1st Entrenching Battalion, a formation used in trench digging and other labouring tasks which allowed new arrivals to gain some experience of the battle front without actually being involved in any fighting. He eventually joined his own unit, alongside seventy eight other reinforcements, on the 16th September 1916 at a place known as 'Brickfields' near the town of Albert, on the Somme.

Since the 8th September the 10th Battalion had been engaged intermittently in a series of defensive operations in the area and on the 22nd September it was ordered back into the trenches to the north of the town. Initially held in support, the battalion was moved up into the front line on the night of the 25th/26th September and over the following forty eight hours was engaged in heavy fighting. It was during this period that Ellis Buckingham was fatally wounded. Suffering from gunshot wounds to his chest, arms and legs he was evacuated from the battlefield to the 49th Casualty Clearing Station near the village of Contay, where he died on the 29th September 1916.

He was buried in the nearby military cemetery at Contay, east of Albert, France, where his grave can be found today.

Ernest C. Buckingham
Private, Ernest Christopher Buckingham, 9991,
5th Battalion,
Oxfordshire and Buckinghamshire Light Infantry

Ernest Buckingham was born in Witney during the second quarter of 1896, the second child and eldest son of Christopher, an agricultural labourer, and his wife Ada (née Pickett). Around 1903 the family moved to Poffley End near Hailey and at the time of the 1911 census Ernest was working on a local farm.

Ernest volunteered for military service within the first few weeks of the war, joining the Oxfordshire and Buckinghamshire Light Infantry (OBLI), and was deployed to France on the 23rd November 1914. His record of medal entitlement shows that he was attached to the 2nd Battalion, OBLI, however the information held by the Commonwealth War Graves Commission indicates that

---

[153] Known to cotemporaries simply as the 'Fighting Tenth' this unit participated in every major Canadian battle of the War.

by the late summer of 1915 he had been transferred to the 5th Battalion, OBLI, part of the 14th Division.

In September 1915 the 14th Division was in Flanders, engaged in the Third Battle of Ypres, or "Passchendaele" as it came to be known. During the night of the 24th/25th September the 5th OBLI, in preparation for an attack, moved into trenches south of the German front line positions at Bellewarde Farm. At around 3.30 a.m. on the morning of the 25th an artillery bombardment of the German lines began. It was to last for approximately one hour before the British infantry assaulted the enemy positions. The orders for the 5th OBLI were that it should attack in two columns – left and right. But not all went according to plan.

Three out of the four guns of the battalion's own artillery battery put shells down on the German lines but the fourth fired short, lobbing at least fourteen shells into the trenches held by the 5th OBLI and around 21 men were killed or wounded as a result. The infantry assault began at 4.20 a.m. when the men of the battalion climbed out of their trenches and, forming up into two columns, advanced on the German lines. The right column overcame the enemy's defences and was able to reach its objective (although it was later driven back by a German counter attack) whilst the left column, coming under merciless machine gun and rifle fire from the outset, disintegrated into confusion and sustained heavy casualties.[154]

It was during this fighting that Ernest Buckingham was killed. His body was never identified and he has no known grave. Today his name is remembered on the Ypres (Menin Gate) Memorial, Ipres, Belgium.

A. Victor Busby
Private, Albert Victor Busby, 7924,
2nd Battalion,
Oxfordshire and Buckinghamshire Light Infantry

Albert Busby, known by his middle name of 'Victor', was born at Lower End, Leafield, during the fourth quarter of 1893, the son of Philip, a general labourer, and his wife Jane (née Willis). Around 1894 the family moved to Ducklington and then again in 1900 to New Yatt. By the time of the 1911 census Victor had joined the Army and was at the Cowley Barracks, Oxford, a soldier of the Oxfordshire and Buckinghamshire Light Infantry (OBLI). In early 1914 he was married to Kate Giles.

---

[154] WO 95/1900

211

It is likely that by the time of his marriage Victor had been discharged from the Army, having completed his regular service, and transferred to the reserves. When the order for mobilisation was issued in August 1914 the reserves were immediately called up and Victor rejoined his regiment. He was posted to France on the 12th September 1914 where he joined the 2nd Battalion, OBLI, part of the 2nd Division.

The men of the 2nd OBLI fought at the First Battle of Ypres (19th October – 22nd November 1914), through the winter of 1914/15 and at Festubert in early May 1915. The following letter, written by Victor to a friend at home, records the events of the 15th-17th May 1915 when the Battalion were at the front near the village of Richebourg Saint-Vaast, approximately 3 miles west of Neuve Chapelle:

"I am pleased to say I am still quite well, and have again escaped injury in the biggest battle in which we have yet fought. I daresay you will have read something of it before now. It was terrible. We were in billets, held in reserve about a mile from the firing line, and the Germans kept shelling us out, killing and wounding some of our number. We had been thus placed for two nights when a rumour went round that we were to make an attack at the same place that one had been made a week before. However it did not take place that night (Friday). An order was sent round to the effect that Holy Communion would be celebrated on Saturday, then we knew what was going to happen. We paraded at 7.30 in full marching order for the trenches. We were to support the Inniskillings in a night attack and you can bet we were troubled with a lump in our throats, though we did not much care about the job; still it had to be done. Most of us shook hands with one another; we knew that many would not return, though we did not expect to lose as heavily as we did. The losses in our regiment alone about 500 men and officers! Oh it was most terrible. How I managed to get through I don't know; my luck, I suppose. It was the Oxfords who took the enemy's trench. I was among the first over our parapet, but I never expected reaching the other end, being straight in front of a machine gun. Every second the groaning and moaning of men struck down was heard on every hand. I reached the first line of the Inniskillings, and you could hear a sergeant or an officer shouting to them to make another dash. I think we must have lost our way, for we were up the side of the German trench instead of going for it. The enemy got in an enfilading fire which caused terrible damage. Along with four others, I jumped into a big hole, and lucky for us we did, or we should all have been hit. As it was the four got wounded, but not just then. We stayed in the hole for a few minutes, then I

suggested we should make another advance. They were up in a moment. Luck again! I took the opposite side of the hole and missed being hit: the other four were all wounded and fell back into the hole. I bandaged them as best I could, but I was in a queer fix with four men who could not move. It was so dark I could not see another man near. I knew I was very close to the German trench, and I thought reinforcements would surely come. I was determined not to be taken prisoner if I could help it. Waiting a short time I was able to distinguish several of our men coming along, and I crept out and joined them. I told them about the machine gun giving its locality as near as possible, and we decided to make a rush for it, making as much noise as possible in order to make our small force seem bigger. There were three Germans and an officer at the gun, and four others quite near, but all went under. My bayonet went through the officer and two rounds point blank at the others put a finishing touch to them. We got the trench, but I have not time to tell you all we went through! The next 48 hours were awful. Shells were fired like rifle fire, indeed, the noise was like continuous heavy thunder. I don't think it can possibly be worse than that. You can imagine what an ordeal it was, and expecting to be killed at any moment. I thank God I am still safe and well." [155]

In September 1915 the 2nd Division went into action during the Battle of Loos (25th September – 18th October). It is likely that it was during this battle that Victor Busby was mortally wounded. He died on the 12th October 1915 and is buried in the Cologne Southern Cemetery in Germany. In 1922 it was decided that the graves of all Commonwealth troops, who had died in Germany, should be brought together in four large purpose built cemeteries, Cologne being one of the sites chosen. It would appear that a wounded Victor had been taken prisoner by the Germans and died whilst they treated his wounds. Most likely buried somewhere in Germany, his grave would have been removed to Cologne after 1922.

---

[155] Letter originally published in the *Witney Gazette*, 26th June 1915.

Isaac Clements
Sapper, Isaac Clements, 216875,
2/1st Cornwall (Electric Light) Company,
Royal Engineers

Isaac Clements was born at Delly End, Hailey, in November 1875, the second son of Jason, a stone mason, and his wife Lucy (née Buckingham). Although, upon leaving school, he was initially employed as an agricultural labourer, Isaac later trained as a stone mason and bricklayer. On the 5th January 1911, at St. John's Church in Hailey, he married Beatrice Millin and their only child, Marjorie, was born in the village a little over a year later on the 1st May 1912.

Isaac joined the Army on the 4th December 1916 and, as a qualified mason and bricklayer, latterly in the employ of local building firm *Messrs Long and Berry*, he was posted to the Royal Engineers (RE), joining the 2/1st Cornwall (Electric Light) Company, RE, at a depot in Falmouth, Cornwall. This unit was one of a number of Fortress Companies all engaged in coastal defence duties. Some were used solely for Electric Light (searchlight) duties and others, such as the 2/1st at Falmouth, also undertook construction and maintenance work of coastal defences.

But Isaac was not a well man, since the age of thirteen he had suffered with dyspeptic symptoms and it was not long before he began making regular visits to the Depot's Medical Officer for treatment. On the 25th May 1917 he was admitted to Falmouth Military Hospital with an inflamed stomach. He told the medical staff there that before he had joined the Army he regularly lost three to four working days each month as a result of his condition. Additionally it was discovered that he was prone to suffer from asthma in wet weather conditions. Clearly he was not fit enough for military service and, following his discharge from hospital on the 31st July 1917, it was recommended that he be discharged from the Army. Two months later, on the 22nd September, the military authorities agreed that Isaac should be released from his military obligations and allowed to return home.

Back in Hailey Isaac had hoped to spend his time tending his two acre allotment but his ailments persisted and on the 26th February 1918 he died. He was buried in the Churchyard of St. John's, Hailey, in a plot he now shares with his wife, daughter and Harold Newell, the son-in-law he never knew[156].

---

[156] Marjorie Clements married Harold R. Newell during the summer of 1939.

Cecil L. Harris
Shoeing Smith, Cecil Lionel Harris, 69014,
17th Heavy Battery,
Royal Garrison Artillery

Cecil Harris was born in Hailey during the late summer of 1876, the son of Albert, a wheelwright, and his wife Ann (maiden name unknown). Upon leaving school he entered into an apprenticeship to a local blacksmith and by the time of the census of 1901, with both of his parents having died during the 1890's, he was living with his elder brother, Walter, and his family at the *Carpenter's Arms* pub in the village and working for himself as a blacksmith. On the 5th February 1902 he married Amy Pratley and their first child, Dorothea, was born a year later in March 1903. Three more children followed; Phyllis in 1904, Ruth 1908 and Joan in 1910.

Cecil joined the Army on the 18th January 1915 and, following his basic training, was posted as a shoeing smith to the 17th Heavy Battery of the Royal Garrison Artillery. He moved with his unit to France on the 7th October 1915 and was to remain on the Western Front for the duration of the war. On the 20th January 1918 he was admitted to a military hospital in Dannes Carniers suffering with myalgia[157] and as a result he was referred to a medical board at Etaples where the decision was taken to redeploy him. On the 2nd February 1918 he was assigned to the 943rd Area Employment (Artisan) Company of the Labour Corps, the unit with which he was to remain until the end of the war.

On the 19th February 1919, following his discharge from the Army and in receipt of a small pension for an eye condition aggravated by shell gas during the war, Cecil returned to Hailey. However, within months of his homecoming he fell ill and on the 30th June 1919 he died of suppurative tonsillitis. He was buried in the graveyard of St. John's Church and his grave, sited to the left of the path leading to the church, is today marked by a Commonwealth War Grave headstone.

---

[157] Also known as muscle strain, myalgia can be a symptom of many diseases and disorders.

James Hill
Private, James Hill, 276900,
20th Battalion,
Durham Light Infantry

James Hill was born in Crawley during the second quarter of 1888, the third son of George, a general labourer, and his wife Amelia (née Barrett). The family moved several times over the next two decades, living in North Leigh, Curbridge and again in Crawley before settling in Hailey. At the time of the 1911 census James was recorded as working on a local farm as a shepherd.

Although his service record has not survived, his regimental number indicates that James joined the Army prior to 1916 and that when he was deployed to France he went as part of the 20th Battalion of the Durham Light Infantry, part of the 41st Division[158]. The Division landed in France on the 5th May 1916 and fought in the great Allied offensive on the Somme later that year. In 1917 the Division was in Flanders during the Third Battle of Ypres ("Passchendaele") and at the end of that campaign it was ordered to the Italian Front. By the 18th November 1917 the Division was concentrated to the north west of the town of Mantua, from where it took over a sector of the front line behind the River Piave. At the beginning of February 1918 the Division returned to France.

On the morning of the 21st March 1918 in the wake of an immense artillery bombardment of British positions on the Somme, the Germans launched a huge offensive. Fast moving enemy troops (stormtroopers) infiltrated the British lines before mass infantry assaults overwhelmed the defenders and forced the British into a large scale retreat across the battlefields of two years earlier.

On the 23rd March 1918, at the Battle of St. Quentin (21st – 23rd March), as the British desperately tried to hold the line before being forced to retire, James Hill was killed in action. His body was never identified and he has no known grave. Today his name is remembered on the Arras Memorial, Arras, France.

---

[158] WO 95/2643

Herbert C. Morton
Private, Herbert Charles Morton, 42653,
1st Battalion,
Worcestershire Regiment

Herbert Morton was born in Middletown, Hailey, during the fourth quarter of 1891, the second son of Charles, an agricultural labourer, and his wife Annie (née Holloway). At the time of the 1911 census Herbert was employed as a 'coach painter'.

He joined the Army at some point after January 1916, initially being posted to the Oxfordshire and Buckinghamshire Light Infantry. Following his basic training, he was deployed to France and reassigned to the 1st Battalion of the Worcestershire Regiment, part of the 8th Division. This is likely to have taken place around the 24th July 1916 at which point the 1st Worcesters, resting out of the line at Beuvry, received a draft of 350 men from other regiments to make good the losses it had sustained in the early phase of the Somme Offensive.

On the 30th July 1916 the 1st Worcesters went back into the line at Cuinchy where they were to remain for the next two months, after which the whole of 8th Division returned to the battlefields of the Somme. On the 19th of October the 1st Worcesters went into the trenches near Gueudecourt. For the first twenty-four hours nothing of note occurred, but on the morning of the second day their positions came under German artillery fire and the men of the 1st Worcesters, already suffering from the cold and wet in waterlogged trenches, were forced to make a partial withdrawal. In this incident the battalion suffered over fifty casualties, one of whom was Herbert Morton.[159]

Officially recorded as having been killed in action on the 22nd October 1916, Herbert's body was never identified and he has no known grave. Today his name is recorded on the Thiepval Memorial to the missing of the Somme, Thiepval, France.

William Painting
Private, George William Painting, 14459,
7th Battalion,
Duke of Edinburgh's (Wiltshire Regiment)

See entry for William Painting on the Witney War Memorial.

---

[159] WO 95/1723

Frederick W. Pratley
Private, Frederick Walter Pratley, 11911,
2nd Battalion,
Hampshire Regiment

Frederick Pratley, known as 'Fred', was born at Lower End, Leafield, during the first quarter of 1893, the fourth son of Walter, a general labourer, and his wife Thirza (née Shayler). In 1895 the family were living in Fulbrook; by 1901 they had moved to Swinford, near Farmoor, where Frederick's father was working as a woodsman and general estate worker, and by the time of the 1911 census Fred and his parents were living at White Oak Green, near Hailey, where Fred was employed, as was his father, as a general labourer.

Fred volunteered for military service soon after the war broke out in August 1914. Initially he was posted to the Duke of Cornwall's Light Infantry but was later redeployed to the 2nd Battalion of the Hampshire Regiment, part of the 29th Division, which was sent to Gallipoli in March 1915.

From his record of medal entitlement it is unclear if Fred served with his new unit before its deployment to Gallipoli or whether he was sent to join it after. It was usual, at least up to 1916, for a soldier's record of medal entitlement to record the date upon which he entered an active theatre of operations. On Fred's record there is no such date and officially he is recorded as having 'died at sea' Therefore one can conclude that he was not with the 2nd Hampshire's at the time of their original landing at Cape Helles on 25th April 1915 and that he was posted later and died on the 13th August 1915[160] whilst en-route to join his new unit.

He has no known grave and is today remembered on the Helles Memorial at Gallipoli, alongside more than 21,000 other names of commonwealth soldiers, who died during operations on that peninsula.

---

[160] The 2nd Battalion had suffered heavy casualties on the 6th August 1915 – the first day of the Allied offensive.

Wilfred G. Smith
Private, Wilfred George Smith, 22768,
2nd Battalion,
Oxfordshire & Buckinghamshire Light Infantry

Wilfred Smith was born at the beginning of 1897 in Poffley End, Hailey, the second son of Charles, a mason's labourer, and his wife Fanny (née Rhodes). At the time of the 1911 census Wilfred was living with his widowed mother and his siblings, and working as a farm labourer.

In the absence of his military record it is unclear as to exactly when Wilfred joined the Army but, from his record of medal entitlement, it is evident that he was not deployed to France until after the beginning of January 1916. Once on the Western Front he was attached to the 2nd Battalion of the Oxfordshire and Buckinghamshire Light Infantry (OBLI), part of the 2nd Division - a formation which had been in France since August 1914.

In mid-July 1916 the 2nd Division joined the Allied offensive on the Somme, which, far from being one huge battle, comprised of a number of separate phases collectively lasting for several months. The 2nd Division took part in the Battle of Delville Wood (15th July – 3rd September) and then the Battle of the Ancre (13th – 18th November) during which it is likely that Wilfred Smith was mortally wounded.[161]

Evacuated from the battlefield, Wilfred was taken to the huge British camp at Etaples where, on the 22nd November 1916, he died of his wounds. Today his grave can be found in the Etaples Military Cemetery, to the north of Etaples, France.

Wilfred's elder brother, Arnold, who initially served with the 6th Battalion, OBLI, was wounded in action on the 3rd September 1916 at Guillemont during the Somme offensive. He returned to the UK to convalesce and was subsequently reassigned to the Labour Corps. However, continuing to suffer from the effects of a nervous debility - later recognised as 'shell shock', he was medically discharged on the 14th September 1917. He returned to Hailey,

---

[161] The Battalion diarist recorded that the total casualties for the period 13th – 18th November 1916 were: *"Officers killed wounded or missing – 13. Other ranks: killed 10, wounded 149, missing 76"*. WO95/1348

where, in 1924 he married Elsie Walker. The couple's first child was born the following year, a son. They named him Wilfred.

Acknowledgments

Throughout the past four years I have had the pleasure and privilege to meet a great number of people who can all claim a connection to at least one of the three war memorials of Witney, Hailey and Crawley. Some are direct descendants of those named, others are more distantly related. Some had been friends, former work colleagues and comrades on the field of battle - on one very emotional occasion, I had the privilege to meet and talk to the man who had pulled one of Witney's fallen heroes, mortally wounded, from his stricken tank on a battlefield in Normandy in 1944 – an account which will be covered in my next book. Many have allowed me to use personal letters, photographs and diaries to tell the stories of those they knew and of those their parents had spoken of. With regards to the men named from 1914-19 I would particularly like to thank Kathy Cass, Julie Leigh, Cathleen Powell, Harry Beale, Willy Townsend, Angela Godfrey, Debbie Betts, Valerie Burton, Steve and Rita Kearsey, Alan Leach and Bob Franklin. Also Cheryl Price (of the Wangaratta Family History Society in Victoria, Australia) for providing me with information I would have been otherwise unable to obtain, similarly the staff of Thames Library, Thames, New Zealand, and staff at the Library and Archives of Canada, John Nash of the York and Lancaster Regiment Museum in Rotherham, and the volunteers at The Soldiers of Oxfordshire Museum in Woodstock. Additionally I would like to acknowledge the help I received from a number of online forums in particular the Canadian Expeditionary Force Study Group and The Great War Forum.

Penultimately I would like to thank my long suffering wife Wendy for putting up with my periodic absences over the past few years, sat for many hours either at the computer or engrossed in old documents and books and for having to listen to my deliberations, ideas and readings of draft biographies. Unfortunately, by the very nature of the project, I never did get to write the 'happy story' she always hoped for.

Finally I want to pay an extra special debt of gratitude to my friend Don Garner. A man who I was fortunate enough to meet whilst researching for this book and someone who subsequently offered to proof read the document for me. Indeed if there is any one person who has read and re read these pages as often, if not more than myself it is Don. His enthusiasm and support for this project has been truly inspirational throughout. Don, I thank you.

Nevertheless, and despite all the assistance I have received, I take full responsibility for any and all inaccuracies that appear within these pages. This has always been and will continue to be a work-in-progress and because of this I continue to seek further information on all those I have researched. If anyone can help I look forward to hearing from you.

Jeff Clements,

e mail: *witneywarmemorial@hotmail.co.uk*

Appendix (i)

List of casualties born or living in Witney or Cogges at the time of their enlistment, who are not recorded on the Witney War Memorial:[162]

Rifleman, Herbert Edward Cyril Lewis, A/201400.
Born in Witney.
Served with the 8th Battalion, King's Royal Rifle Corps.
Killed in action, Flanders, 24th August 1917, aged 19.

Private, Edward Arthur Pickett, 646.
Born in Witney.
Served with the 1st Battalion, Northumberland Fusiliers.
Died 8th November 1914.

Private, Sylvester Frederick Richardson, 1379a.
Born in Witney. Emigrated to Australia with his family after 1911.
Served with the 18th Battalion, Australian Imperial Force.
Killed in action, Gallipoli, August 1915, aged 21.

Private, Charles Weaver, 16/1631.
Born in Witney.
Served with the 16th Battalion, West Yorkshire Regiment.
Presumed killed in action on the Somme, 1st July 1916, aged 24.

Lucy Harris, No.23686, Women's Royal Air Force.
Born in Cogges.
No.1 Stores Depot, Kidbrooke.
Died 1st November 1918.

---

[162] Taken from Broome, J.A., <u>Roll of Honour of Servicemen and Women from Witney and Cogges who lost their lives during the 1914-1918 and 1939-1945 World Wars</u>, unpublished, copy held at the Witney and District Museum.

Private, Edward Henry, Pearse, 5062.

Of Cogges.

Served with the 1/4th Battalion, Oxfordshire and Buckinghamshire Light Infantry.

Killed in action on the Somme, 14th August 1916, aged 19.

Appendix (ii)

Lucy Harris, 23686,
Women's Royal Air Force

Lucy Harris has the distinction of being the only woman from Witney to be recorded on the Commonwealth War Graves Commission (CWGC) web site and yet she is not mentioned on either the town's memorial or on the memorial plaque in St. Mary's Church, Cogges. Nor is her grave marked by a CWGC headstone. Nevertheless as Witney's only female casualty of the Great War she deserves to be remembered here.

It is believed that she was born at Newland, Witney, in the third quarter of 1887, the illegitimate daughter of laundress, Emily Haley. In the spring of 1892 her mother married Albert Launchbury and over the next few years the couple went on to have three children together; Catherine, Alice and Charles – himself later to become a fatality of the Great War. Towards the end of 1898 Lucy's mother died and the following year Albert, with one step-daughter and three young children of his own to care for, married again to Elizabeth Pickett.

Around the time of her mother's death and her step-father's re marriage, Lucy, a former pupil of the original Cogges School, passed into the care of her widowed Grandfather, Charles Haley, of Oxford Hill Road. Charles died in March 1906 and Lucy went to live with her Uncle, William Haley, and his family in Stanton Harcourt Road. At the time of the 1911 census Lucy, still living at Cogges, was working in the town's woollen industry as a blanket weaver. In September 1917 she moved from Witney to London following her marriage to wheelwright, Percy Harris of Forest Gate, Lewisham.

In April 1918 the Women's Royal Air Force was established. Initially aimed at providing female mechanics in order to release men for active service, the WRAF soon attracted huge numbers of women applying to fill other positions such as drivers, clerks and fitters. On October the 16th 1918 Lucy enlisted with the WRAF to work at the No1 Stores Depot at Kidbrooke (later RAF Kidbrooke). However it is likely that she was never to attend her place of work. Her death certificate indicates that she was ill with influenza at the time she joined the WRAF and after a fortnight this had developed into pneumonia. She died on 1st November 1918.

Her body was brought home to Witney and buried in the churchyard of St. Mary's Church, Cogges, at the feet of her Grandparents; Charles and Catherine Haley. Originally her grave was delineated by a very low border of iron railings but these were removed many years ago when they had become worn and broken. Today the grave is unmarked and does not appear on the churchyard plan.[163]

---

[163] St. Mary's, Cogges, churchyard plan accessed at www.coggesparish.com

Appendix (iii)

Roll of Honour, Holy Trinity Church, Woodgreen. Witney.[164]

George Henry Long
Howard Charles Long
Charles Edward Launchbury
Charles William Pimm
Stephen William Smith
James William Martin
John Martin
Alfred Samuel Tallett
Cyril Walter Shurmer
John Painter
Ernest Walter Pratley
Frank Ernest Buckingham
Harry Richards
Alresford William Engelfield
Sydney Humphris
Arthur Guy Mace
Ernest George V. Brotherton

Albert Benjamin Brain
Herbert E. Long
Ernest Jesse Grant
Frederick Percival Pimm
Albert Job Horne
George Ernest Martin
Fred Sherbourne
Albert Pickett
Harry [Henry?] Painter
Walter Richard Bridgman
William George Stroud
Ernest Stephens
Ernest Jospeh Fowler
Ernest J. Rose
George William Painting
William Edward Goddard

---

[164] Taken from Broome, J.A., <u>Roll of Honour of Servicemen and Women from Witney and Cogges who lost their lives during the 1914-1918 and 1939-1945 World Wars</u>, unpublished, copy held at the Witney and District Museum

Appendix (iv)

Roll of Honour, St. Mary's Church, Witney.[165]

James Hanks
S. Collett
A. Arnold
Job Horne
A.E. Brooks
John Foreshew
G. Fowler
Sidney Miles
C. Hodgson
Fred Brooks
George Jones
Edwin Elliott
Aaron [Alfred?] Townsend
Walter Winterbourne
James Godfrey
Percy Bustin
Ernest Fowler
Fred Amery
Hariph Young
George Burford

---

[165] *ibid.*

Appendix (v)

Roll of Honour, St. Mary's School, Church Green, Witney.[166]

F. Turner
A. Pickett
W.S. Paintin
F. Sherbourne
W. Miles
A. Townsend
H. Evans
G.H. Long
H.E. Long
H. Long
E.J. Fowler
G. Harris
F. Buckingham
H. Richards
A. Haggit
L. Hinton
G. Hooker
C.E. Launchbury
H. Townsend
H. Gardner
C. Edwards

R. Moore
S. Miles
F. Bennett
W. Stroud
T. Clack
A.S. Tallett
C.J. Sirett
H.E.C. Lewis
G.N. Buswell
J. Hanks
F. Brooks
G. Wright
H. Hooper
H. Morris
A. Johnson
S. Beale
F. Pratley
A. Pinfold
L. Whitcher
A. Pearce
H. Castle

J. Cox
W. Dix
W. Hall
D. Castle
J. Turner
H. Sherbourne
W.T. Richards
J. Townsend
W. Bridgman
G.W. Burford
C.M. Warren
I. Walker
S. Humphris
B. Clements
T. Keene
W. Weaver
E. Godfrey

---

[166] *ibid.*

Appendix (vi)

Roll Of Honour, Henry Box School, Church Green, Witney (formerly known as the Witney Grammar School)[167]

William Heathcote Blackaby
Herbert Frank Boggis
Francis Buckingham
Herbert Florey
Ernest Joseph Fowler
Archibald Grant
James Edward Lewis Hinton
Sidney Miles
William Hugh Miller
Reginald Moore
Robert Craig Murray Nisbet
Tom Powell
Matthew Strong
Ernest William Tarrant

Note: In 2010, whilst researching in preparation for the school's 350th anniversary celebrations, local historian, Jane Cavell, discovered two more names of former pupils who had lost their lives during the Great War - Archie William Hutt and Walter Frederick Oakley.[168]

---

[167] *ibid.*

[168] As reported in the *Oxford Mail*, 10th June 2010.

Appendix (vii)

Index of the units in which the war dead of Witney, Crawley and Hailey served:

Army Service Corps
    168th Lab. Coy. *54, 208*
    206th Lab. Coy. *35*
    1st Auxiliary Horse
    Transport Coy. *75*
    904th M.T. Coy. *150*
    Mechanical Transport *102*
    No.1 GHQ Reserve M.T.
    Coy. *39*
    943rd Area Employment
    (Artisan) Coy. *215*
Cheshire Regiment
    1/4th Bn. *76*
Devonshire Regiment *54, 208*
    4th (Res) Bn. *90*
Duke of Cornwall's Light Infantry
218
    1st Bn. *66*
Duke of Wellington's (West Riding
Regiment)
    13th Bn. *22*
East Surrey Regiment
    1st Bn. *167*
Essex Regiment
    1st Bn. *58*
Gloucestershire Regiment *55*
    8th Bn. *59*
    14th Bn. *140*
Grenadier Guards
    1st Bn. *111*

    2nd Bn. *125-126*
    4th Bn. *125*
Hampshire Regiment *141*
    2nd Bn. *24, 218*
Herefordshire Regiment *41*
    1st Bn. *88*
Household Cavalry & Cavalry of the
Line
    12th Royal Lancers *184*
    17th Lancers *34*
    Queen's Own Oxfordshire
    Hussars *51, 83, 94, 147*
    19th Hussars *149*
King's Own (Yorkshire Light
Infantry)
    2nd Bn. *62*
    12th Bn. *89*
London Regiment
    1/9th Bn. *20*
    23rd Bn. *12*
Machine Gun Corps
    56th Coy. *110*
    105th Coy. *55*
Middlesex Regiment *184*
    11th Bn. *185*
Oxfordshire and Buckinghamshire
Light Infantry
*23, 24, 54, 79, 104, 110, 128, 132,
217*
    1st Bn. *158*

2nd Bn. *28, 47, 50, 63, 65, 73, 80, 86, 97, 131, 138, 212, 219*
5th Bn. *37, 57, 67, 78, 85, 146, 172, 178, 187, 210*
6th Bn. *14, 29, 100, 121, 125, 161, 174, 196*
7th Bn. *26*
8th Bn. *188*
1/4th Bn. *42, 53, 68, 70, 75, 99, 106, 109, 114, 117, 119, 120, 136, 148, 154, 162, 163, 165, 166, 171, 182, 197, 224*
2/1st Bn. *61, 122, 177*
2/4th Bn. *46, 91, 116, 117, 142, 156*
3/4th Bn. *208*
Prince of Wales' (North Staffordshire Regiment)
1/5th Bn. *135*
Princess Charlotte of Wales' (Royal Berkshire Regiment)
1st Bn. *74, 195, 199*
6th Bn. *39*
8th Bn. *107*
Rifle Brigade (The Prince Consort's Own)
3rd Bn. *51, 186*
6th Bn. *51*
13th Bn. *31*
Royal Army Medical Corps
37th Field Ambulance *175*
87th Gen. Hospital *95*
Royal Defence Corps
24th Protection Coy. *169*

Royal Engineers
26th Labour Coy. *123*
57th Field Coy. *104*
89th Field Coy. *105*
2/1st Cornwall (Electric Light) Coy. *214*
Royal Field Artillery
87th Bty. 2nd Bde. *33*
"D" Bty. 65th Bde. *38*
"A" Bty. 84th Bde. *173*
"B" Bty. 124th Bde. *82*
"B" Bty. 152nd (Notts) Bde. *199*
"B" Bty. 190th Bde. *30*
"D" Bty. 298th Bde. *157*
Royal Garrison Artillery
17th Heavy Bty. *215*
132nd Heavy Bty. *159*
Royal Horse Artillery
2/1st (Berks) Bty. *27*
Royal Irish Fusiliers
1st Bn. *153*
Royal Marine Light Infantry
2nd Bn. *93*
Royal Scots
1st Bn. *127*
Royal Warwickshire Regiment
15th Bn. *184*
2/8th Bn. *137*
Seaforth Highlanders
1/4th Bn. *19*
Somerset Light Infantry
1st Bn. *40*
6th Bn. *134*
South Lancashire Regiment

8th Bn. *152*
Tank Corps
6th Bn. *56*
The Queen's (Royal West Surrey
Regiment)
3/4th Bn. *45*
Welsh Regiment
13th Bn. *41*
Wiltshire Regiment *134*
7th Bn. *79, 128*
Worcestershire Regiment *41*
1st Bn. *217*
2nd Bn. *129*
3rd Bn. *135*
4th Bn. *114*
10th Bn. *112, 141, 175*
York and Lancaster Regiment
12th Bn. *132*

Royal Air Force *23*
No.3 Sqn. *101*
Women's Royal Air Force
No.1 Stores Depot *223, 225*

Royal Navy *44*

Australian Imperial Force
37th Bn. *69*
18th Bn. *223*
Canadian Expeditionary Force
Alberta Regt.
10th Bn. *209*
Eastern Ontario Regt.
21st Bn. *143*

Quebec Regt.
42nd Bn. *16*
Canadian Engineers *206*
New Zealand Expeditionary Force
Canterbury Regt.
1st Bn. *43*
New Zealand Engineers
Div. Signal Coy. *181*
Ceylon Planter's Rifle Corps
58
South African Overseas
Expeditionary Force
1st Regt. (Infantry) *179*

Abbreviations used:

Bde.	Brigade
Bn.	Battalion
Bty.	Battery
Coy.	Company
Div.	Division(al)
Gen.	General
GHQ	General Headquarters
Regt.	Regiment
Sqn.	Squadron

233

Sources and select bibliography

The National Archives, London:

Various battalion and unit war diaries, as identified in the text, from the record series WO 95
Medal index cards in the record series WO 372
Individual Army service records in the series WO 363
Army pension records in the series WO 364
Individual Royal Marine service records in the series ADM 159
Individual Royal Naval service records in the series ADM 188
Individual Royal Air Force service records in the series AIR 76

Newspapers:

Witney Gazette, held on microfilm at Witney Library
Western Mail, held on microfilm at Cardiff Library
Eastbourne Chronicle, held on microfilm at Eastbourne Library
The London Gazette, accessed online at www.london-gazette.co.uk

Books:

Broome, J.A., <u>Roll of Honour of Servicemen and Women from Witney and Cogges who lost their lives during the 1914- 1918 and 1939-1945 World Wars</u>, unpublished, copy held at the Witney and District Museum
Callwell, C.E., <u>The Dardanelles</u>, Constable & Co., London, 1919.
Cavell, J., <u>The Henry Box School – Its Place in History</u>, The Henry Box School, Witney, 2009.

Coombs, R.E.B. MBE, Before Endeavours Fade, Battle of Britain Prints International Ltd, London, 1994.

Dyer, G., The Missing of the Somme, Phoenix, London, 1994.

Gilbert, M., Somme, John Murray, London. 2007.

Holmes, R., Tommy – The British Soldier on the Western Front 1914-1918, Harper Perennial, London, 2005.

Jenkins, S.C. (Ed), Historic Witney, Mill House Publications, Witney, 2002.

Keith-Falconer, A., The Oxfordshire Hussars in the Great War (1914-1918), London, John Murray, 1927

Liveling, E.G.D., Attack – An Infantry Subaltern's Impression of July 1st, 1916, Macmillan, London, 1918.

MacDonald, L., They Called it Passchendaele, Penguin, London, 1993.

Majendie, V.H.B. Major D.S.O., A History of the 1st Battalion The Somerset Light Infantry, Goodman & Son, Taunton, 1921

Marwick, A., The Deluge, British Society and the First World War, MacMillan, London, 1991

Masefield, J., Gallipoli, Macmillan, London, 1916.

Middlebrook, M., The First Day on the Somme, Penguin, London, 1984.

Oliver, N., Not Forgotten, Hodder & Stoughton, London, 2005.

Rose G.K., The Story of the 2/4th Oxfordshire & Buckinghamshire Light Infantry, B.H. Blackwell, Oxford, 1920.

Wolff, L., In Flanders Fields, Longmans, London, 1959.

Electronic resources:

Ancestry (*www.ancestry.co.uk*)

Australian Military records and unit diaries (*www.awm.gov.au*)

Canadian Expeditionary Force Study Group (*www.cefresearch.ca*)

Canadian unit diaries and individual service records (*www.collectionscanada.gc.ca*)

Downloadable ebooks from the Gutenburg Project (*www.gutenburg.net*)

Find My Past (*www.findmypast.co.uk*)

Transcribed diary of the 1/4th Oxfordshire and Buckinghamshire Light Infantry

March 1915 – March 1919 (*www.weymouthsands.co.uk/diary/oxbucks.htm*)

New Zealand Military Records (*www.archway.archives.govt.nz)*

The account of Private 41946 Charles Victor Holman, with the 1st Battalion Essex Regiment (1916-1919) (*www.hellfire-corner.demon.co.uk/holman.htm*)

The Commonwealth War Graves Commission (*cwgc.org.uk*)

The Great War Forum (*www.1914-1918.invisionzone.com*)

The Long, Long Trail, the British Army in the Great War of 1914-1918 (*www.1914-1918.net*)

The National Archives (*www.nationalarchives.gov.uk*)